the
geek gap

ADVANCE PRAISE

"Having both business people and developers work on projects collaboratively and effectively is an important skill for any company. By letting these two groups understand how each other thinks, acts, and works, *The Geek Gap* provides the keys to let teams succeed at the essential task of choosing and implementing the right technologies for their business."

—Adam Gross
Vice President, Developer Marketing, Salesforce.com, Inc.,
San Francisco, California

"Having spent almost thirty years bridging the communications gap between engineers and the rest of us, it's great to finally have a 'how-to' survival guide to the forever-united worlds of business and technology. Pfleging and Zetlin make a powerful team. Read this book!"

—Larry Weber
Chairman/CEO, W2Group, Inc., Boston, Massachusetts

"There are very few of us who understand both camps and can communicate and persuade both camps. *The Geek Gap* enables those without such a background to more effectively communicate with and lead the technical staff if they read the book and truly listen to what is being said. A marvelous job that presents some real jewels!"

—Jeff Chasney
EVP Strategic Planning & CIO

"Geeks and suits seem to inhabit parallel universes separated by language, clothing, work habits, office décor, and the definition of success. *The Geek Gap* entertainingly explores the business consequences for both sides, drawing on history, anecdote, and personal experience for scores of examples that are comical, dumbfounding, and also, unfortunately, familiar."

—Steve Kemper
author of *Code Name Ginger* and *Reinventing the Wheel*

the
geek gΛp

Why Business and Technology Professionals Don't Understand Each Other and Why They Need Each Other to Survive

Bill Pfleging & Minda Zetlin

Prometheus Books

59 John Glenn Drive
Amherst, New York 14228-2197

Published 2006 by Prometheus Books

Inquiries should be addressed to
Prometheus Books
59 John Glenn Drive
Amherst, New York 14228–2197
VOICE: 716–691–0133, ext. 207
FAX: 716–564–2711
WWW.PROMETHEUSBOOKS.COM

10 09 08 07 06   5 4 3 2 1

Library of Congress Cataloging-in-Publication Data

Pfleging, Bill.
    The geek gap : why business and technology professionals don't understand each other and why they need each other to survive / by Bill Pfleging and Minda Zetlin.
        p. cm.
    Includes bibliographical references and index.
    ISBN 13: 978-1-59102-415-6
    ISBN 10: 1-59102-415-3 (hardcover : alk. paper)
    1. Information technology—Management. 2. Communication of technical information. 3. Communication in management. I. Zetlin, Minda. II. Title.

HD30.2.P487 2006
306.3'6—dc22

                                                                        2006008263

Printed in the United States of America on acid-free paper

The authors lovingly dedicate this book to

Thaddeus "Teddy" Klingman, 1948–2005: practical joker, raconteur, and surrogate big brother, you are sorely missed,

and

Bill and Erlinda Brobston, our first and best readers.

CONTENTS

8 CONTENTS

ACKNOWLEDGMENTS

M any people helped us in various ways to create this book. Our thanks to our agents, Sheree Bykofsky (who gave the book its title) and Janet Rosen; to Linda Regan, our editor, as well as Jill Maxick, Chris Kramer, and everyone at Prometheus who made this happen; and to Cathy Lewis, who has been hugely helpful with publicity. Thanks also to the literally hundreds of business and technology professionals who have taken the time to talk to us about their experiences at work on either side of the Geek Gap. Special thanks (and rubber-band snaps) to the Tripod gang, who showed how it *can* work. And finally, our thanks to Robert Egert, Neil Van Zile Jr., and James Klingman.

PREFACE

When my economics professor, Dick Sabot, and I decided to collaborate on an Internet company we called Tripod, our plan was to provide useful information to college students who were doing things such as renting an apartment or buying health insurance for the first time. I knew this information was best delivered on the Internet, but I didn't know how to install a browser on my computer, so I figured I'd better get some technical experts involved. That's when I hired Ethan Zuckerman to head the programming team.

Ethan and I soon learned that there were significant differences in how we worked. What I do depends on other people agreeing to do things with me. Ethan and his team, on the other hand, spend all of their time trying to get a machine to do what they want it to do. Every day they can make an incremental amount of progress, whereas in my case, I can fire a lot of blanks before finally hitting my target.

It can be difficult for each of us to see the value in the work of the other because the process for getting a result is so different. When Ethan sits down and says, "We're going to build this," I may be able to see the value of the finished product but it can be hard for me to see the value in each little step along the way.

And it's equally hard for geeks to see the skills involved in raising

11

money or managing. "Oh, it's all about who you went to prep school with and how good you are at golf," they say. Which is partially true, but only partially. This inability to see and appreciate each other's skills and contributions—in other words, the Geek Gap—is an ongoing problem throughout the business world.

Closing the Geek Gap comes down to a question of trust. Do I trust the geeks I work with? Do they trust me? In situations where that trust is lacking, the working relationship can turn into a total disaster. But when you do have that trust, and you can elegantly combine the work modes of geeks and suits, you can create something very powerful. It requires a sort of Kierkegaardian leap of faith.

I have always considered it important to let the geeks do what they want to do and do it in their own way. Geeks are so good at what they do that it scares me, and I make sure to know just enough about their work to scare them. Just enough so that they won't be able to convince me a project will take two months to complete when I know it can be done in three weeks. Over time, as they learn to trust me, they stop trying to fool me. I am also careful never to insist that geeks stay focused on a single project. It's the nature of how they work to be working on ten different things at once, some of which have nothing to do with any of their actual assignments. In fact, that's how the geeks at Tripod came to create our Homepage Builder, which empowered users to publish whatever they wanted on the Web. The Homepage Builder rapidly became our most important product and was the basis on which we sold Tripod to Lycos for $58 million.

No matter what type of organization you work in, if geeks and suits are working together, there must be trust in order for there to be productivity. *The Geek Gap* provides an excellent blueprint for building that all-important trust. Let Bill Pfleging and Minda Zetlin's book help show you how it's done.

Bo Peabody
Managing General Partner
Village Ventures
www.villageventures.com
Cofounder and ex–Chief Executive Officer of Tripod

FOREWORD

In 1994 I was a twenty-one-year-old graduate student at Rensselaer Polytechnic Institute in Troy, New York, spending roughly eighteen hours a day exploring the possibilities of a new technology called the World Wide Web, and the language it was written in, HTML. I got a phone call from a college friend, who asked me if I'd be interested in making some money developing a Web site for a new company starting up in Williamstown, Massachusetts, my college town. Being paid $18,000 a year to write HTML sounded like a better deal than paying $10,000 a year to study HTML. I said yes.

A few days later, I met my new boss, Bo Peabody. I disliked him immediately. Despite the fact that we were roughly the same age, from the same part of the country, and had graduated from the same college, we had nothing in common. We had different friends, different pastimes, different goals, different values. Despite the fact that he was wearing a baseball cap and rope sandals, he was a "suit." And while I'd just spent the past year in West Africa studying xylophone music, I was clearly a "geek."

Bo was building an online information service for college students, but didn't know a thing about computers. I took on the first task he gave me and spent several days building a complex, hyperlinked text mock-up of the site. When I presented it to him, he declared that I was "just another fraud" and threatened to fire me. He'd expected flashy animated graphics and got blue text on a white background—clearly I was taking him for a ride, like the geek he'd just fired, who had taken him for $50,000 without producing a usable line of code.

We didn't have the words for it, but we were beginning to explore the Geek Gap together. How could two people with so much common background misunderstand each other so badly? Why did Bo mistrust me—a nice guy—so much? Why did I dislike him—a nice guy—so profoundly?

Through countless late nights, early mornings, cases of Diet Coke and stacks of cold pizza, we developed a grudging respect for each other. I had no idea what the hell he was doing with those spreadsheets and endless phone calls, and he had no idea how many hours I spent turning piles of printed text into Web pages, but we could both see that the other was putting his whole heart into accomplishing . . . something.

Over time, I began to trust that, whatever Bo was doing, he was doing it uncommonly well, and I spent much of my time convincing the geeks who worked with me to trust him as well. Bo, for his part, let the inmates run the asylum—my programmers slept in the attic, worked barefoot and in pajamas, played Metallica at ear-shattering volumes as they coded . . . and generally felt like they were getting paid to do work they'd do for fun.

The trust that geeks and suits can develop for one another can get you through very tough times. A year into our work together, I dedicated much of my staff's time to developing a new technology platform for online conversation. It was revolutionary! Brilliant! Paradigm-shifting! And absolutely and totally incomprehensible to anyone other than the programmers building it. Bo tried valiantly to learn how the new tool worked, spending a dozen evenings by my side as I took him on a tour through the intricate online world my team was building.

Finally, one night he put his hand on my shoulder and said, "I'm so sorry. I can tell that what you're doing is really exciting and interesting. But I can't understand it, and I can't use it. And if I can't use it, I can't sell it." I got it. We killed the project and refocused on tools that made sense to the suits as well as to the geeks. And Bo moved another step closer to being one of my most trusted friends, his suit status aside.

A few months later, it became clear to me that one of these tools—a tool that let any user build a Web page on our server—was more popular than anything else we'd ever built. I made the crazy suggestion that we abandon the business we'd worked so hard to build and refocus around this new tool. And Bo made an amazing leap of faith, throwing out the business plan he and other suits had worked so hard on, to work on one based on a new idea from the geeks. That idea ended up being worth $58 million to Bo, me, and all the other suits and geeks who worked on it.

Not every Geek Gap gets bridged, and it's a rare suit who can sell that bridge for millions of dollars. But the problems Bo and I faced—the ones that almost caused me to quit and him to fire me—are the same ones Bill Pfleging and Minda Zetlin detail in this excellent book you're now reading. Indeed, more than a few come directly from Tripod, where Bill had a ringside seat for several key geek-and-suit dramas.

Bill and Minda have excellent practical advice for geeks and suits alike in recognizing Geek Gap issues and strategies for working through them. Most important, they identify the key ingredient—respect—that lets geeks and suits genuinely enjoy working together.

The Geek Gap can be bridged, and those bridges can take you places you can barely imagine. Let this book help you get there.

Ethan Zuckerman
Cofounder, Global Voices
www.globalvoicesonline.org
Research Fellow, Berkman Center for Internet and Society,
Harvard Law School
Former Vice President, Research and Development, Tripod

INTRODUCTION
THE ELEPHANT IN THE CORNER

This book is not about hidden problems. Everyone we've spoken to about the Geek Gap has vigorously nodded when we discuss the basic premise of the book: that poor communications between business and technology professionals is the root of a large percentage of costly failures in business. No, this problem is right out in the open.

We don't claim to be casting light on something no one else can see. We're just looking at what we all know to be true, only from a different perspective. Seeing the Geek Gap is a bit like looking at one of those Magic Eye 3-D pictures. You can't see it unless you look from the right distance, squint, and cross your eyes just so. Suddenly, it's clearly there, and you wonder why you didn't see it in the first place.

Whenever we're called on to describe the Geek Gap project, we use a variety of comparisons to help the listener understand the scope of the problem. But our favorite phrase, the "elephant in the corner," probably describes it best. Everyone knows it's there, but no one knows what to do about it, so no one talks about it. It's a generally recognized problem without an actual name. After discussing this issue with literally hundreds of business and technology professionals, we believe the Geek Gap is so embedded in the psyche of the business world that, to both workers and management, it is simply part of the landscape. The business world just negotiates around it, figuring into projects the probability of losses, difficulties, and delays caused by the lack of efficient communication between the technology workers and the rest of the company.

When we first thought of writing this book, we searched for any other books on this topic. We found books about the communication problems between lower-level employees and higher-level employees. There are books for managers about how to supervise technologists, and books for techies about how to create presentations that business people will understand. But none addresses the actual culprit behind many of these problems, the cultural clash between technology workers and business workers which we've dubbed the Geek Gap.

Why not? It's not that geeks and suits don't know they have trouble working together. Talk to either about the other and you'll hear a host of complaints. It's as if business people believe that the problems they have working with techies are like taxes or the common cold—something they dislike but must live with—and geeks believe the same about their business counterparts. But it doesn't have to be that way.

Once we began looking at the Gap from an outside perspective, we found that it can indeed be managed efficiently, by changing some assumptions and adopting different methods of interaction. Losses can be reduced, projects don't always have to run over budget or outright fail, and companies can in fact benefit from a better working relationship between business executives and technologists.

Think of this book as a wake-up call. The elephant in the corner is there. It costs businesses billions of dollars every year, and leads to failed projects, job frustration, and damaged careers. But it is possible to do something about it, to address the problem everyone has but no one ever names.

A Word about "geeks" and "suits": When we set out to write this book, we knew what to call technology people for short: "geeks," a term that was once pejorative, but has come to be worn with pride by techies, who know perfectly well they are different from everyone else. But we struggled to find an equally monosyllabic word for the geeks' counterpart—the business professionals.

After some trial-and-error, we settled on "suits." Though less common than "geeks," it has a more or less equivalent position as a slang term for business executives. Please note that we do not mean this term literally—any more than we literally mean geeks to be people who bite the heads off chickens, which is the dictionary definition of that term. In our usage, a suit is anyone whose orientation is business rather than technology. For instance, one of the authors considers herself a suit for the purposes of this book, but actually wears a business suit only a few times a year—which is quite enough for her.

CHAPTER 1

WHAT IS THE GEEK GAP?

A nutritionist had started a small but successful business selling all-natural supplements to doctors' offices, along with providing information on how best to use them. Taking the business online would be a natural way to expand, everyone agreed. And so, in 1999, with the dot-com revolution at its peak, he launched an online version of the company.

The concept was a success. Within a few months of the launch, the company had active discussion boards, with health-conscious computer users eagerly downloading nutrition articles, and this translated into healthy early sales.

So he hired a technology expert to build and maintain the new site. Almost from the beginning, there was tension between the two. The CEO's business was inspired by his own love of good nutrition and healthy living, a philosophy that permeated everything he did. He liked holding yoga classes in the company's common area during lunchtime, for instance, and once a month he'd host a vegan potluck for employees and their families. Most of the company's staff shared his nutrition-conscious background, and they loved the yoga and vegan food, sharing a common interest in health and nature. The technologist, however, never joined in the yoga classes, or cared to learn anything about using supplements to fight health problems. Most lunchtimes, he could be found at his desk, munching on potato chips and a tuna sandwich while reading *Computerworld*.

He did, however, know a lot about building a successful Web site, and he tried to teach some of what he knew to the CEO, discussing the pros and cons of different chat and message board software, or different ways of handling online shopping carts. The response tended to be, "Just make sure it works, that's all I need to know."

"Going into the CEO's office was an odd experience, considering he headed an Internet company," notes one former employee. "There were plants everywhere, and posters of the rain forest. All the furniture was natural wood and cotton. The only technological item was his laptop, which he kept open, sitting by itself on his conference table. And even that would be closed up and put away whenever he wasn't using it."

Within the company's first few months, the people who worked there began noticing strained relations between the techie and the boss. "Any time you saw them converse in the hallway they would both walk away rolling their eyes in disgust," recalls another former staffer. "If you went into either of their offices afterward, each one would go into a long complaint about the other. The tech expert would say the company was in serious trouble because the boss had no idea what technology it needed to survive, and the boss didn't want to learn about it. The CEO would complain that the technologist didn't know what it took to make a business profitable, and would happily spend money on all the latest hardware and software, with no regard to what the business needed and could afford."

Then came the company's first Christmas. The CEO received an animated holiday greeting in his e-mail. He thought it was charming, and forwarded a copy to each of the company's employees—thus infecting his entire staff with a computer virus. The techie sprang into action. Leaving his family to enjoy Christmas Eve without him, he managed to clear all traces of the virus out of the company's servers before any real harm was done.

Before he went home to a well-earned rest, he sent an e-mail out to the entire company. "With a lot of hard work, the virus appears to be out of our system," he wrote. "But it is imperative to avoid such mishaps in the future. That's why, from now on, no one is to download any material from Web sites or e-mail. If you feel you need a downloaded file in order to do your job, notify a member of the Information Technology staff and we'll take it from there."

Reading this e-mail, two days later, the CEO was furious. "What makes you think you can issue an edict without my permission?" he demanded.

"*I've* got a lot of nerve?" the technologist shot back. "I just spent Christmas Eve fixing a problem that never should have happened, and wouldn't have if you ever listened to your tech staff about how to use the Internet. Sending out that e-mail was the bare minimum required to keep our servers safe. And instead of thanking me, you're complaining about it!"

He stomped back to his office. The CEO said nothing, but a few days later sent an e-mail of his own to the entire company. "I've decided that the Internet is an inefficient way for me to communicate," he wrote. "As you know, I strive for simplicity in my life, and reading through hundreds of e-mails each day has worked against this. So I'm going to stop doing it. If you need to communicate with me, send a note or pick up the phone. These are my only forms of communication from now on."

The company's technology staff chuckled at the thought that the head of their Internet company was refusing to communicate online. But they had little to laugh about. They were more and more swamped with work, as late nights and working weekends became the norm. This was partly because the company's visibility was growing, and there was more traffic to the site every day. But the bigger factor was a series of new projects and initiatives they were ordered to create on a rush basis.

"It would happen like this," a former staffer says. "The techie and the CEO would be sitting in a strategy meeting, brainstorming new ideas. The techie would say something like, 'You know that database of vitamins and supplements with cross-referenced recommendations from prominent health experts? We could put access to that on the Web site so that customers could find the recommendations directly.'

"The CEO would say, 'Great idea! Go ahead.' And a few days later, he would send out a press release to all his media and nutrition contacts about how all this great information would be available on the site, and they should go there to check it out."

Meanwhile, the IT staff was still working out the security and integration problems involved in making what had been a proprietary corporate database available to the Internet at large. "Visitors would come to the site and click on the link for the database," the staffer recalls. "And it wouldn't work. It would hang up, or their search would yield no results. These were our regular, loyal customers and investors. It looked to them like we didn't know what we were doing."

The problem, he adds, is not that the CEO intended to make their lives harder. He thought, once he'd given the go-ahead, all it would take was a few mouse clicks to make the new database link a reality. He'd failed to learn how the technology worked, and his IT staff had failed to teach him.

With his employees overworked, the techie repeatedly requested funding to hire additional staff. "You don't understand," the CEO replied. "We can't just keep raising spending till the company goes into the ground. You'll just have to make do with what you have till we can turn revenues around."

The techie went away fuming, but the boss did indeed have his back against the wall. Funding for the company was running out. To make matters worse, though traffic at the site was up, actual sales revenues had never reached their projected levels and were now falling. How much of this was because the overworked tech staff couldn't make the site work the way it was supposed to? It's hard to say. But whatever the reason, the company was in serious trouble.

Over the next several months, everything unraveled. The site developed more and more glitches as, one by one, the overworked tech employees found other jobs and left. Sick of the constant need to fill vacancies and train new people while struggling with an overgrown workload, the head technologist left, too. After a few desperate attempts to branch out into health food recipes and nutrition counseling, the CEO was forced to face reality, and he shut down his company. It had been killed by changing economic times—but also by the inability of its corporate and technology leaders to communicate effectively or work together for the common good. That inability is what we call the Geek Gap.

"WHY CAN'T YOU MAKE YOURSELF CLEAR?"

Talk to any businessperson about the technology people he or she deals with, and you'll likely hear lots of frustration. Talk to any technology person about his or her business colleagues, and you'll hear the exact same sentiment. This schism was brought home to us a month or two ago when we attended a talk by a software developer, and he started the presentation by reading aloud a memo he'd received about accounting software he'd installed.

"'This is the kind of the thing that happens all the time,'" he read, his voice fairly dripping with aggravation. "'I ask the software to write a check to pay a receivable account. Then I need to void the check. When I write it again, all the information about the receivable account has disappeared!'"

"Here's my return memo," the developer said.

"'If this kind of thing happens all the time, why haven't I heard about it before now? What exactly do you mean when you say you "void" a check? If you're deleting the record and starting a new transaction, then of course account information from the previous transaction won't be there. What exactly did you do? What exactly did the software do? And why can't you make yourself clear when you ask these questions?'"

The solution, the developer concluded, is for the companies who buy his software to have their staff trained in how to use it so that they'll know exactly how it works and won't ask bonehead questions. After all, they're using it to run their business. The customer in question wasn't present, but if he had been, he probably would have said something like this: "We don't have the money and especially not the staff time to invest in a lengthy training process. After all, we're running a business."

And that's the whole problem. It's not just that business and technology people have different backgrounds, although they usually do. It's not just that they use different terminology, although they do that as well. It's not even that most business people have a limited understanding of how technology actually functions, and most technology people have a limited understanding of how a business actually functions—although that's a big stumbling block. It's that, on an even more fundamental level, geeks and suits each see what they do in a different light. They have different priorities, different agendas, different criteria for defining success, and different views of how the world works. And most of the time, they don't trust each other to have each other's best interests at heart.

The effects of the problem are far-reaching. The Geek Gap plagues companies large and small, high-tech and "old economy," in the United States and all over the world. It has cost businesses billions of dollars in wasted IT spending. It has contributed to the demise of many dot-com companies—as well as the boom-and-bust history of e-business in general. In short, the Geek Gap is an enormous problem.

$55 BILLION A YEAR

According to researchers at the Standish Group, only 34 percent of all IT projects in the United States are successful. The rest either fail completely or are "challenged"—that is, are seriously late, substantially over budget, or both. In total, they say, this cost American businesses about $55 billion in 2003, the last year for which figures are available.[1]

Chances are that most of those projects would not have failed—or would not have been started in the first place—had there been clearer communication between IT and business. And even that huge number doesn't tell the whole story because it doesn't include the thousands of projects that are completed but never used. These are successes from an IT standpoint (they're tested and they work), but failures in the larger view of business, either because they don't deliver what users need, or else because users never learn their benefits. These problems, too, could be avoided, through clearer communication.

Sometimes the cost is more than financial. The Geek Gap was a factor in at least one major national disaster—the explosion of the space shuttle *Challenger*. (The more recent explosion of the shuttle *Columbia* seems to us a different matter because it was caused by a fundamental design weakness with no obvious solution: the foam that insulates shuttles on reentry is vulnerable to damage from debris.) In the case of *Challenger*, there was a simple work-around: since the O-rings that sealed its rockets became brittle and ineffective in cold weather, NASA could simply have avoided launching on unusually cold days.

The *Challenger* launched on January 28, 1986, after a night when temperatures dipped into the twenties, a most unusual occurrence in Florida. The shuttle's solid rocket boosters, built by the company Morton Thiokol, were made in segments and sealed together by O-rings composed of fluorocarbon rubber. Each seal had two O-rings, one as a backup for added safety. Nevertheless, the rings turned brittle in the cold, both primary and backup failed, and the shuttle exploded seventy-three seconds into its flight.[2]

In the following weeks, disturbing reports emerged about the decision process that had led to the launch. It turned out Morton Thiokol engineers were well aware of the dangers of launching in cold weather. One of them was so sure it would be a "super colossal disaster" that he asked his adult daughter to watch the liftoff with him while he prayed. These engineers had done their level best to warn their bosses of the danger. Why hadn't anyone listened?[3]

When first researching the incident for possible inclusion in this book, we hoped to discover that something about the way the engineers communicated their concerns was too technical, too open to misinterpretation, or too arcane to be understood. But then we read some of their memos, and the message was all too clear, even to a lay reader.

For instance, Roger M. Boisjoly, a Morton Thiokol engineer later credited with blowing the whistle on the company, had conducted tests a few months earlier that showed the O-rings did not seal correctly at temperatures below 53°. "If the same scenario should occur in a field joint (and it could) then it is a jump ball as to the success or failure of the joint," he wrote. "The result would be a catastrophe of the highest order—loss of human life."[4]

Nothing ambiguous about that.

But one moment in the decision process was especially haunting. On the evening before the launch, Morton Thiokol and NASA executives met by conference call to make a final decision about whether to go ahead. A dozen Morton Thiokol engineers joined in the conference and unanimously called for delaying the launch. They spent hours explaining why launching in cold weather represented an unacceptable risk, backing up their position with test results and photographs of burning at the O-ring sites from what was then the shuttle's coldest-ever launch the previous January.

After the engineers spoke, the NASA officials purportedly expressed their outrage. They'd never been told before that night that cold might be a concern. The flight had already been delayed twice, and they were under enormous pressure not to postpone again. Though no one mentioned it, renewal of Morton Thiokol's contract was clearly at issue. Nonetheless, the NASA executives said, they would not launch without a formal go-ahead from Morton Thiokol.

At this point—nearing midnight—the Morton Thiokol executives asked for five minutes to confer privately, and pressed the mute button on their speakerphone. Of the four managers present, three were in favor of giving the go-ahead. The lone dissenter was Bob Lund, vice president of engineering. According to testimony, senior vice president Jerald Mason turned to him and said, "Take off your engineering hat, and put on your management hat." Lund gave in, and *Challenger*'s fate was decided.[5]

Whether or not this remark amounted to coercion was much discussed at the subsequent inquiry into the explosion.[6] Nobody questioned the underlying assumption, though, so let's question it now: *Why would changing from an engineer's viewpoint to a manager's viewpoint mean wanting two different things?* The notion that it did—so ingrained that it wasn't even worth mentioning—is the very essence of the Geek Gap.

However, there really must have been a communication problem between the managers and the engineers, because in this instance they did want the same thing. It is simply not possible that the Morton Thiokol executives could have wanted what happened. Even if they'd been callous enough to place their company's profitability ahead of the astronauts' lives, the explosion was a disaster for their company as well. It exposed them to billions of dollars in lawsuits, devastating publicity, and a federal investigation. The firm eventually split into Morton and Thiokol (later renamed Cordant Technologies, and later still, acquired by ALCOA). The executives themselves were reassigned or had to retire. If nothing else, recommending the launch was a terrible business decision.

So why did they do it? It must have been, in part, wishful thinking. Consider the awful choice these managers faced. Recommending against the launch would have brought down the wrath of NASA on their heads, exposed them to the charge that they weren't living up to their commitments, and would possibly cost them their livelihood and the survival of their company. As things turned out, they've been branded by many as monsters who put corporate profits ahead of both human lives and national honor. Clinging to the idea that the shuttle really was safe was their only hope of escape from this dilemma.

But to cling to that idea they had to disregard every word that the engineers said to them. How could they do that? Perhaps their thinking went something like this: "These engineers want everything to be perfect, and safety to be assured to an absolute certainty. They don't understand that in the real world of business, there are schedules to meet and customers to satisfy, and that if we don't do these things thousands of our employees will be out of work. So, while it's their job to lobby for absolute safety, it's our job to determine when they're going too far, and when something that may not be absolutely safe is still safe enough."

If that's what they believed, then telling Lund to think like a manager rather than an engineer makes perfect sense. And it was that thinking that prevented them from hearing what the engineers were trying to tell them: not that they wanted absolute certainty that the shuttle could fly safely, but that they knew to a near certainty that it couldn't. The managers' assumption that the engineers could not have Morton Thiokol's best interests at heart allowed them to make the decision that caused the catastrophe. That, too, has everything to do with the Geek Gap.

EVERY PROBLEM COMES DOWN TO THIS

We gradually became aware of the Geek Gap over years of writing articles on business and technology. It seemed every problem we were writing about came down to this: business and technology professionals have trouble communicating effectively with each other, which has led to a lack of both respect and trust between the two groups.

Business people complained to us that the technologists they worked with cared more about getting the "latest and greatest" software or device than about actually doing their jobs. Geeks responded that the business people had no respect for the technology and what it could do. Suits griped that technologists spoke gobbledygook and could not make themselves clear to mere mortals. Techies shot back that the business people couldn't be bothered to learn even the most basic elements of the systems their companies depended on, and that explaining these concepts to someone determined not to learn them was impossible.

Over and over, we heard frustration from both sides. When we mentioned to new acquaintances that we were writing about this topic, they often responded with a rueful laugh. "Yes, we have that problem where I work," they would say. Ultimately, we found, the Geek Gap came down to three basic issues:

1. *Geeks and suits don't communicate well.* It's often noted that technology people don't seem to speak the same language as everybody else. But there's much more to it than that. First of all, the lack of understanding goes both ways, and a programmer may be just as confused by someone talking about targeted marketing or accrual accounting. And it's not just that the terminology is unclear on both sides—it's also that the fundamental concepts and priorities may be at odds. If one person thinks that the most important task facing an organization is to stay up-to-date, so it doesn't get left behind in the modern world, and another person thinks the most important task is to minimize costs and maximize profits,

each may have a legitimate point of view, but each is starting from assumptions that may not make sense to the other.

2. *Geeks and suits don't respect each other.* This mutual lack of respect becomes painfully apparent whenever one spends any real time alone with either group. We once worked with an executive who referred to his company's IT person as "the technology weenie." He meant it kindly, but try to imagine a high-level manager saying "the marketing weenie" or "the finance weenie," and you begin to see the problem. Implicit in the term is the idea of expertise, but also that the expertise is in a trivial area, not of fundamental importance to anything. Then there's the insult implicit in the word "geek" itself, though technology people have proudly made it their own.

Technology people respect their business counterparts just as little. Consider their frequent references to the "pointy-haired boss." This is, of course, the boss from Scott Adams's comic strip *Dilbert*, a suit so heartless that he demands one subordinate work 178 hours a week (there are only 168 hours in a week), and so clueless about technology that when told he needs Unix programmers, he hears it as "eunuchs" instead.[7]

The programmer and essayist Paul Graham speaks for most geeks when he comments: "I think most people in the technology world not only recognize this cartoon character, but know the actual person in their company that he is modeled upon."[8]

3. *Technology people and business people don't trust each other.* This would be a natural enough result of the above two issues. But to make matters worse, business people and technology people today work together in a climate that seems almost deliberately created to foster suspicion on both sides.

First, the two groups typically work in different physical spaces with completely different atmospheres and norms. Most suits work in environments where décor and dress codes are designed to foster a serious working atmosphere and project a professional image to clients or other outsiders who may visit. There, they perform the "real" work of the organization. Most techies are relegated to separate areas, fulfilling a function none but they understand, and only find themselves in contact with their non-techie coworkers when something has gone wrong.

Then, the downsizings of the last few decades forever put to rest the notion of job security, or of giving one's allegiance to a company with the expectation that it would take care of you. In this new world of work, experts advised, job security came not from years of service to an employer, but from developing your own "skill set" to the utmost—taking an entrepreneurial approach to one's own career. Some technology people took this lesson fully to heart. Many reasoned that their best career strategy was to keep their skills as up-to-date as they could, whether or not this best served their employer's needs.

This makes sense from their point of view, but it gives some credibility to business people's complaint that technologists seek ever-newer systems and devices, and don't care what the company needs. For their part, they tend to see technologists as beings akin to witch doctors, performing strange, mystical operations that sometimes work and sometimes not, and about as deserving of their trust.

A PERSONAL VIEW OF THE GEEK GAP

The authors also encountered the Geek Gap in a very personal way. Bill and Minda met just before Christmas in 1995. Bill was a computer consultant, Internet community expert, and a dyed-in-the-wool geek. Minda was a professional freelance writer, business expert, and barely a technology user.

She had been using computers to write for over a decade, but was only on her second one. In fact, that's how they met. Her venerable laptop, which had accompanied her all over the world and even fallen down a flight stairs, finally acknowledged the limits of its indestructibility when she tripped over its power cord and it hit the floor hard and upside-down.

A friend recommended that Minda call Bill, who took the thing apart, tried in vain to repair it, then provided an equally outdated, and thus very cheap, replacement. After that, he gently set about coaxing Minda out of the backwater of command-line DOS (remember, it was 1995) and into the modern world of Windows and the World Wide Web. He also refused to be paid for his initial repair attempts, except by a dinner out. Which led to another dinner, and another, and another and eventually, marriage.

Meanwhile, the world of technology and the Internet was revving into overdrive. Dot-coms were blossoming in garages across America, while even the most old-fashioned corporate giants suddenly found they needed a Web presence. In this new world, Bill's Internet community expertise was a very valuable commodity. And so, for the first time since a brief stint at IBM in the 1970s, he found himself working in the corporate world.

Internet community takes place in chat rooms, message boards, e-mail lists, user reviews of products, and anyplace else where groups of people communicate directly online. While Bill knew his subject area well, he found the business issues that drove his company's decisions bewildering.

"They're talking about how community should pay for itself!" he lamented one day. Minda nodded, thinking that she'd often heard of companies seeking to make each of their departments prove their value by showing how they contributed to the bottom line. But the directive to analyze what he did and find how it could help profits drove Bill straight up the wall.

He would, of course, talk to Minda about these problems. Being a business writer, she would point out that the primary purpose of most businesses is to make money. He would respond that while that might be true, some business functions, such as customer service, were not direct profit centers but could still contribute to the overall good. Minda would retort that most customer service efforts were ultimately viewed as marketing efforts.

As they debated these issues, it struck them both that they were looking at them from completely different perspectives. One day, for instance, Bill came home in a fury because of a suggestion from one of his company's marketers. The company he worked for then was largely supported through advertising. Users who were looking at any of its pages or posting in its chat rooms and message boards were presented with ads across the top and along the sides of the window. The marketing person wanted the ads in the chat rooms to respond to the words people were using in chat. For instance, if somebody typed "vacation" or "Florida," an ad for Orlando might appear. Or, if someone typed "car," an ad for Ford might pop up.

Minda thought this was an interesting idea, and a good way to tap the Internet's enormous potential for matching sellers with buyers who might be interested in their products. Bill thought it was an outrage.

"It's a complete invasion of privacy!" he stormed.

"But they're planning it for public chat rooms, which aren't private," she countered.

"It's not the same thing," he said. "It's one thing to think that other people might join the chat room. But they don't expect that the company is listening in."

"Well, there won't be anyone actually listening in, will there? It's just software making note of the keywords they use."

"It's a terrible precedent. If they use it for that, they can use it for other things."

"Maybe, in theory. But no one's talking about using it for other things. And think how much more effective it'll make the advertising, and more useful for the people in the chat rooms, too: they'll be more likely to see an ad for something they might actually want."

They (or more accurately, we) argued for a long time, but never did agree. Slowly, we realized how completely differently we saw the exact same issue. That started us thinking more about what we would come to call the Geek Gap.

"Many companies, especially big ones, don't understand or care about technology," declares one disgruntled techie. "All they understand is cutting costs."

While this may not be a fair accusation, it is true that business managers often see technology as a means to an end, a very powerful tool that can do incredible things—but nothing more than that. They believe too many technology projects take on a life of their own, divorced from the needs of the users they were created for. They believe that business concerns should drive the use of technology, and not the other way around.

"Technology people get fascinated with 'the shiny object,'" one executive complains, and most business leaders would seem to agree. "They're not interested in the success of the business, they're only interested in technology for its own sake."

That's not fair either, at least not about most technology people—though there are some who really are interested only in the coolest new hardware or software. The majority do care about the success of the businesses they work for. But they see technology as not only a means to an end, but an art form in itself, with its own intrinsic value. They believe (as Bill's outrage illustrates) that technology has integrity of its own, and that it's wrong to misuse it. They believe in technology's power to reshape businesses, as the Internet has done and continues to do. They believe technology projects deserve, if not a life of their own, then a certain respect for their power and complexity. And that constantly altering them to suit the business priorities of the moment is a very bad idea.

Who's right and who's wrong? Both—and neither—just as both of us were right in the debate about the chat rooms, and at the same time neither of us was. The point is not to declare a winner in this struggle; the point is that as long as both sides are struggling, everyone loses.

At the company where Bill worked, the idea of tailoring ads to words used in chat rooms was quickly abandoned, in part because of his objections to it. No one explored alternatives that might have been more palatable. Perhaps it was the right thing to do, or perhaps a chance to make the business more financially viable was lost.

It's interesting to note that at the Internet community site RemarQ, software was put in place that turned certain keywords, which users typed in message boards, into links to advertisers' sites. That is, if you typed "eBay" that word might appear as a hyperlink when you posted it, and if someone clicked on it, it might take that person to the eBay site.[9]

Users were outraged. Imagine how you'd feel if you were writing an angry post about how annoyed you were by a company's bad service, and your complaint contained a link to that company's site, whether you wanted it there or not? The linking software was quickly removed, under howls of protest.[10] On the other hand, Google and other well-respected search engines routinely show advertising to users in direct response to the words they include in their e-mail without a peep of protest from anyone.

These situations are not precisely parallel. But the Google example shows that business and technology people can both meet their goals if they find the right ways to work together. And the RemarQ one shows how badly things can go wrong when they don't.

MORE DEPENDENT ON EACH OTHER

Finding the right way to work together will become more and more important over the next few years, as the Geek Gap becomes a larger issue for American businesses. Which it will, for several reasons.

As time goes by, business people are becoming more and more dependent on technology people, a trend which is, if anything, accelerating. The fate of dot-com companies and the prestige of the Internet itself may wax and wane, but all the while, e-commerce has continued to grow. According to the market research firm eMarketer, e-commerce spending was about $84.5 billion in 2005 and will reach $139 billion by 2008.[11]

At the same time, Corporate America's use of the Internet is growing. It's increasingly used for "mission critical" systems. These days, there's a trend toward the use of collaboration and/or "knowledge management" software that allows people in many different locations to share information freely, work on projects together, and pick each others' brains. All of this essential information flows back and forth over the Internet, on company intranets, and through various sorts of networks. Most companies would limp badly, or grind to a halt altogether, if the networks that kept them connected to each other and the world ceased to work. Whatever suits may think of techies, they need them, and most know they need them.

Meanwhile, technology people are more and more dependent on business people. The thinking which led to the boom-and-bust of the dot-com world of 1999 to 2001 can be stated as, "If you build it, they will come." Many dot-commers believed that anyone who could create a Web site sufficiently prominent and appealing for Web surfers to visit in meaningful numbers had done everything necessary to launch a successful business. Issues of cash flow, return on investment, and profitability were set aside during that heady time. For as long as venture capital money poured in and technology stock prices climbed, there was the illusion that these entities were making money.

When the bubble burst, many technology people found themselves at sea in a sink-or-swim business world where they suddenly had to prove how many dollars the technology that they wanted would earn for the company, or help it save. Not only did this require their learning new ways of looking at their jobs, but also learning a whole new language, and a whole new style of communication, in order to sell business people on what they wanted to do. This trend, too, will continue for the foreseeable future, as companies struggle to earn profits and save money wherever possible.

Even as this mutual dependence is growing, the number of technology people available to do the job is shrinking. Layoffs of recent years have cut IT staffs to a bare minimum, and they aren't over. The outplacement firm Challenger Gray & Christmas reported more than ninety-nine thousand high-tech jobs cut in the first six months of 2005 alone.[12]

This means that the remaining tech folk, who routinely work twelve-hour days and longer, will find themselves even more swamped with what technology author Ed Yourdon calls "death march" projects—that is, projects that must be completed to meet near-impossible deadlines, and which allow the geeks who work on them little time to sleep, let alone see their families.[13] Many techies see themselves today as overworked, underappreciated lackeys of corporations that couldn't care less about either them or technology. Ballooning workloads will only deepen this attitude.

With all these factors working to deepen the culture gap between business and technology people, the time to start doing something about it is now. Before the Mars and Venus books,[14] there were any number of books written for women about what was wrong with men and how to deal with them, and an (admittedly smaller) set of books for men about what was wrong with women and how to get along with them. John Gray's inspiration was to look at the problem from both sides at once, identify the areas where the two genders failed to communicate, and blame neither for the problem.

The same philosophy applies here. Whether you're a techie who's never understood what business people are thinking, or a business professional who knows what a market base is but not a database, you need a clearer view of how the other half operates and why they do the things they do. The purpose is not to find fault or to learn how to manipulate the other side into giving you what you want. The objective is to know what the other half needs so that you can fulfill those needs and wind up with a better, more effective working relationship. By doing so, you can help create a whole that is stronger than either of its parts.

CHAPTER 2

A BRIEF HISTORY OF THE GEEK GAP

Misunderstandings between those in technology and the people they work for have existed since well before the first computer, since even before Benjamin Franklin first experimented with electricity. At issue is not what technology does or how it works, but how it is perceived. Through the ages, geeks have investigated and learned, building ever new and better devices, to advance knowledge and technology. Meanwhile, their employers have concerned themselves only with the practical—and sometimes political—effect of new inventions or discoveries. Each group has been right, in its own way. Rarely has either understood the needs and values of the other, and often this has meant trouble for both.

In seventeenth-century Rome, Galileo Galilei was sentenced to spend his last years under house arrest for daring to publish a work suggesting that the Earth revolves around the sun. He was also forced to publicly retract what he'd written. It was a disaster for Galileo—a humiliating end to an illustrious career—but no less of a humiliation in the long run for the Catholic Church, which is still trying to live down this injustice more than three hundred years later, though it recently reversed its decision.

Ironically, as a teenager, Galileo was a novice in the Camaldolese Order, and might have lived out his life as a monk, except that his father forced him to leave—because he wanted Galileo to go to medical school instead.[1] But Galileo was an uber geek of his time, and though not interested in becoming a doctor, was firmly focused on such matters as the movement of pendulums and planets, the physics of falling objects, and the designing of ever more powerful telescopes.

Roman Catholic Church leaders in the seventeenth century functioned, to some degree, as managers who had oversight over Galileo's work, just as today's technology folk are overseen by company leaders with different views and priorities. Most significantly, while Galileo was focused only on the accuracy of his science and discovering the truth about the physical world, the Church leaders, much like today's suits, were also aware of different implications of his work. In their case, it was Church doctrine.

This is why, in 1616, when Galileo first argued that the Earth was moving, the Church felt the need to take up the matter in a formal court proceeding, known as an Inquisition. (The Roman Inquisition of the seventeenth century was much less ruthless than the infamous Spanish Inquisition of the fourteenth and fifteenth centuries.) The inquisitors decreed that Copernicus's sun-centered view of the universe was heresy, and Galileo was warned not to write or even talk about it.

But here begins one of the greatest technology/nontechnology misunderstandings in history, because a few years later, Maffeo Barberini was elected Pope Urban VIII. Barberini was an admirer of Galileo, and had made a show of defending the scientist's views on floating bodies against a powerful cardinal during a court dinner. The new pope had six audiences with the astronomer, and assured him that he *could* write about Copernican theory, as long as he made it clear that it was only hypothesis and not reality.[2]

Galileo did—but only sort of. In his *Dialogue Concerning the Two Chief World Systems* (1632), Simplicio and Salviati debate Ptolemy's view that the sun revolves around the Earth versus Copernicus's notion that things are the other way around. Both are just theories, but Copernicus's view is supported by many more scientific arguments and Simplicio, the Ptolemic supporter, comes off as, well, simple. Worse, Simplicio repeats some of the arguments that the pope had made to Galileo during their discussions of Copernican theory. And so, within months of its first printing, the *Dialogue* was banned, and Galileo was summoned to Rome to stand trial for what he'd written.

It's easy to imagine what the pope had in mind during his audiences with Galileo. He admired Galileo as a scientist and didn't want to constrain him from publishing his theories. At the same time, he could hardly encourage him to propound Copernican theory, which was heresy as a matter of Church law. Telling Galileo, with a wink and a nod, as it were, to write what he wanted as long as he called it hypothetical must have seemed like a reasonable compromise. Add to that the pension he bestowed on Galileo during the writing of the *Dialogue*, and you have to admit the pope gave Galileo the best deal he could offer. When he saw his own comments coming from Simplicio's mouth, he must have felt betrayed and outraged. This may be why Urban VIII resisted all subsequent proposals to pardon Galileo.

It's harder to guess what was going through Galileo's head. Later generations have sometimes seen him as a revolutionary. A rumor persists that he muttered "eppur si muove" (*and yet it moves*) after publicly recanting his work. But in fact, he spent most of his long career staying on the Church's good side, not to mention taking its money. It's possible he thought that, as a discussion between two debaters, the *Dialogue* fulfilled the letter, if not quite the spirit of the pope's instruction. Thus he might have expected it would not get him in trouble. He might have changed the *Dialogue* or skipped writing it altogether, had he realized what the consequences would be.

It's easy to cast the Church as arbitrary and tyrannical, which is also how many modern-day geeks view the management to whom they must report. Of course, the seventeenth-century Church *was* arbitrary and tyrannical; Giordano Bruno, another proponent of Copernican astronomy, had been burned at the stake in 1600 for his beliefs.

But this assessment misses the larger picture. While Galileo was focused only on persuading readers of the truth that the Earth moves around the sun, the Church was grappling with different implications of his theory. Late in the *Dialogue*, Simplicio asks Salviati to explain, if indeed there are vast empty spaces between Earth and the other planets and stars, what divine purpose they serve—why would God want them there?

Salviati's (and thus Galileo's) answer amounts to the idea that man should stop presuming himself to be the center of the universe. "It seems to me that we take too much upon ourselves, Simplicio, when we will have it that merely taking care of us is the adequate work of Divine wisdom and power," he says.[3]

It's hard to imagine a scarier proposition for priests and cardinals raised on the belief that the Old Testament description of the universe was literally true, and that Man himself—created in God's image—was the center of everything. No wonder they struggled so hard to contain and then refute this viewpoint.

THE BIG IDEA VERSUS THE REAL WORLD

Less than two hundred years later, the English mathematician Charles Babbage would prove himself to be centuries ahead of his time with his invention of the computer. That is, if drawing up the plans for something can qualify as inventing it. Actually building a computer turned out to be an insurmountable problem, thanks to some serious personality problems, and a worse-than-usual case of the Geek Gap.

In 1822 Babbage wrote to the British government, describing his idea for a "Difference Engine."[4] This device was intended to fix something that had long irked him: the high number of errors in mathematical and astronomical tables. In those days, more than a century before the arrival of mechanical calculators, scientists and mathematicians referred to written tables to find answers to complex calculations. (Think of these as similar to those printed sheets restaurants use to calculate tax.)

These tables had been created by hand—tedious, boring work. Since human error was inevitable, the tables were notoriously inaccurate. Babbage was sure a machine could do better. The Difference Engine that he envisioned would calculate and print more perfect mathematical tables by using a system of levers and dials.

In 1823 he was granted £1,500 to start work, so he and Joseph Clement, the engineer on the project, worked on it in Clement's workshop. By 1829 they had spent all the money but had not yet succeeded in building a working Difference Engine. Babbage was sure the government had promised more money if it was needed. The government had no recollection of any such promise. Babbage found himself financing the Difference Engine out of his own pocket.

That year, some of his friends persuaded the prime minister to give the Difference Engine another chance, and Babbage got £3,000 more. Instead of immediately completing the project, though, he spent his time and funds building a fireproof workshop in his house where work could proceed. But Clement refused to move it out of his own workshop. This was just one of many disputes between the two men, most of which centered on money. They never completed the Difference Engine.

Babbage seemed fairly unconcerned about the progress or lack thereof on the machine, however. He was too busy coming up with bigger plans. When work on the original Difference Engine bogged down, he simply began designing a better one. The earlier machine would have calculated polynomials to the sixth place; the new concept would have gone instead to twenty places.

In 1834 conflict between Babbage and Clement boiled over. Accusing Clement of extravagant demands, Babbage refused further payment to him. Clement responded by firing his crew and abandoning the project. With his work in ruins, Babbage again applied for help from the government—but not with the Difference Engine. Never mind the Difference Engine, he told them. He had thought of something a whole lot better: the Analytical Engine.

Whereas the Difference Engine was good only for making tables of polynomials for use in logarithms and trigonometry, the Analytical Engine would be able to answer any mathematical question put to it, he explained. Powered by steam and using punch cards (familiar to anyone who worked with computers in the 1970s), it was the first design for a programmable computer. Augusta Ada King, the Countess of Lovelace and daughter of the poet Lord Byron, actually understood Babbage's design, and wrote some programs for it, thus becoming, in a sense, the first computer programmer.

Babbage then urged the government to forget all about the Difference Engine, and fund his work on the Analytical Engine instead. But this displayed the complete disregard for real-world concerns that plagued Babbage throughout his life. By the time he proposed the Analytical Engine, Babbage had spent $17,000 of the government's money, and about an equal amount of his own on a project that he now wanted to throw in the trash.

The government, understandably enough, refused. Babbage was instructed to finish the Difference Engine before they would even discuss the next project.

Matters were at an impasse, and there they remained, pretty much, for the rest of Babbage's life. He never finished the Difference Engine, from which the government formally pulled the plug in 1842. He also never stopped asking for funding to build the Analytical Engine. Babbage went down in history as an eccentric figure worthy of ridicule. He never actually built any of his inventions.

Others, however, did. Swedish inventors Georg and Edvard Schuetz built the first Difference Engine in 1855, from Babbage's 1834 design. The British government even bought one four years later, which must have been galling, considering how much it had already paid Babbage for the exact same thing.

Babbage's failure to understand how the British government would respond to his endless requests for money was matched only by the government's failure to understand how to work with him. His government sponsors left him to carry out his project by working with a machinist who was under his direction, but this was a recipe for failure. What Babbage really needed was a partner, or even a manager, to keep him on schedule, force him to meet deadlines, and actually finish building an invention before moving on to the next. Whether such a person could have gotten along with the notoriously misanthropic Babbage is not certain. Nor is it clear whether even the most talented manager could have helped Babbage overcome his "people problems" long enough to save his inventions from abandonment and himself from obscurity. But at least he might have had a chance.

For years, historians believed that Babbage's work was moot—that Victorian-era manufacturing was not precise enough to build a working Difference Engine as he envisioned it. But they were proven wrong. In

1991 the London Science Museum built a machine from the plans for Babbage's Difference Engine No. 2, using only Victorian-era materials and manufacturing techniques. They tested it, and it worked perfectly.

This raises interesting questions about what might have been had Babbage avoided becoming a casualty of the Geek Gap. The author B. V. Bowden speculated that Babbage's decision to start designing the twenty-place Difference Engine, when he couldn't get the six-place one built, set back interest in his ideas by one hundred years.[5] If Bowden is right, then this one mistake dramatically altered the course of history. Because Babbage's next idea, the Analytical Engine, was nothing less than a prototype for the computers we all use today.

Imagine, for a moment, that Babbage had been more practical, more efficient, and better able to deal with the world around him. Imagine that he had finished his Difference Engine and shown the government how useful it could be. Then, when he proposed the Analytical Engine, the response might well have been an enthusiastic yes. What sort of world would we be living in today if the invention of computers had happened one hundred years earlier?

THE GENIUS AND THE MONEY MEN

The name Nikola Tesla is unfamiliar to many people today. For those who do know it, it conjures a vague image of a tall, highly eccentric foreigner, with a phobia of germs who staged strange demonstrations in which electricity crackled around him. All of this does indeed describe Tesla, but it tells only part of the story, and the smaller part, at that.

The bigger part is that when most people plug in any electrical device, from a pencil sharpener to a laptop computer, they're using something Tesla invented. If the device happens to be a radio, they're using two of his inventions instead of one. Of all the inventors who reshaped our world at the end of the nineteenth century, Tesla is the most unappreciated and least remembered. His story is a good illustration of what can happen, both good and bad, when inventive genius in one person collides with financial prowess in another.

Tesla, a Serb born in Austria-Hungary, arrived in New York in 1884 with almost no money. He however had a big idea about the benefits of alternating current, and a letter of introduction to Thomas Edison, whose direct current (DC) electricity was all the rage at the time.[6] (Though history knows Edison as an inventor, and he might thus be considered a geek, it was his skills as a businessman that led to his immense success.) Tesla showed Edison his plans for AC power. But Edison was already perched atop a hugely successful business that had been built entirely on DC power. Edison could see great potential expense and no particular benefit in switching it all over to AC.

Instead, he hired Tesla to make improvements to his existing generators, and promised the inventor $50,000 if he succeeded. Now, $50,000 in 1885 was worth more than $1 million today, and a modern-day geek told by his or her boss, "I'll give you a million dollars if you can fix this," might or might not take that statement seriously. Whatever the intent, Tesla took this as a literal offer and spent a year designing twenty-four new standard machines that were used throughout Edison's plants. Then he went to claim his money, and was outraged to be told the promise had been intended as a joke.

"When you become a full-fledged American, you will appreciate an American joke," Edison reportedly answered. A more sophisticated geek of today might have considered hiring a lawyer, or at least trying to negotiate some sort of bonus commensurate with the immense benefits his work had created. But Tesla, showing the same degree of financial good sense he would display throughout his career, quit in a huff instead.

Soon afterward, a group of investors offered to finance Tesla if he could invent a better arc light. They gave him the chance to start a company in his own name. He set to work, and the resulting light was put into immediate use for factory and municipal lighting. But—in a deal that may seem familiar to anyone employed in the dot-com industry at the end of the 1990s—Tesla was compensated for his patents not in money or royalties, but in stock certificates with potential but no actual value. He spent the following year digging ditches and laying stones.

Things were about to get better, however. A. K. Brown of the Western Union Telegraph Company offered Tesla the chance to develop AC current in a laboratory of his own. In Tesla's case, "developing" something merely meant building the functioning model that had existed for years in his brain, so it didn't take long for him to produce the first AC motor, which he then demonstrated to a great reception.

Tesla's alternating current attracted the attention of George Westinghouse, an industrialist and Edison's rival in the race to bring electricity to market. Westinghouse believed—correctly—that AC could be instrumental in facilitating long-distance transmission of electricity. He paid Tesla $60,000 for his patents, but in the form of $5,000 cash and 150 shares of Westinghouse Corporation stock. He also agreed to pay a royalty of $2.50 for every horsepower of electricity Westinghouse sold. Tesla used much of this money to build himself the lab he had wanted, and set about creating machines for large-scale production of AC.

Thus began the "current war," a long and vicious battle between Edison's DC and Tesla's Westinghouse-backed AC for dominance of the electricity market. Edison did everything he could to make the public think AC was more dangerous than DC—though this was the opposite of the truth. He hired Professor Harold Brown who did awful demonstrations electrocuting dogs and elderly horses—and even one unfortunate ax murderer—to prove the horrors of AC. (William Kemmler, a convicted ax murderer, died horribly on August 6, 1890, in "an awful spectacle, far worse than hanging." The technique was later dubbed "Westing-housing.")[7]

But such stunts couldn't overcome basic economics: AC was simply much less expensive. This became evident when the two companies bid against each other to bring electric lighting to the 1893 World's Fair, called the Columbian Exposition, in Chicago. General Electric (which had taken over Edison's company) bid $1 million for the job, in part because DC current required a huge amount of copper wire to use. AC didn't, and Westinghouse's bid was about half that amount.

Needless to say, Westinghouse and Tesla won the contract and when the exposition opened, hundreds of thousands of lights illuminated the fairground's graceful buildings. High-frequency, high-voltage lighting as designed by Tesla produced brighter, more efficient light with less heat than General Electric's Edison lamps. Tesla also displayed another of his inventions: phosphorescent lighting powered without wires by high-frequency fields, the precursor to present-day fluorescent lights. Some twenty-seven million visitors attended the fair that year, and by the time it was over, the future of electric current was decided. AC had won.

The partnership flourished, and Tesla and Westinghouse went on to harness the power of Niagara Falls later that year. But there was trouble ahead. The financier J. P. Morgan, who dreamed of dominating the lucrative new world of electricity, began manipulating stock prices in an attempt to corner Westinghouse in a takeover. Drained by the DC versus AC war, Westinghouse Corporation's finances were in disrepair and its investors insisted George Westinghouse do something about it. What he did was appeal to Tesla for relief from the royalty payments promised him. "Your decision determines the fate of the Westinghouse Company," Westinghouse reportedly said.[8]

The inventor's response was vintage Tesla: impulsive, flamboyant, and financially suicidal. Tesla tore up his contract with Westinghouse and declared him free of royalty obligations from then on. "You have always been my friend," he told Westinghouse. "You will save your company so that you can develop my inventions."[9]

Noble and selfless, to be sure. But was this over-the-top reaction really necessary? Westinghouse's company survives to this day—clearly, its financial troubles were only temporary. Why couldn't Tesla have come back with an equally temporary response? He could have deferred the royalty payments for a time. Or he could have tied them to the company's success, receiving payment only after it became solidly profitable. He could have negotiated a reduction in his royalties. There were probably hundreds of solutions that would have allowed the company to survive without meaning ruin for the inventor, but Tesla evidently didn't suggest any of them.

Maybe he didn't know any better. Tesla had arrived in the United States with no money at all. He'd had to resort to building sidewalks for a living. He also came from an Old World society, where intellectuals were not supposed to sully their hands with money dealings. So it's quite possible he lacked the sophistication for a complex business negotiation.

But Westinghouse did not. He had all the smarts to see the enormity of what Tesla was giving up. And, he was supposed to be Tesla's friend. Why didn't he suggest a more equitable solution to the crisis, one that would let him save his company without depriving Tesla of money he both needed and had earned?

Perhaps part of the reason was the era they lived in, when robber barons ruled and fair play was a rarity in the business world. Or perhaps the pressures from his investors left him little choice. A century later, it's hard to know, but the questions this incident raises go right to the heart of the Geek Gap. Did Westinghouse betray Tesla's friendship by letting him tear up the contract? Or did Tesla, who was working in the business world, bear some responsibility for understanding it? In any case, Westinghouse kept the royalty money, and Tesla struggled with poverty for the rest of his life.

Tesla's next big idea was for transmitting electricity wirelessly, much as radio waves are transmitted today. He never quite had enough money, though, to give it a proper try. He worked on the experiment for a while in Colorado Springs, where he believed the thinner air would make transmitting electricity easier—and there are some reports that he succeeded, wirelessly lighting vacuum tubes at Pikes Peak from several miles away. On the other hand, this apparent success might have been an effect of the highly conductive ground in that area.

Tesla returned to New York, where J. P. Morgan offered him $150,000 to build a transmission tower for radio signals and a power plant. Tesla took the money and then set about building a tower for transmitting electricity. But even in 1901, the sum Morgan had provided was not enough to finish the giant tower that Tesla envisioned. Meanwhile, word came that Guglielmo Marconi had succeeded in transmitting the letter S across the Atlantic, though Tesla said Marconi used seventeen of his patented concepts in doing so. Morgan refused to give Tesla further funding, and in 1905, the inventor had to abandon his experiment for want of other investors.

Tesla always insisted that the transmission of electricity was possible, though, and that the solution existed as clearly within his brain as the alternating current motor had years before. "It is not a dream," he wrote. "It is a simple feat of electrical engineering, only expensive."[10] What if he was right? Imagine a world in which you could set any device from a personal computer to a desk lamp down on a table and switch it on without bothering with power cords and outlets. Where laptops and cell phones never fail for lack of battery power. Where batteries are obsolete because devices from pocket cameras to children's toys could receive their power wirelessly. Could this have happened? We'll never really know.

Tesla continued to generate interesting ideas throughout the rest of his long life, and when he died in 1943, Yugoslavian and American government officials converged on his hotel room, hoping to get their hands on his notes. A few months later, the Supreme Court finally upheld his patents on radio transmission technology, voiding Marconi's claims.

THE SCIENTIST AND THE GENERAL

In August 1939 Albert Einstein sent a letter to President Franklin D. Roosevelt, urging the US government to fund research for building an atomic bomb—and in particular, to secure uranium for this purpose—before the Nazi government did it first. Einstein wrote the letter at the urging of Leó Szilárd, a Hungarian-born scientist who had been Einstein's student at the University of Berlin, and then collaborated with him on various projects, including the Einstein-Szilárd refrigerator. Indeed, the letter had been drafted with Szilárd's help.[11] Though he is relatively unknown, especially compared with his colleagues Einstein, Oppenheimer, and Fermi, it was Szilárd who first envisioned that a neutron chain reaction could produce atomic energy and/or atomic explosions.

The government eventually provided the $6,000 the scientists needed to get started, and Szilárd went to work, along with Fermi and the physicist Herbert Anderson, trying to make the first chain reaction a reality. Now that their research was part of a military project, they found themselves under the watchful eye of a military that found Szilárd—who had emigrated from Germany—particularly untrustworthy.

But Szilárd, who was Jewish, had left Germany precisely because he recognized as early as 1933 the threat that the Nazis posed, and indeed predicted they would one day rule Europe. He was determined that the United States should develop an atomic bomb as quickly as possible. He knew that the threat of atomic retaliation would prevent the Germans from launching an atomic attack against the United States if they managed to build one of their own.[12] So he led his fellow scientists in a movement to build the bomb, insisting on utmost secrecy in the hope that his group could beat out its German counterparts and build the first one.

There's a common complaint that technologists develop a kind of tunnel vision—they focus only on their own projects and fail to comprehend the bigger picture. But Szilárd was the precise opposite. A man of incomprehensible genius, Szilárd, who had no medical training, would in later years cure his own bladder cancer, by rejecting the treatments offered by doctors and designing his own radiation therapy instead. And, though he was very much a geek, he was uniquely able to foresee the long-term results of both his actions and the events unfolding around him. Thus, Szilárd held the then unique view that the greatest use of a nuclear weapon was *not* to detonate it, but to use it instead as a deterrent, much as the United States and Soviet Union would later do throughout the cold war.

In fact, Szilárd foresaw the cold war itself: he predicted that an escalation of building ever greater weapons of mass destruction between the United States and the USSR would inevitably result, if the United States actually used its atomic bomb on an actual wartime target.[13] This is one argument he used again and again against their use. He believed the bombs should be used only as demonstrations of the destructive power that such weaponry could unleash.

After Germany surrendered in 1945, Szilárd began a concerted lobbying effort to dissuade first Roosevelt and then Truman from dropping the bomb on Japan. He sent a petition, signed by sixty or so of his colleagues on the Manhattan Project, through official channels to the president. He realized it would do little good, but wanted the scientists' views to be part of the historical record.

Part of the problem is that Szilárd was trapped by the role he'd been assigned. He was supposed to be a geeky scientist working to solve a complex physics problem, and the bosses he reported to could not or would not see that he was also a world traveler with an uncanny sense of how global conflicts would play out over time. They wanted him to do the science and not interfere in issues of foreign policy—which makes sense, if you think about it. He'd been hired as a scientist; if they'd been looking for an ethicist or a military strategist, they would doubtless have chosen someone else.

A bigger part of the problem was that from the beginning, Szilárd locked horns with Gen. Leslie Groves, who oversaw the Manhattan Project. Groves was a notorious autocrat and hated by many who worked for him. Szilárd had little use for military ways, so the two were bound to come into conflict—and they did, from the very first time they met. At their initial meeting, which included several key scientists in the Chicago portion of the project, Szilárd publicly corrected the general's mistakes when discussing the technology, and otherwise made clear his disdain for Groves's limited grasp of science.

Things went from bad to worse when Groves explained that communications among scientists on the project would have to be strictly controlled. This was, no doubt, a perfectly normal step to take on a project whose secrecy was of such paramount importance—or so it must have seemed to Groves. To Szilárd, it was an outrage. He'd known these scientists, in some cases for years, and they all were accustomed to working together in an informal brotherhood that disregarded boundaries among their various specialties. Besides, the secret bomb designs that Groves was trying to protect existed primarily in Szilárd's mind, and his colleagues were the only ones who could remotely understand what he was thinking about. As soon as Groves left, he exclaimed to his colleagues, "How can we work with people like that?"[14]

To a decorated general whose career had been a long list of triumphs, Szilárd's behavior must have seemed like the rankest insubordination. Groves tried to fire him right away, but was told by his superiors that Szilárd was popular among his fellow scientists and his dismissal might lead to general revolt. He remained Szilárd's sworn enemy, however.

When he discovered Szilárd had had the gall to circulate his antibombing petition, an infuriated Groves actually began writing to his military colleagues, looking for any evidence that could show that Szilárd had discussed anything top secret with any of his colleagues outside the

Manhattan Project. Had he found such evidence, he could have had Szilárd jailed under the Espionage Act, but he could never find anyone to say the scientist had ever revealed anything he shouldn't. The whole exercise was absurd to begin with, since it was Szilárd himself who first brought the idea of an atom bomb to the US government, and that he himself had urged secrecy from the start.

But even if Groves couldn't find a way to throw him in jail, antagonizing the general cost Szilárd throughout the rest of his career. According to William Lanouette, coauthor of the Szilárd biography *Genius in the Shadows*,[15] Groves arranged to have all commendations taken away from Szilárd, and prevented him from working in government nuclear research after the Manhattan Project. Since there was no nongovernmental nuclear research, this meant Szilárd was barred from his chosen profession, one that he had helped to create. Even after Szilárd's death in 1964, Groves was still at it, contacting encyclopedias to recommend that they shorten their entries on the scientist, who, he claimed, was only a minor figure in the A-bomb's development.[16] And it worked. Today Szilárd is most often mentioned only in passing in historical works about the period, which is why he is far less known than the others who helped create the bomb.

As for Szilárd, he told a *U.S. News & World Report* interviewer in 1960 that the world might have been a very different place, if only he'd been able to get someone in power to listen. "I think, if we had not dropped the bomb on Hiroshima and instead demonstrated the bomb after the war, then, if we had really wanted to rid the world of atomic bombs, I think we could probably have done it," he said.[17]

It's hard to envision a world without stockpiles of nuclear weapons, one in which all nations had agreed not to develop these weapons before the arms race ever got started. From today's perspective, the whole thing seems unlikely. On the other hand, Szilárd was right about so many of his predictions. Maybe he would have been right about this one as well.

Szilárd's story is also an illustration of how badly things can go wrong when technologists lock horns with those who employ them. Szilárd was highly unusual in having a broad view of international relations, and how the countries of Europe would interact in the decades after the war. But, in other ways, he was a stereotypical geek. He was brilliant in physics, but inept at everyday tasks, and, in particular, short on social graces. Where someone else might have worked to find a way to ingratiate himself with a new boss, or at least arrive at an amicable working relationship, Szilárd alienated Groves, and shut himself out of any political power, not to mention future employment, in the process.

For his part, Groves behaved like the worst of all possible managers, imposing rules without understanding how the technologists he was overseeing actually worked. Though Szilárd's conduct must have seemed galling from his viewpoint, another man might have summoned the maturity to see that he could not expect atomic physicists to behave like well-trained soldiers. Banishing Szilárd served only to hurt the country he had sworn to defend, since the government thus lost the services of one of its most imaginative scientists. In the end everyone lost, and the loss was entirely due to the Geek Gap.

CHAPTER 3
GEEKS GAIN LEGITIMACY

G eeks like Leo Szilárd were trapped in the roles assigned to them: they were supposed to be scientists and technologists, not high-level managers. It was considered inappropriate for them to take a hand in making policy. (Oppenheimer was an exception, but his leadership role in the Manhattan Project was highly unusual for a scientist.) But attitudes eventually began to change. As computers and technology became more and more integral to the functioning of businesses, governments, and all types of organizations, the roles of the people who understood that technology evolved as well.

Twelve years after World War II, the 1957 movie *Desk Set* offered some insight into the changing perceptions of technology as well as its place in the workplace. Spencer Tracy, trying his best to appear geeklike, plays Richard Sumner, a technology expert who arrives to install a room-sized computer in the office where Katharine Hepburn heads the research department. By this time, technology and technologists have taken on a status of their own: the big boss actually offers Sumner a corner office, which he cheerfully refuses.

When, later in the film, it appears Hepburn and her coworkers have been let go—presumably to be replaced by Sumner's computer—he calls the boss to shout, "You broke a promise to me!" Apparently this geek has enough authority to tell the CEO whom he can and can't fire.

The firings, of course, turn out to be an error by the computer Sumner has installed in payroll. In the world of this film, a computer can apparently replace a department full of people, but can't print paychecks without accidentally firing everyone. The geek who created it can't be bothered to wear matching socks and needs a woman's hairpin to fix things when the machine goes haywire. Still, he's entitled to a corner office and to treat the big boss as an equal. It's a perfect snapshot of the evolving perception of technology and technologists in the late 1950s.

Throughout the 1950s and 1960s, one of the biggest private-sector workplaces for technologists was IBM. The international business machines that gave the blue-chip giant its name referred originally to such items as typewriters and adding machines. As the company made its transition to computers, it also created a separate class of pure technologists—programmers and engineers who were on the cutting edge of that time's technology, as they often are today.

Throughout its history, Big Blue has been a suit-oriented company. Its leadership has mostly consisted of executives who started out in sales and who, for the most part, cheerfully wore the company's blue-suit-white-shirt-and-tie uniform and bought homes at subsidized mortgage rates in IBM-approved neighborhoods.

But, especially as the 1960s arrived, these "Beemers" formed a stark contrast to the growing cadre of geeks working, often in secret, on the company's computers and technology products. These were mostly offbeat types who found their own creative ways of following IBM's white-shirt-and-tie dress code—one fellow we came across, for instance, wore a white shirt and bolo tie to work. This group loved both inventing and playing early versions of computer games.

How did these two groups interact? For the most part, they didn't. Many of the geeks actually chose to work overnight shifts to minimize their contact with the company's business executives. And many of the suits appeared to view the geeks with disdain.

"The first thing to know about geeks is that they can't write," one retired IBM suit told us of the relationship. "The second thing to know about geeks is they can't spell." What's more, in his view, most of them were no good as managers because they could relate only to science, not people.

"I knew one instance where someone's house burned down and he called and left a message for his engineer boss, saying his house had burned down. He didn't come in to work for several days, and when he did come in, the manager wanted to know where he'd been.

"He said, 'My house burned down! I had to find a place to live, and I had a few other things to do!' The manager said, 'You should have explained it better.' How much should you have to explain that when your house burns down you might miss a few days' work?"

Still, IBM management had the good sense to know that it was growing increasingly dependent on technology—and the people who created it—for the company's continued success. "Marketing was very high on T. J. Watson Senior's list," the retired IBMer says (T. J. Watson was IBM's founder). "It was also high on T. J. Watson Junior's list. However, Junior could see there was a technical revolution coming down the pike and he needed engineers just as much as he needed salesmen."

So Watson Jr. created a whole separate hierarchy for the company's technical people. It was similar to the Marine Corps within the Navy—a group with its own agenda, traditions, and marching orders—but no less important. They both served the same ultimate goal, yet had very limited contact and even less trust between them.

To reward these separate-but-equal geeks, Watson Jr. created the IBM Fellows—specially recognized engineers who had demonstrated both past and future value to the company and were bestowed with a great deal of status and autonomy. An IBM Fellow retained that designation throughout his or her tenure at IBM, and would become an IBM Fellow Emeritus upon retiring. Appointed by the CEO, only a few were chosen every year, and becoming a fellow was the highest technical achievement possible at Big Blue.

The company is careful to phrase it that way: "the highest technical achievement" at IBM—not "the highest achievement possible for a technical person." But there is some truth to the second version as well. IBM has had eight CEOs throughout its ninety-two-year history and although IBM is a technology company, not one of them rose to the post via a technological career. With one notable exception, all of them started out in IBM sales or marketing. Even Watson Jr., who followed his father's lead, first worked for the company as a salesman in one of its Manhattan offices.

The exception is Louis Gerstner Jr., CEO from 1993 to 2002, who is widely credited with turning IBM around from moribund giant when he took over to an industry powerhouse by the time he retired. But this is an exception that very much proves the rule—the rule being that it's more important to understand business than technology when running a giant high-tech corporation. Gerstner did not come up through IBM's sales organization, but he didn't come from its engineering side, either. Indeed, his background in technology was nil. Before running IBM, he'd been CEO of RJR Nabisco, and his earlier career was at American Express and the consulting firm McKinsey & Co.

Sam Palmisano, the current CEO, is widely praised for his knowledge of technology and the fact that he actually understands the products and services his company offers. But he arrived at Big Blue with a degree in behavioral sciences and started out as a sales rep in the company's Baltimore office. As for ambitious technologists, they still have the IBM Fellows program, which remains mostly unchanged to this day.

GLASS HOUSES

Meanwhile, through the 1960s and 1970s, more and more companies were finding that, to run effectively, they had to have computers, and thus needed some technology people in-house. At first, these computer technicians were relegated to strange and unknown areas where computers the size of the average living room chugged away in solitary splendor in chilly and immaculate rooms. These were called "glass houses" because they were surrounded by windows so operators could see what was going on inside.

Computers in those days were used almost exclusively to support their companies' financial operations. Though ready access to computer-ized financial data provided a powerful tool for these money people, the technologists who ran the computers were anything but high profile.

"In the 60s and first half of the 70s, we were DP [data processing] managers. We worked for the controller and did all the back-office stuff. Nobody in the company even knew where we were," said Charlie Feld, executive vice president of portfolio management at the IT consultancy EDS.[1]

Then, in the 1980s, desktop computers began making an appearance, often followed by a lone and harried-looking geek who would try his best (it was almost always a he) to keep them all running smoothly, no matter what foolish things the users did to them. In terms of status, these folk were about on a par with the copier repair guy. And many companies rated them even lower.

Sometime around the mid-1980s, a woman, whom we know, worked at the headquarters office of a Fortune 500 company. She had started out there as a secretary. Over ten years, she had worked her way to a job as the company's office manager, primarily because she was exceptionally organized and had a flare for interior decorating. Her domain included choosing carpet colors, overseeing office moves, and dealing with the phone company. She had no technological training whatever, yet it fell to her to purchase and deploy the company's first desktop computers. Of course, they would be delivered not to the top executives, who viewed all typing with disdain, but to their secretaries, most of whom had never seen a personal computer—or any computer—in their lives.

A popular acronym among today's geeks is RTFM, which stands for "Read the Fucking Manual!" The secretaries in our friend's company would have no other choice. In those days before help desks and on-site training, they likely were on their own, and there was certainly no one in the office manager's department who could provide expert help. Luckily for them, the computers were mainly used for word processing—simple, secretarial tasks—so the users could usually find their own way without much trouble, and could always go back to typewriters if necessary.

Things got more interesting over the next few years, as computers came to occupy a more essential role in the workplace. There were also more of them. As desktop computers became affordable, more and more employees found themselves working on one. Part of the reason for the computers' rising popularity was the advent of point-and-click Graphic User Interface (GUI) technology. This innovation helped lessen the stigma of using a keyboard for those who wanted to make sure nothing they did smacked of clerical work. We remember running across an early tutorial that explained how to write an entire letter without touching a single key, using the mouse to cut-and-paste letters and words. Sounds silly, but it probably helped many an executive and aspiring executive get over the mind-set that only pink-collar workers use keyboards.

It's hard to remember, from a twenty-first-century perspective, how valuable computers were even before the Internet became widely available, but up through the late 1980s and early 1990s, users were generating reports, working with databases, and creating spreadsheets on them. These desktops were also linked through an in-house client-server system that allowed multiple workstations access to the same software and databases, as well as in-house e-mailing and messaging. Suddenly, computers were no longer replaceable by typewriters, and it really did matter if they stopped working. Companies began assembling technology staff, and thus a new career path was born.

By this time, DP had long ago morphed into MIS (management information systems) and some large companies were starting to add CIOs (chief information officers) to their list of "C-level" executives.

"The first time the title CIO was used anywhere was in 1980," said Paul Strassmann, special assistant to the administrator for information management at NASA.[2] "Bill Synnott was then the head of management information systems at the Bank of Boston where the CFO had complete control over IBM mainframes. When loan officers arranged to get their own DEC (Digital Equipment Corporation) minicomputers they needed somebody to legitimize their acquisitions. They got Bill Synnott promoted to the same level as the CFO and anointed him with the title of CIO for better effect. This is an example of how information politics influences the careers of information technologists." Suddenly, those nerdy guys everyone looked down on in high school could start aspiring to corner offices.

CODING WELL IS THE BEST REVENGE

Things were starting to look up for geeks, but the new marriage between technology and business was shaky at best, and about to get a lot shakier. When the Internet began gaining popularity in the mid-1990s, it became painfully apparent just how different the worlds inhabited by geeks and suits really were.

In 1995 Rod Fournier had just completed a project for his employer Kmart Corp. He had proved that the same computer that handled cash register sales and stocking could run the company's shipping and receiving system. This saved Kmart millions of dollars, but eliminated his own job in the process. The company decided to reward him with a plum assignment: designing its new corporate home page. His qualifications for doing so were that he'd built a personal Web site, with pages describing himself and his work and showing pictures of his family and pets.

Today, no matter how good a job he'd done, a system architect with one personal site to his credit would never be given the task of designing a Web site for a major corporation. It's simply too central to corporate identity to be left to an amateur. The job would likely be given to a reputable Web design firm, after a careful review of several proposals from different competitors. Such firms existed in 1995, though they were certainly fewer and less sophisticated. But Kmart didn't use one because management had not yet begun taking the World Wide Web seriously. It was a lesson they were about to learn the hard way.

As for Fournier, he went off and created a home page for Kmart. At first it seemed fine. "Everything we did was approved by a committee," he says.[3] He also included a link to his personal home page concealed in a period on the site. He claims that this, too, was approved by the committee, and that he explained it was usual for a Web site to include a link to information about its builder.

Kmart claims it was a violation of corporate policy to link its site to a personal site at all.[4] At the heart of the issue was a single page on Fournier's home site. Preceded by promises of salacious content to be viewed there, visitors who clicked that link found what appeared to be a sexually explicit picture mostly obscured by a large black square on which *CENSORED* was written in big red letters. Whether this was offensive or not is a matter of opinion, but it certainly wasn't in keeping with the corporate image that Kmart sought to convey. When the link to that page was discovered, Kmart shut down its Web site and fired Fournier.

What happened next is legendary. Fournier went home and created a page titled "Kmart Sucks,"[5] which recounted his firing and invited others to post their own gripes about the chain. "Kmart sucks!" is a line from the 1988 movie *Rain Man*, in which Dustin Hoffman plays an autistic man, and Tom Cruise plays his brother who, among other things, upgrades Hoffman's wardrobe from Kmart casual to a snazzy suit. The retail giant had lived down the movie, and here the phrase was back again to haunt it.

Unfortunately for Kmart, when it fired Fournier, it lost its employee who best understood the Internet, so he was able to register Kmart Sucks with search engines so that it came up ahead of the company site created to replace his. After the company complained that the K in his "Kmart Sucks" logo looked too much like its own K, Fournier switched the name of the site to "The Mart Sucks." And there it remained, unchanged, for years, a David-and-Goliath symbol to anyone who felt mistreated by a giant corporation, and a warning to business managers that they ignore the Web at their own peril.

Looking back, Fournier and Kmart both said the other should have known better. Kmart representatives stressed that its no-links-to-personal-sites policy had been in place for about six months before Fournier was asked to build Kmart's site, and that he was informed of it before he started. Besides, they felt it should have been obvious to anyone working in business that linking a family-oriented company's Web site to anything with even a whiff of sexuality would be unacceptable.[6]

Fournier countered that it is common practice for a Webmaster to include a link from the sites he builds to his own home page—and anyhow, he contended that the executives who approved his work knew that the link was there. Besides, he felt it should be obvious to anyone working on the Internet that everything links to everything else, informality and humor are the norm, and users can easily distinguish between the online identity of a large corporation and the personal Web site of the guy who built it.[7] In the end, it was a lose-lose situation: Fournier lost a job at a time when his wife was eight-and-a-half months pregnant, and Kmart suffered a public humiliation that took years to die away.

Kmart was far from the only company to suffer in the 1990s for not realizing soon enough the potential of the Internet. In 1994 Intel—which, as a technology company should have known better—spent months ignoring scientists' online complaints that its new Pentium chip had trouble with some calculations and that the chip maker was dragging its feet when asked for replacements.[8] News of Intel's transgressions spread rapidly, since the science community was among the Internet's earliest users. By the end of the year, then CEO Andrew Grove was forced to offer an abject and very public apology.

At the end of it, he pledged: "We will try to be more sensitive to the needs of customers, including the customers on the Internet."[9] This would become a watchword for many suits over the next decade.

WHY 2K?

Throughout the later 1990s, as the New Economy boomed, many "bricks and mortar" suits gained a new appreciation of the technologists they worked with and their strange new world of the Internet. ("Bricks and mortar" refers to non-online companies, i.e., they have an actual physical operation.) But during the same period, the advent of the year 2000 problem began changing the relationship for the worse.

A few lone voices were sounding the alarm about the year 2000 problem as early as the 1970s. (The year 2000 problem, or "Y2K," referred to potential malfunctions caused when software with only two digits for the year reset the clock to "00.") But most technology people didn't begin worrying till around 1995, when some software that used five-year increments began encountering the Y2K software bug. Thanks to the Geek Gap, their suit counterparts didn't have a clue that anything might be wrong until around mid-1997, when consulting firms such as the Gartner Group, which covered technology but catered to suits, began sounding the alarm.

Of course, we all now know that a lot of the panic was unfounded. Thousands of people bought generators and candles in anticipation of power failures and other disruptions that never happened. And while it seems clear that the worst expectations were exaggerated, it's hard to know what would have happened in the absence of the massive Y2K remediation efforts undertaken around the globe.

Ultimately, whether it was a disaster wisely avoided or a tempest in a teapot, or some combination of both, Y2K was a very real event in the lives of many companies and the technology folk who worked for them. An estimated $500 billion was spent worldwide to fix the Y2K bug.[10] Much of this paid for huge, hurried remediation projects that either dragged companies into upgrades that they didn't really want, or, conversely, put all new technology on hold until the old software could be fixed.

Many people on both sides of the gap were eager to blame someone—anyone—for the Y2K problem, but the truth is, it was no one's fault. Most of the two-digit years had been written into antiquated software created in the 1970s or 1980s which no one thought would still be in use by the turn of the century. (In some cases it was still in use; in others, the original code had been used to create newer generation programs.) Certainly, almost no one still working in technology by the late 1990s had had anything to do with creating the problem. Nonetheless, many suits wanted to blame technology—and technology people, as a whole. Their trust in the geeks they worked with was broken.

"People spent two years thinking the whole technology house of cards was going to come tumbling down at midnight, and the whole thing proved to be a non-event," notes Karin Albert, educational research and design leader at Granite Construction Inc.[11] "Left the whole industry with egg on its face."

But technology folk had their grievances, too. For many of them, trust in the suits they worked with and the companies they worked for had been broken years earlier, during the widespread downsizings of the 1990s. Now they were being asked to work endless hours to fix a problem not of their making. Worse, they were expected to use antiquated programming languages that might leave them without a marketable skill once the Y2K repairs were completed. The goal of all this effort was not to create a new system or technology (which always excites geeks) but merely to ensure the survival of a company that might decide at any moment it no longer required their services.

Ironically, Y2K itself led many suits to the conclusion that they could indeed get along better with fewer geeks on the premises. Furious that they'd spent huge sums on what appeared to be a nonproblem, many CEOs began to wonder just why they needed to have IT departments in the first place. Many corporate managers believed they had well-functioning IT departments, only to be told they had to spend millions on year 2000 remediation or else risk having everything fail. The result is that many lost confidence in their in-house techies well before the year 2000 itself arrived.

"Most CEOs know they need to focus on their organizations' core competencies," said Ian Hayes, president of Clarity Consulting, in a 1998 interview.[12] "What Y2K proved—spectacularly—is that IT is not a core competency in many organizations." As a result, he predicted, there would be a sharp increase in outsourcing. Whether or not the ramifications of the millennium bug were the cause, that prediction has certainly come true.

"SOMETIMES I GET FRUSTRATED"

In the years since the Y2K fizzle and then the dot-com bust that changed the workplace status of many geeks, a funny thing happened. While naysayers predicted the death of the Net, technology quietly took over. Information and communications technology spending worldwide is growing faster than the economy at large and is projected to reach nearly $3.8 trillion in 2008, up from $2.1 trillion in 2001, according to WITSA, the World Information Technology and Services Alliance.[13] Today, more than three quarters of technology spending is on workplace technology. This means that even suits with no interest in technology are now dependent on it, for nearly every aspect of their jobs, and on the people who keep it running. The result is a gradual, but unmistakable, shift in the power relationship between geeks and suits.

When talking about the Geek Gap with both technology and business people, we often ask each to tell us their biggest complaints about the other. In the last year or so, we began hearing the word "arrogant" more and more often to describe technology types who are perceived to be looking down on anyone who doesn't share their technical knowledge.

One friend of ours, who works at a local pottery plant, describes the situation this way: "Our company bought some software to help us track and fulfill orders. It was a new system, used company-wide. Everyone who works in the office had to understand how to use it."

The software was installed by a local consultant who had adapted it to work on this company's systems. So when the installation was complete, he spent a day on site to train the staff in the new software's use. At least, that's what was supposed to happen. In fact, whenever the secretaries, order takers, and salespeople who worked at the pottery company asked him a question, they were met with such withering sarcastic responses that they never dared ask another. They knew no more about how to make the thing work when he left than they had when he'd arrived.

For the geeks, this growing impatience is directly related to the rapid growth of people using computers. This means that the few clueless questions they used to get are now multiplied many times over.

"I was at a movie with a friend one night when my brother calls long distance with a computer problem," recalls Bruce Miller, contributing editor of *Puget Sound Computer User* and a technology consultant.[14] (He's also the Webmaster for the American Society of Journalists and Authors, where one of the authors is on the board.)

Miller went out in the hall, told his brother he'd call back, and returned to the film. On the way home, since he wasn't the one driving, Miller returned the call and walked his brother through solving his problem. No sooner had he hung up than his cell phone rang again. The caller was a friend—wanting help with a computer problem. "Some days I've literally had calls backed up from friends wanting computer help," he says. "I generally try to be helpful. Sometimes I get frustrated."

Miller was among the many techies who felt vindicated in February 2004, when the venerable *New York Times* published a front-page story with the headline: "Geeks Put the Unsavvy on Alert: Learn or Log Off."[15] At the time, the MyDoom computer virus was causing devastation on hard drives everywhere. It was a virus that could only be caught by downloading an e-mail attachment—something most geeks believe you have to be really stupid to do, unless the attachment is something you're specifically expecting. For many of them, the rapid spread of MyDoom was just one more proof that most computer users were a menace to themselves and others.

The bigger issue, though, is the increased number of people wanting guidance these days. One technology professional interviewed for the *Times* article found that helping them had gone from fun to drudgery. "Not so long ago, he took pleasure in showing people around the brave new digital world that he moved in with such ease," it read. "Now that everyone has a technical question, he says, being a tour guide has lost its charm." That sentiment, in one form or another, is something we've heard from geeks again and again. This may be contributing to some of them coming across as arrogant.

"OUTSIDE LOOKING IN"

John Martin, an IT executive in telecommunications, has what he calls a "slightly different perspective" on the evolution of the geek/suit relationship.[16] "I think that in the past, the techies were on the outside looking in. Whereas now there is a certain expectation that all business people have some technical knowledge. So it is the business people without some technology knowledge who are on the outside looking in. I'm not sure whether the problem is bigger or smaller, but it has shifted from one population to another."

In every business setting, knowledge always equals power. But it may be a phenomenon of the future that, in the business world, technological knowledge may equal corporate power. At least, that's how many people see it. Recently we were at a technical college giving a presentation about the Geek Gap and talking to some of the students about their experiences and plans. At the end of the presentation, one young woman stood and told us that she was studying electrical engineering. But her ultimate goal was not to be an engineer; it was to become an upper-level corporate manager. She believed that the engineering degree would offer a career path to that goal.

In the business environment that's coming, she might be right. "At the beginning of the last century there was a thriving business in home motors," notes Jonathan Spira, CEO of the technology consulting firm Basex.[17] Each of these motors was used to run several different home appliances that could be hooked up to it in turn. Thus it might run a vacuum cleaner one day and a washing machine the next. "Thousands of them were sold," Spira says.

Nowadays, he points out, motors in the home are so ubiquitous we're barely aware that they're there. They can be found in everything from heating systems to electric mixers and even can openers. Users rarely give them a thought: they're simply part of how our appliances function. They're completely integrated, and the same, he believes, will be true of computer technology, and technologists, in years to come. "With the exception of people maintaining systems within an IT center, IT people should become business experts who can also interact with high-level IT functions."

"Any time you have visible differences between two groups of people, coupled with breakdowns in communication, you get the suits vs. geeks syndrome," Albert notes.[18] "It's almost human nature to want to identify an 'in' group and an 'out' group. Moving forward, as IT becomes more embedded into daily life, that barrier will have to come down."

So while the IBM Fellows program seems to represent the highest aspiration for an engineer in that company, many of tomorrow's engineers will have their eyes set on a bigger prize. "Maybe that's the measure to look for," Albert says. "When a geek comes up through the technical ranks and makes CEO in a *non*-technical company, we'll know the Geek Gap has really been bridged."

CHAPTER 4

WHO'S TO BLAME FOR THE DOT-COM BUST?

A friend of ours is a technology writer married to a programmer. In 1998 they moved to a small town that happened to be the home of a hot new Internet company. It was a heady time, she recalls: "I kept thinking that this must have been what it felt like to be in California during the great gold rush. People in their twenties were buying lavish houses, riding around town in fancy sports cars, taking vacations all over the world."

Part of the reason she and her husband had agreed to relocate was that real estate prices in this sleepy village had been attractively low, but by the time they were ready to buy a few months after they had moved there, everything had changed. Company staff who wanted to buy were now faced with the choice of commuting fifty miles from a neighboring state, or paying top dollar for a tiny run-down home in town.

Noting the company's long work hours, our friend vetoed having her husband drive an hour to get home in the middle of the night. So they bought in town—scraping together some family money to do so. But the only house they could afford was smack up against a state highway, right on a dangerous curve. Their cat, no longer allowed outside, took revenge on their carpets and furniture. Still, they figured, in a few years, they'd sell and look for something better. They were bound to make a profit—prices just kept going up and up.

Besides, they were sure they would have plenty of money. Our friend's husband seemed to get a new promotion every six months or so, and he was regularly solicited by headhunting firms. Our friend herself had never seen a better market for her technical articles. She was accustomed to spending part of her time looking for freelance work, but she now found herself turning it away. They both thought things would go on this way forever, but, of course, they were wrong.

Less than two years after the couple relocated and bought their new house, the company that employed our friend's husband was gone. The company's initial investors had sold their stock before the downfall. They made money, as did the first group of people who had joined the company. But most of the people who worked there had to find new jobs.

A surprising number wound up in professions that had nothing to do with technology—managing a retail chain store or selling commercial real estate, for instance. One went off to write a cookbook. Others wound up working as carpenters or handymen. A few tried starting their own dot-com companies but mostly without much success.

350 POINTS IN A DAY

It was 2000, the year the dot-com boom went bust, the year thousands of people, who thought they would get rich off the Internet, abruptly learned otherwise. That April, the NASDAQ "over the counter" exchange, where most tech stocks are traded, fell 350 points in a single day, losing more than 9 percent of its value. It lost more than 25 percent of its value over the whole month.

Suddenly, investing in tech stocks no longer seemed like a hot idea. This was dire news for most Internet start-ups, very few of which had earned any kind of profit. They had started life with venture-capital (VC) funding, kept going with second and third rounds of funding, and had intended to go public, selling their stock at an initial public offering

(IPO), at prices that would provide enough cash to pay off the venture capitalists and keep the doors open for a good long while; that is, until the company finally figured out how to make money on its own.

With investors suddenly gun shy, many high-tech IPOs failed to bring in the cash that the company's founders had anticipated. Others saw the writing on the wall and canceled their IPOs, hoping for better times to come. Many of these firms now had no meaningful source of funds except for the VC firms that had given them life in the first place. But the VCs were watching the stock market and they, too, became reluctant to keep pouring money into dot-com companies with the prospect of a payback that seemed now highly uncertain. Some dot-coms managed to get themselves bought by larger, more financially stable companies. Many of the rest, though, with no way to pay their bills or their employees, had no choice but to shut down.

By the time 2000 was over, 210 Internet companies had closed their doors[1] and thousands of people were out of work. Some, like our friend and her husband, had reorganized their lives and their financial plans around jobs that turned out not to be as permanent as they'd assumed. Others had worked extreme hours for mediocre salaries, counting on stock options to provide a secure financial future, then discovered that what they had instead were worthless pieces of paper.

Investors suffered too. One friend of ours who'd planned to retire in 2001 found that her newly reduced stock portfolio made that inadvisable and wound up staying at her job another five years. In all, according to a 2002 estimate, investors lost more than fifteen billion dollars on the dot-com bust.[2] Everyone involved felt like a victim. Everyone wanted someone to blame.

"PIZZA KIDS"

For many business people and investors, the fault seemed to lie with the geeks who had—seemingly on purpose—led everyone astray. Early in 2001, journalist Douglas Rushkoff attended a conference of Internet investors. Its purpose was to figure out who was to blame for the disaster.

"By late afternoon, they had agreed upon a common enemy—those pimply 20-something hackers who work in makeshift studios over their garages, eating pizza, drinking Coke and writing code late into the night," he reported. "'It's those pizza kids who fooled all the investors,' an Internet strategist explained. 'They didn't care about your money at all.'"[3]

Technology folk also thought they had been taken for a ride, but in their view it was business people doing the driving. As Bill Lessard and Steve Baldwin wrote in *NetSlaves 2.0*, "[F]or the most part, those wily CEOs, venture capitalists, Wall Street analysts, and investment bankers made it out of town with the loot, and we the people who built the Web are the ones who got screwed."[4]

Lessard and Baldwin refer to the dot-com boom as a "Ponzi scheme,"[5] and in a way, this brings us closer to the truth. The Ponzi scheme was named for the Italian-American con man Carlo Ponzi, who promised to double investors' money in ninety days.[6] He made good on his promise with early investors. What they didn't know is that they were being paid with later investors' money. They told their friends about the wonderful deal they'd found, word of mouth spread, and money kept pouring in. Eventually, the scheme collapsed under its own weight, but not before the charismatic Ponzi had engaged in a life of conspicuous consumption that would put modern-day Internet millionaires to shame.

A "Ponzi scheme" is a fair description of the dot-com boom and bust. The basic principle was the same: venture-capital firms supplied Internet start-ups with their first funding, to be paid back when the company launched its initial public offering (IPO), selling stock to the general public. Not only the venture capitalists, but also the company's early employees would make huge profits from stock options whose value would quickly rise as the stock sold. In effect, later investors—the stock purchasers—were paying the early investors' returns, and, just like Ponzi's customers, they figured everyone would keep making money forever. Until the whole thing got too large and unwieldy for new investors to keep footing the bill, and then the dot-com boom collapsed, just like Ponzi's empire.

The obvious difference is that Ponzi, though charming, was a crook who deliberately set out to bilk people, whereas the venture capitalists and start-up CEOs of the dot-com boom were well intentioned, and truly believed that everyone involved would make money on their ideas. They forgot a fundamental truth: sooner or later, in order to be successful, a company needs to sell something—other than its own stock—that people want to buy. This may seem self-evident, but in that topsy-turvy time, unproductive ad revenues were all that most dot-coms had that could bring in cash, and many not even that. A few were all hype and actually never sold anything other than their shares.

The question is, Why did they forget? We can understand technologists setting aside their understanding of basic business principles when blinded by love for a wonderful new innovation, but certainly money people—venture capitalists, Wall Street types, stockbrokers—ought to have known better.

We think there are two reasons for everyone's collective amnesia. The first is that those who understood e-business recognized a real fact: companies that got going quickly and achieved critical mass early on would have a valuable head start in what would come to be a crowded world of online services and products. America Online and Amazon are two examples of companies that owe their success in part to their status as early entrants.

MAGICAL THINKING

The second reason has more to do with the Geek Gap. We believe a big part of the problem is that business people and technologists view each other's disciplines with what child psychologists and anthropologists call "magical thinking." This is the kind of unscientific view of cause and effect that leads children to carefully avoid sidewalk cracks, and convinces adults that wearing a lucky shirt will help them land a job or win a game. Magical thinking underlies the I-don't-want-to-know-how-it-works-I-just-want-it-to-work view of technology. That may be a viable attitude for business people who don't want to take the time to understand their desktop computers, but it makes for a lethal combination when geeks and suits try to build businesses together.

We think technologists believed that their business colleagues had a near-magical ability to create cash out of thin air. It's not surprising—the best entrepreneurs do appear to have that ability. Bo Peabody, cofounder of Tripod and a master salesman and entrepreneur, wrote in his book *Lucky or Smart?* that he had a standing bet with the programmers at his company that he would be able to configure a Web server before any of them would be able to raise one million dollars.[7] The stakes were attractive—his founder's share of the company against their small ones—but no one ever took him up on it. The lesson seemed clear: stick to what you know and leave the money stuff to the experts who understand it.

This seems like a logical approach, and yet we believe it made for a dot-com crash that was worse than it might have been, as technology folk went about their business, creating and refining new software, building irresistible Web sites, banking on their stock options, and assuming that there would be plenty of money for everyone. For the most part, they chose not to look behind the curtain at the workings of the financial engine that was supposed to be keeping their companies moving forward. Consequently, they felt shocked and betrayed when they suddenly discovered those engines were running on empty.

But had they looked behind the curtain, there's a chance they might have figured it out. It shouldn't have taken an MBA to notice an obvious fact that any number of business experts have gleefully noted since the bubble burst: dot-coms were always headed for trouble because most of them never actually earned much money. They may have made big profits selling their own stock, but most never came out with an actual product or service that significant numbers of customers were willing to pay for. (In a brilliant twist, the online travel agency Travelzoo capitalized on the appeal of dot-com investing by offering three free shares of its stock to the first seven hundred thousand visitors to its Web site. The strategy worked: Travelzoo is a dot-com survivor.)

If geeks didn't stop to ask themselves how their dot-com employers were going to turn a profit, it's more surprising that suits didn't either. After all, technologists might assume that money would somehow automatically appear in corporate coffers, but business people are supposed to know better. They should have known that investors were investing in their companies in the expectation that they would someday generate enough cash from their own operations to pay back those investments and more.

But it was a heady time, when traditional ideas about valuation were generally ignored ("valuation" is the science of determining how much a company—and therefore its stock—should really be worth). "The bubble years were like the last days of the Roman Empire—business practices were totally weird and dysfunctional," commented Greg Galanos, managing director of Mobius Venture Capital.[8] But he made this observation from the vantage point of 2002, by which time it was all too clear that mistakes had been made. In the late 1990s, most observers, ourselves included, thought the good times would never end. Why did so many people get it wrong?

We believe there was magical thinking on the part of business people, too, when faced with the awesome potential of rapidly advancing technology, and, in particular, the Internet. They may not have understood what the World Wide Web was, or how people were going to use it, but it was clear that the rules of commerce were being rewritten for all time. They were also awed by the numbers that the Internet could bring in— hundreds of thousands or even millions might visit even a modest Web site every year. If hundreds of thousands of people visited a store every year, it would be certain to make money. It seemed reasonable to assume that the same must apply—somehow—to a Web site.

Besides, many people were afraid of missing out. We remember a friend who was furious when her mother died and left her a nest egg that was mostly invested in bonds around that time. She felt she'd been cheated out of the much larger fortune she could have had if her mother had only been sensible enough to play the high-tech stock market. In an atmosphere like this, business executives, who turned their backs on the moneymaking power of the Internet, feared they did so at their own peril.

It's interesting to note that one of the winners in the dot-com game was Bo Peabody, who, with his partners, sold Tripod to the Lycos Network for $58 million. (Lycos itself is a good example of how the "survive-by-getting-big-fast" strategy can work. After an acquisition binge that resembled a game of Pac-Man, Lycos was purchased by the Spanish communications firm Terra.)

Peabody made the sale in 1998, near the height of the boom, when everything looked rosy. Not only that, Peabody himself had become a poster child for twenty-something Internet success: he was featured in business magazines, newspapers, and on TV looking sporty and relaxed, wearing a baseball cap and a tan, looking on top of the world.

"Had I actually begun to believe what was said about me in the press, I would never have sold Tripod when I did," he writes. "I would have reasoned, instead, that I was in fact a genius, and that I should take complete credit for the great things happening to my company. Never mind that Tripod had little revenues, no profits, and an unproven business model; we should take this horse public!" If he had, he adds dryly, the company would likely have failed and everyone involved would have lost a lot of money.[9]

FROM UNKNOWN TO VERB

In the years since the Internet bubble burst, observers have often reported an obvious fact: Internet use itself has continued to increase. In fact, during 2000, the year so many dot-coms met their demise, Nielsen/Net Ratings reported that for the first time, more than half of all households had Internet service in twenty-one of thirty-five key American cities.[10] In 2004 e-commerce accounted for more than $69 billion in annual US retail sales, or just under 2 percent of all retail sales, according to the US Department of Commerce. By May 2005, that number had climbed to just over 2 percent. In fact, despite the dot-com turmoil, e-commerce use has been climbing steadily since 1999.[11]

Obviously, there is a market out there for companies with the wisdom to tap it. For instance, consider the search engine Google, which was founded in 1998. One technology writer we know remembers doing an in-depth article in 1999 about gaining search engine prominence. He spent a lot of time studying the details of how successful search engines organize information. He talked to experts who earned big consulting fees helping to put the sites of their client companies higher on the results list. The name "Google" was never even mentioned.

Less than a year later, he left a phone message for an expert he wanted to interview. When she called back, the first thing she told him was, "I googled you to make sure you were legit." In less than a year, Google had gone from an unknown name to a commonplace verb, and was dominant in the world of search.

Google is very much a company created by and for geeks, so much so that the company goes out of its way to emulate the working atmosphere at the best technology universities. For instance, there are typically two or three people to an office. "If you go to the Stanford computer science building, you'll see two, three, or even four people in an office. That model is familiar to our programmers and us because we were all in those offices too," CEO Eric Schmidt says. The company also starts meetings a few minutes after the hour, harking back to the common college practice of starting morning classes at 9:05 or 9:10 am.[12]

As you might expect, Google's success rests squarely on the strength of its technological innovations: its software just searches better. Earlier search engines used software that would examine the content of a Web page, including both meta-tags (invisible labels that provide keywords) and actual text to guess how closely it might correspond to a user's search.

Google rendered both these methods pretty much obsolete with a simple solution: it ranks pages according to how many other pages contain links to them. The logic is simple and powerful: if a Web designer building a site thinks some other site is useful enough to include a link to it, there's a good chance that a user searching on that topic will find it useful as well. The result is that Google search results are consistently more satisfying than other search results, and Web users quickly caught on.

This story so far could resemble a fairly typical Internet start-up tale that ends in failure, had the Google team been satisfied with simply building something better than its predecessors. This is the magical thinking that led many business people astray: something that people find useful should automatically make money—but it doesn't always work that way. Search is a great example of something most Web surfers use daily, but would never dream of paying for. Fortunately for them, Google execs understood this, so they focused their vast geek acumen on the very suit-like goal of selling Internet advertising.

"ARE YOU A PRINCESS?"

This in itself was hardly a new idea. Many troubled dot-coms turned their hopes to selling ads as a way to stay afloat. After all, they reasoned, the thousands or hundreds of thousands of eyeballs that gazed at their pages had to be worth something. Not so, responded the advertising industry, which by and large declared Internet advertising a huge disappointment.

"Advertisers and marketers have become disenchanted with the Internet for many reasons," according to Hongsik John Cheon, assistant professor, Department of Marketing and Finance, College of Business, Frostburg State University in Frostburg, Maryland. Reasons for ineffectiveness include the "cluster-bomb" nature of much Internet advertising, and "banner blindness"—users' tendency to direct their eyes away from anything that looks like a banner ad on a Web site. He notes that click-through rates for Internet ads declined from 2 percent in 1995 to 0.6 percent or less in 2003.[13] Faced with statistics like these, many dot-coms that had thought advertising sales might be their salvation had those hopes dashed. They found instead that advertisers snubbed them and turned back to more familiar media, or agreed to buy only at bargain-basement prices.

This is something of a pet peeve for us, because it strikes us as unfair. It seems none of these advertising experts have ever stopped to consider the likelihood that most Internet advertising fails because most Internet advertising is horrendously bad.

Anyone who uses the Web knows what we're referring to here: Brightly flashing banners that make it impossible to see or concentrate on anything; ads that pop up and meander around the computer screen so that it's nearly impossible to click on the little x quickly enough to close them; banner ads made to mimic Windows warnings, telling users their computers are not secure. One of our favorites, circa 1999, was a banner that asked: "Are you a princess?" with links to click for "Yes" or "No"—

and no other information of any kind. (Sure, we thought, we'll drop what we're doing in the middle of a busy workday to find out if we're a princess or not.)

Many of these ads were created by respectable agencies on behalf of respectable organizations that would never have dreamed of using these kinds of shenanigans in the pages of a local telephone directory, let alone a print magazine. They treated the Internet as something trivial, then professed disappointment when it failed to deliver serious results.

The reason this is a pet peeve is not only that we ourselves, as intensive Internet users, have been as annoyed as anyone else by traditional Web advertising. But worse: we believe that some of the failed dot-coms might have been saved by the proper use of advertising.

Google, however, realized the potential of Internet advertising and found a completely new way to exploit it. It eliminated pop-ups, glitz, and graphics of any kind—all its ads are text-only. Then it changed the financial model: advertisers pay only when their ad is clicked, so an ad that is ineffective costs little or nothing to run. Finally, it began selling ads in relation to keywords users searched (and later, to keywords included in e-mail messages on its mail system Gmail), increasing the likelihood that users might actually be interested in the product or service offered. The formula proved successful, so Google expanded it, offering owners of other Web sites the chance to include Google advertising as well.

Here, too, the customer pays only if an ad is clicked, and Google shares the income with the Web site owner. A site with few visitors would see little revenue, but a popular site might see lots. For instance, Matt Daimler, a Seattle networking engineer and frequent flier, created Seat-Guru.com to help himself and others identify the best and worst seats on airplanes. It started as a hobby, but then he signed up to receive travel-related ads from Google advertisers.

The site proved popular, becoming a Yahoo! pick of the week, and nominee for a Webby award. At last count it drew about 1.3 million page views a month.[14] Daimler isn't selling anything of his own on the site; it's strictly supported through advertising. Thanks to Google, he says, it's turned into a $120,000 a year business.[15] Ironically, a few years after the dot-com bust saw many well-loved sites fold for lack of income, the dream that a popular site could pay for itself has come true.

Google is still banking on its technological mastery to create even better targeted advertising. "Take any large consumer packaged-goods company," Google CEO Eric Schmidt says. "How many products do you think they have? Probably millions, by the time you take into account all the geographic variants. We want every one of those products to be advertised in the appropriate market within Google in the right country and so on."[16]

"ME-TOO WANNABEES"

If the Geek Gap helped create the overblown Internet stock market that inevitably led to a crash, Google's example shows how overcoming the Gap—blending both business and technology priorities and expertise— can lead to success for the next generation of dot-coms. And a growing number of Internet executives seem to understand that is what's required. In fact, some say they're happier working in a rational world where a company is expected to actually earn money. They feel they're better off now that the "me-too wannabees with stupid business plans," as one tech exec put it, have gone elsewhere.[17]

Recently, we read about a business executive who helped start an online company to handle Internet sales transactions.[18] When it went belly-up, he concluded that his lack of technical expertise was partly to blame, so he enrolled at the University of California, Berkeley, to study computer languages. Meanwhile, his partner, the technical brains of the enterprise, headed for business school.

"This time, we got caught up in the rush of the excitement, but next time, we'll be more prepared and we'll do it right," he says. We don't know if these two partners' next project will succeed or fail, but we believe they're headed in the right direction.

CHAPTER 5
FUNDAMENTAL DIFFERENCES

Afew months ago, we stayed in one of those bed-and-breakfasts where a half-dozen guests sit around one big table for their morning meal. We all chatted amiably about our various jobs, and we mentioned our discussion of geeks and suits in an upcoming book.

"How do you tell the difference between a geek and a suit?" one guest asked.

"We have our methods," we said, then added: *"All your base are belong to us."*

Sure enough, the one true techie at the table—a gentleman who'd just described in exhaustive detail his most recent IT project—burst out laughing. The other guests stared in obvious surprise, first at him, then at us.

"All your base are belong to us" is not only an inside joke in the techie world, but a good illustration of the differing viewpoints between the geek world and the world of commerce.

The phrase, sometimes acronymed as AYBABTU, was originally a (badly translated) line from the 1989 Japanese video game *Zero Wing*, spoken triumphantly by an alien general after the player has lost a space battle. The line became a fad around the Internet in the late 1990s and early 2000s, with users all over the Web inserting the phrase into

81

images, posting it on message boards, and using it as a battle cry in more up-to-date games.

"All your base are belong to us" has been used in popular songs, rolled across a character's watch in the enigmatic animation feature *Waking Life*, and is the name of a cyber cafe. On April 1, 2003, some young geeks even put up signs sporting the phrase around Sturgis, Michigan—an April Fool's joke that went over badly, in view of the recently begun invasion of Iraq.

Observing this widespread fad, advertising executives might well have started thinking about how they could use the AYBABTU phenomenon to lend a cool factor to the products they were marketing. But, in a stunning display of geek disdain for all things commercial, an Irish Web employee named Vincent O'Keeffe prevented any such move by creating the Web site allyourbrand.org and filling it with imaginary advertising that featured the AYBABTU theme. (A fake ad for a sports channel, for instance, reads "All Your Husband Are Belong to Us.") According to the text on the site, the idea is to "inoculate" consumers and make them less receptive to advertising using AYBABTU. And to make sure that something geeks thought of as their own would never be used for so crass a purpose as to sell products.[1]

Whether or not they're fans of AYBABTU or even video games, geeks have their own culture that is definitely distinct from that of the business world. Nowhere is this as obvious as in what they choose to do for fun. These choices reflect the different thought processes and their values, which also influence how they do their jobs. They contrast sharply with the predilections of the suit world.

"I AM THE MAN!"

It's spring 1999, and at 2 am in Williamstown, Massachusetts, the front offices of Tripod.com are dark and silent. The last official workers to leave for the day had shut off their monitors and left the building at 8 pm, locking up for the night. All the overhead lights are out; only the dim night lighting remains, showing the honeycomb outlines of row after row of cubicles. Here and there among the darkened workstations, however, a light glows, and the occasional squeak of an office chair indicates that the old factory space is not quite empty.

Suddenly, groans and curses erupt from several cubicles at once. From one of the center cubicles a head with bushy hair and shoulders sporting a Hawaiian shirt pops up, and proclaims "Survival of the fittest, you peons! I AM the man! Leftover pizza before we dive back in, anyone?"

The dozen or so Tripod employees in their various cubicles are enjoying their weekly—or whenever they can—late night LAN party, using the company's otherwise dormant computer network to connect with each other and create a multiplayer game environment. Across the network, players can see, hear, and especially kill one another within the same game, each on his or her own computer.

LAN (Local Area Network) parties have been steadily growing since geeks started playing them in the mid-1990s. They meet in garages, basements, abandoned warehouses, cyber cafes, malls, and even stadiums in countries across the globe. Among the biggest is The Gathering, a five-day extravaganza held in Norway's Viking Ship Olympic Arena, which draws about 5,200 gamers every spring, each playing on a separate-but-networked computer. The Gathering was recently beaten out as the largest by DreamHack, which takes place in Sweden, accommodates up to 6,270 at its Winter games, and even publishes its own *DreamHack Daily* newspaper during the event.

Many LAN parties charge admission at the door and offer cash prizes for winners at the end of the night. Apparently, in Japan and Korea, there are even a few professional gamers who actually live off their LAN party winnings.[2]

LAN parties began at places like Tripod, where employees could commandeer a bevy of networked computers after work hours. But they've evolved into BYOC (Bring Your Own Computer) events, and we're not talking laptops. Instead, these highly committed geeks lug entire desktop setups to the designated gathering place. They set them up and plug the different components into the computer box—monitor, mouse, and, usually, headphones, often with microphones, so players can talk to one another. Then they plug everything into a power source, connect their computers to whatever network is available, and check that all these connections are working properly.

Getting everything hooked up and working can be a lengthy process, and may involve some trial-and-error, as anyone knows who has ever assembled these components and plugged them into a network. Only once it is complete is anyone ready to actually play.

Why, in this age of tiny processors, portable computing, and wireless everything would anyone transport a desktop away from home? The answer is for power, speed, and screamingly good graphics, three things most tech folk find impossible to resist.

Since they are lugging their desktops from place to place, these techies make the most of it. Forget the usual standard-issue gray metal boxes. LAN parties are a chance for gamers to show off their newest hottest "case mods"—modifications made to the computer's outside skin and—despite the name—internal components as well.

Companies now exist whose sole customer base is gamers who build their own tricked-out machines—much like hot rods for old-car enthusiasts. Think custom cases with lights flashing in sync to the game music or MP3s and overclocked chips that run so hot that they actually need liquid coolant. There are even specially constructed straps and cases just for hefting a desktop from place to place.

Even if it were to make sense to lug a desktop computer and its peripherals to a LAN party rather than merely pop open a laptop, why does it make sense to go there at all? To sit in front of a computer, staring at the screen, listening through headphones—isn't it exactly the same as they'd be doing at home? If the fun of going out to a party is spending time with people face-to-face, then why does face-to-face contact seem to be the last thing these gamers are interested in?

For LAN party gamers, the effort and aggravation of dragging a desktop computer to a remote location is more than made up for by the intense satisfaction of being able to combine their online gaming world with real life, or "RL" as they call it. While RL has its appeal, it definitely falls short in certain ways when compared to the constant excitement, bright colors, and magical abilities available in the virtual world.

"There are no respawn points in RL!" laments a gaming-obsessed character in one popular online video series. Asked for a translation, a game-savvy geek explained, "In many games, players earn 'respawn' points for accomplishing tasks such as killing bad guys or monsters, so that when they themselves are killed, if they've accumulated enough of these points, they can get another life. Obviously, RL lacks this advantage." Just one of the many ways life can seem like a poor substitute to those accustomed to living through computer games.

These gamers are digital natives—or if not, they aspire to be.

The term *digital native* was coined by the game designer and guru Marc Prensky in 2001[3] to describe those born into the world of computers and the Internet, who thus are completely comfortable there. A "digital immigrant," on the other hand, is someone who has arrived later in life in the digital world, either because that person was not exposed to or drawn to computers at an early age, or simply grew up before these things were widely available. Digital immigrants, like those who emigrate from one country to another, speak with "accents" in their new home.

"There are hundreds of examples of the digital immigrant accent," Prensky writes. "They include printing out your email (or having your secretary print it out for you—an even 'thicker' accent); needing to print out a document written on the computer in order to edit it (rather than just editing on the screen); and bringing people physically into your office to see an interesting Web site (rather than just sending them the URL)."[4]

One key to understanding geek culture is that a geek born too late to be a digital native will still try hard to become one. The ambition is to be fully at home in the new digital homeland, and speak with as little an accent as possible. And, like all immigrants, the geek will want his or her children to be completely assimilated.

"I might have immigrated, but I immigrated very young," says Mark Oehlert, director of learning innovations at The MASIE Center, a technology and learning think tank.[5] "I have a five-year-old son, and he's a digital native. He's on his third computer. He understands going to cartoonnetwork.com. He knows you can take pictures with your phone. He's at the technological point I was when I was twelve." There's unmistakable pride in his voice, mixed with a touch of envy.

For geeks who seek to be digital natives and have learned to live and relate in the virtual world as easily as the real one, face-to-face interactions can feel limited in certain ways. We know one group of geeks who spent many years working in online community, supervising chat rooms, and the like. This team was constantly conversing online, in chats, or private instant messages. They spent many, many online hours talking together, and they got to know each other very well, although they'd never physically met.

Conversing with someone in typed text is, of course, different in many ways from talking to that person out loud, and one of the differences is that typed text offers the opportunity for nonverbal communication of its own sort: symbols created with keyboard characters that have a graphic rather than textual meaning, which techies refer to as emoticons. The most common emoticon, and the one nearly everyone has seen is this one: :-), which indicates a smile, and is often used in conjunction with something that might seem harsh or critical: it lets the person at the other end know that the comment was meant in a friendly or jocular way. But, though less widely known, there is a wealth of other emoticons like :-? for puzzlement, ==:-0 for shock, and :-x for "I'm keeping my mouth shut!" Over the years, chat users in the many online communities throughout the Internet had developed these symbols and many more quite freely, often to convey sentiments in a more subtle way than they could through words alone.

Then, one day, some of the team decided to take a road trip so they could meet their online colleagues in person. They all met in a roadside diner, where they sat together at a booth, sipping coffee, and talking together for hours about their jobs, their lives, the world at large, and everything else they could think of.

As their talk progressed, they found the conversation oddly hampered. Sitting at a table and talking they had no way, or at least no easy one, to use emoticons in the discussion. Ridiculous as it seemed, they found themselves actually saying "LOL!"—while they were in fact "laughing out loud." They also wound up pulling a pile of napkins from the dispenser in order to scribble the emoticons they could no longer type to each other.

SOLVING PROBLEMS VERSUS INFLUENCING PEOPLE

Cultural differences between geeks and suits can run deeper than how they spend their free hours, which affects how they interact with each other in a work setting. One of the most congenial suits we know is Bill Brobston. A graduate of the Salisbury Prep School and Wharton, he became a leader in the cement industry, like his father before him.

Brobston headed Alpha Cement many years ago, in the early days of computing, the days of mainframes and minicomputers attended by technical experts in some far-away basement room. Alpha had a computer, and a technology person who ran it, but Brobston found he could make little use of what was generated.[6]

"Every day, he would bring me a big pile of printouts," he recalls.

What was in them, we asked?

"Everything you could possibly want to know about how the plant worked," Brobston told us. "Utilization rates and production rates and monthly projections and cost." Potentially useful stuff, he admitted. "But there was simply no way I could take the time to go through that whole stack every morning. I would try to get him to tell me about it instead, but he never wanted to do that. He wanted me to take an interest in the computer itself." Even more frustrating for Brobston was that he couldn't seem to connect to the geek on a personal level. He tried to make friends, but the technologist only seemed to want to discuss the computer.

The company tennis tournament came up, and Brobston and the geek found themselves partnered for doubles. Brobston was very athletic, the geek wasn't half bad either, and between the two of them, they won. Having sweated and prevailed together, Brobston was sure that he and his technical employee would share more of a bond, and that their working relationship couldn't help but improve. He was wrong, however. To his astonishment, once back at the office, the geek acted exactly as before.

Brobston was up against one of the most significant differences between suits and geeks: strengths in *problem solving* versus strengths in *influencing people*. He had built his career on his sales successes. In the commoditized world of cement, where both the price and the composition of the product were identical from company to company, the decision to buy from Alpha rather than some other supplier was entirely dependent on which sales rep customers liked best.

And so Brobston had learned to be likable. Mostly, he says, he did it by listening to his customers' problems, letting them open up to him and offering words of encouragement. Nearly everyone he met warmed to him in this way, and so his career flourished. Influencing people—the ability to connect with others and make them feel understood—was his stock in trade.

Why did none of this work on the techie? We never met him, but we can make an educated guess. In his world, success depended not on selling a product or influencing a customer's perceptions, but on how well the technology he created and maintained was working. This was likely a difficult task in those early days of gigantic and intensely sensitive computers. Success for all geeks is less a matter of exerting influence on those around them, and more a question of fulfilling the technological tasks in front of them—in short, solving problems, as opposed to influencing people.

To the techie, the computer was the important part of the equation. He probably spent nearly every waking hour, and some of his sleeping ones, thinking about it. Brobston had unknowingly committed one of the great errors of managing technologists by not at least feigning interest in it. Because his employer did not appear to value the technology to which this man had devoted his life, he probably felt that he himself was not greatly valued either.

As for the tennis tournament—it was good exercise and a fun diversion from the everyday world of work. But he likely saw no more significance in it than that. Another big cultural difference between suits and geeks is their respective approaches to team sports.

Some technology people like sports, others don't. For their own pastimes, they may tend more than suits to gravitate toward solo sports, such as snowboarding. But whether they enjoy team sports or not, they rarely see them as more than just that: games that are fun to watch or play on a weekend afternoon. They don't consider them a test of character or a metaphor for their jobs or their lives.

To suits, interpersonal dynamics and the ability to work effectively with a diverse range of people are essential. Perhaps for this reason, many of them have a reverential regard for team sports. They hire retired pro football players—even those with little business experience—for high-level business leadership positions. And they even speak in sports metaphors, saying things like "I'd like to be the quarterback on this project," or "He hit that one out of the park."

PROCESS VERSUS PRODUCT

Another fundamental difference between techies and business people has to do with the preference of process as compared to product—the act of creating something as opposed to the usefulness of the finished product created.

"What's the bottom line?" You hear suits ask this question quite often, and they're not always talking about financial matters. It means, what's the upshot, the moral of the story, the final effect, when all is said and done, of an event or a project or a decision.

For geeks, this question makes a whole lot less sense, because it's not necessarily the bottom line itself that interests them, it's the getting there. As Paul Glen notes in *Leading Geeks*, technology folk love solving puzzles, and the fact that their jobs feel like puzzle solving most of the time is what keeps them at their desks for hours after most sane people have gone home. "To a geek, a puzzle is an opportunity to exercise the mind, prove competence, or foil the puzzle master who formulated the question. It doesn't matter if that challenge is a simple math problem or President Kennedy's call to put a man on the moon," Glen writes. When it comes to technology, he adds, "[T]he passion is not so much what technology can do, but the joy in understanding how it works."[7]

"One of my earliest memories is taking apart an old alarm clock my mother had thrown away to see what was inside," one of our geek friends told us recently. Nearly every grown-up technologist has a similar story to tell. One geek we know, given a free evening, will likely spend it disassembling a laptop, not to diagnose or repair it, but simply to learn how the inside parts fit together. The act of making something, figuring something out, creating something is more compelling than the thing itself.

This was illustrated for us when a married couple, made up of a suit and geek, decided to watch the Japanese animated feature *Ghost in the Shell*. Geeks seem to share many of the same tastes. Among them are science fiction, particularly the writings of Neal Stephenson, the old Thunderbirds puppet show (which was actually rerun on the old TechTV), and the beautifully elaborate Japanese animations that aficionados call "anime." Believe it or not, the word is short for "animeshon"—a Japanese corruption of the English word animation. *Ghost in the Shell*, one of the crown jewels in the world of anime, was first a comic book (called a "manga"), then a movie, then a TV series. The protagonist of all these is Motoko, a cyborg with a human soul or "ghost," which is where the work gets its title.

"Just watch this," the geek said to his suit wife, sitting her at his computer and fitting its headphones over her head. "These next three minutes— that's why I love anime." She watched, and what followed was not a battle sequence or any kind of action, but a montage of images of the crowded and futuristic city in which the story takes place. With the movie's haunting choral theme in the background, Motoko rides along a canal between city streets as it begins to rain. Drops land in puddles, rippling the reflections of the buildings above. A group of school children, each with a yellow umbrella, trots across a road in the distance. Passing an office building, Motoko looks up into a window to see another woman who looks exactly like her looking back out. Since her body was made in a factory, and is not one-of-a-kind, this makes sense in the story line.

But the point is this: had those exact same images been filmed rather than drawn, they wouldn't have made such an impression on our friend the geek. It is the artistry—the careful and computer-aided calculations, required to give each of these moments realistic detail and perspective— that makes it so appealing. And, of course, the story—which asks the same questions in many different forms: Can machines think? If they can, do they have rights? And if human bodies can be improved by technology, where exactly is the line between human and machine?

There was a reason, however, that our friends had to watch this gorgeous animation one at a time on a computer monitor, instead of together on their televisions. The geek had found a version of it that they could watch online on his computer. The trick now was to find a way to transfer it to the television in the living room a few yards away. This is exactly the kind of puzzle geeks love, so he dived in head first, disappearing into his office for an entire evening.

"I think I'm zeroing in on it," he told his wife late that night as she headed upstairs to bed. She hoped so: she had loved the little snippet she'd seen sitting at his computer, and was eager to see the rest—in the more comfortable setting of her living room. But several days passed and he still hadn't figured out how to play the movie on the television.

Finally, she simply went out and bought the DVD, satisfying her desire to watch the movie but spoiling his fun at the same time. He was a geek, mainly interested in process. She was a suit, mainly interested in product.

In a workplace environment, this process-versus-product dichotomy means business people often start taking interest in a technological innovation just at the moment that technology people are losing interest in it. For instance, let's say the IT team is hard at work creating an in-house knowledge-management system. This system will allow everyone to share files, documents, e-mails, memos, instant messages, contact information, even images and sound files, freely across the entire organization.

For the tech folk, this project provides a number of fascinating challenges. It means integrating a wide variety of documents and document types into one platform, using the in-house intranet, the Internet, or some combination of both to allow for easy communications to deal with issues of security and reliability, and creating a user interface that is easy to understand, yet offers the full functionality of the software. Exactly the kind of puzzles geeks love.

Meanwhile, the organization's business staff may be vaguely aware that IT is working on something that could be very useful when it's finished. (*If* it's finished, since, as we've seen, many technology projects don't meet their goals.) Knowing this, and busy with their own jobs, the business folk are likely to pay the new project little mind, assuming they'll have plenty of time to learn about it when it is deployed.

Now, let's say the project is successfully completed. The IT staff and a team of beta-testing users have played with all the links and buttons and everything seems to be running smoothly. The new software has been successfully installed into the company's servers, and it's ready to go.

This is the point in the process when suits are likely to start taking an interest in the software—when it appears they will be able to use it to do their jobs more effectively. Meanwhile, the geeks, having successfully solved the puzzle, are ready to celebrate and then move on to the next puzzle. The only task left here is that of teaching the business users exactly how the software works and the new capabilities it offers—which is the aspect of their jobs that most technology people enjoy least.

The seesaw will tilt back the other way if it turns out the new software isn't working properly, and has bugs that need to be resolved. Then fixing it becomes a whole new puzzle to grab the geeks' attention. Meanwhile, of course, suits who see that the technology isn't delivering what was promised are likely to lose interest in it again.

WAR DRIVING VERSUS PAYING FOR WIRELESS

Since one of us writes a technology column for the local paper, we're often on the receiving end of phone calls airing people's fears and concerns about all things technological. Lately, several of these have had to do with the sanctity of both home and office wireless networks. Did we know, the callers ask, that with an open wireless network, outsiders can get in and use their Internet connection?

Yup, we did. In fact, this is the basis for a favorite geek activity: war driving. The online tech glossary Wordspy.com defines "war driving" as: "A computer cracking technique that involves driving through a neighborhood with a wireless-enabled notebook computer and mapping houses and businesses that have wireless access points." To geeks, it can also be a heck of a lot of fun.

In the 1983 movie *War Games* a young techie uses a (then state-of-the-art) computerized phone dialing system to look for computers with modems so he can find bulletin boards with games to play. He accidentally ends up connecting directly to a high-level military computer that, when he starts playing what he thinks are games, gains control over the US nuclear arsenal. This phone search for modems came to be called *war dialing,* which is where the terms *war driving* and *war walking* came from.

Here's how it works: One day, a geek friend found himself with time to kill on a sunny day in Manhattan. He headed down to Chinatown for a dim sum brunch, then meandered up through the Lower East Side toward Greenwich Village, stopping in the occasional clothing or housewares store. He was enjoying the fine spring weather and New York City's unparalleled opportunities for people watching. But he was also looking for wireless access, and he was toting along a laptop.

Every few blocks, he'd stop at a bench or lean on a building and start up the laptop, hoping its wireless antenna would pick up a signal. Sometimes he tried plugging in his "cantenna," a special, round cylindrical antenna, about the size and shape of a Pringles potato chip can, which would amplify any wireless signal it managed to find. Being busy and lazy, he'd purchased his cantenna ready-made, but there are instructions on the Internet for building your own—using an actual Pringles can, which just happens to be a usable size and shape for the project.[8]

Even with the cantenna, he came up empty until he neared the New York University campus at Washington Square. Here, he figured, with so many tech-savvy college students around, there were bound to be some wireless access points, and he was right. From nothing at all, he suddenly found himself picking up eight signals at once, of widely varying strength. The strongest seemed to come in best inside a basement-level Laundromat he happened to be passing. And so, he sat on the plastic benches in the Laundromat while the students stuffed their clothes into the machines around him and read his e-mail.

Another variant on war walking is *war chalking.* Drawing on a centuries-old tradition in which hobos left coded markings for each other to indicate a place where, for instance, a free meal might be had, war-chalkers look for wireless networks and then leave information about what they've found in code for other war chalkers.[9]

To most business managers though, the whole idea of people looking for wireless connections seems like a real headache. Outsiders breaking into their networks? Yikes! If warchalk marks appear near your company (common ones include a circle with a w in the middle, or two joined half-circles), *Computerworld* columnist Frank Hayes advises bringing them directly to the attention of the CEO, and informing him or her that "the hackers already know where your wireless nets are—and if you don't secure them, they will be hacked."[10]

Well, maybe not. First of all, with a proper firewall in place on each computer and a password protecting the wireless network, the only thing that the average wireless seeker will be able to do is exactly what our friend did in that basement Laundromat: piggyback on the company's Internet connection for a while. Legally speaking, this might be considered theft of services, but some might respond that this is like complaining that a stranger who enters your living room is stealing your air. It would take a whole lot of people before you ever noticed any difference in your connection speed. (Still, we don't support stealing, and the safest course is to ask politely before accessing someone else's wireless network.)

And the geeks may only stay connected for moments. In a classic act of choosing process over product and use, many war walkers and war drivers don't stop to actually use the wireless networks they discover. All the fun is in finding them.

In fact, war driving has spawned a number of spin-off games, such as AP Hunt, in which competitors race against time to locate as many access points as they possibly can (which, of course, leaves no time for stopping to use them). The largest of these is WiGLE (Wireless Geographic Logging Engine, www.wigle.net), a project with the ambitious goal of mapping every single wireless network in the world. Started in 2001, WiGLE had already logged more than five million networks as this book was going to press. Another is the Wardriving Contest that covers a fifty-mile radius during Las Vegas's annual DefCon convention (DefCon claims to be the world's largest "underground hacking" event).[11] Now in its fifth year, the AP Games had to add some smaller, short-term games, since most serious Wardriving Contest competitors had to miss the actual conference in order to spend their three solid days driving around on a wireless search. Contest rules specify no flying allowed.

If it seems like this whole notion is all fun and games to the geeks who play it, it is—but there's an underlying streak of seriousness, too. Finding and mapping out access points gives people the opportunity to use the wireless Internet for free, which is what many technologists believe it should be. It comes down to another fundamental difference in the way geeks and suits view technology. The suits believe it should serve a specific purpose, and since in some cases, that purpose could be to earn money, they see nothing wrong with pay-for-access services, such as those available at various coffee and bookstore chains.

For many geeks, it's an article of faith that wireless access, like the Internet itself, should be freely available. Like all technology, it has value and beauty in its own right and is its own justification. They know the means exist to make whole towns, whole cities, perhaps even whole nations into one giant wireless zone, where anyone anywhere could sign on at will. Because it can be done, many geeks believe it should be done.

Suits envision a future where the Internet is part of commerce, an essential and infallible means to keep the wheels of the world in motion. Geeks envision a future in which all people, at all times, and in all places, are always connected.

CHAPTER 6
GRIPES ABOUT GEEKS

In the move *Ghostbusters*, a couple of geeky scientists find themselves ejected from academia. "You don't know what it's like out there!" laments one to the other. "I've worked in the private sector. They expect results!"

Unfortunately, many business people feel this sentiment perfectly describes how techies approach their jobs: all they want to do is play with their newfangled toys; to accomplish anything is beside the point. Justified or not, these kinds of complaints come up again and again when we talk to suits about their experiences with technologists. Here are some of their most frequent gripes, which will be balanced by a look at the issues from the techie point of view.

1. GEEKS DON'T UNDERSTAND—OR WANT TO UNDERSTAND—ANYTHING ABOUT THE BUSINESSES THEY WORK IN.

When we attended large technology conferences in the late 1990s, we heard the phrase "the business side" for the first time. It took us a while to understand what was meant. What business side? Is it a separate side? Eventually, we realized that this was precisely what the technology speakers we were listening to were saying. They did indeed see their companies as having two distinct sides—with themselves on one side, everyone else on the other, and a huge barrier in between. They even talked about "throwing things over the wall" to their business colleagues. It would never have occurred to them to learn anything about how the business people functioned.

Some technologists would surely ask: Why should we? They were hired for their ability to write code or manage a database, not devise a marketing plan or restructure the company's debt. Why should techies—most of whom already work very long hours—spend the time and effort to learn about something that isn't even part of their jobs?

Because it is part of their jobs to have a view of all parts in order to understand the whole, even if they never actually work on the "business side." Here's an example of why: A young technology worker complained to us recently that the company he worked for rushed its projects to delivery as the end of the quarter approached, sometimes sacrificing quality in favor of speed.

"Can you think of any business reasons why this might be the right decision?" we asked him. The obvious interpretation, and likely the right one, is that the company's managers must make out a quarterly report to investors or creditors in which it works to their advantage to show work as completed. Getting those projects delivered and the invoices out shows the company in a better light on paper. But what if the company is cash poor, and completing the work before the quarter ends means having enough to make a quarterly loan payment that is about to come due? Or even payroll? Knowing the right questions to ask might help a curious technology person better understand where the quarter-end urgency is coming from.

"Why is it the geek's job to ask involved questions, instead of the suits' to provide the information he needs?" asked a technology expert we know, upon hearing this suggestion. We agree: it shouldn't be the geek's job, and the business people he's working with should freely supply all pertinent information, including the reasons for the quarter-end crunch, so they might be able to schedule their time better throughout the quarter.

Unfortunately, in most working environments—for tech and nontech jobs alike—not all needed information is provided up front, so asking the right questions is a key survival skill. This can be doubly true for technology people, whose business managers may subject them to the "vending machine" approach. The "vending machine" approach refers to the belief by some business people that they can drop in money and instructions, and the technology they want will pop out as if from a dispenser. They don't see the necessity to discuss the wider question of why they need this particular technology or what goal they hope it will meet, any more than they would discuss their chocolate cravings with the machine supplying the M&M's. For technologists facing this sort of attitude, one defense is to understand the business they're working for and be able to ask the questions that will help them see their work in a larger context.

From the technology people's point of view, it may not seem reasonable to have to invest much time or energy in learning about the business world. It's difficult for nongeeks to comprehend the fact that people who work with technology are in a constant and neverending race to stay current. Even working on a project as part of a job can leave a technology person at a disadvantage, if the project in question uses last year's version of software, or a programming language that's not the very latest. So tech folk who ask how they're expected to find the time to learn about business may have a legitimate objection.

Nevertheless, more and more geeks are managing to find the time to do just that—because, increasingly, they know they need those skills in order to advance in their careers. In part, this is a legacy of the dot-com bust of 2000 and 2001. When the bottom fell out of the NASDAQ, many technologists found themselves forced to justify the cost of their projects for the first time. They learned the acronym ROI (Return on Investment) for the first time. Now ROI appears often in session titles at technology conferences and geeks who work in the corporate world are used to the idea that they will have to make a business case for the technology projects they propose.

But even without the dot-com bust, the likelihood is that many technology people would have started learning about business anyway. Increasingly, these are skills they need, as the technology field itself continues to evolve. Thirty years ago, when mainframes ran the world, technology professionals spent their careers locked away from the rest of the company, tending to computers in their glass houses. Their interaction with the company's business management might go no further than dropping a daily stack of printouts on someone's desk.

Today, geeks can be managers, not just of other geeks, but of cross-functional work teams that might well include members from "the business side." Ask a CIO or other top executive what qualities make a good technology manager and the answer will always include understanding of the business world. The message has not been lost on techies, many of whom are now seeking business training in an effort to broaden their horizons.

This will become only more necessary over the coming years, as business and technology become more intricately intertwined. As companies come to rely on computers and the Internet for everything, from conveying messages to keeping track of bookkeeping to sales, marketing, and customer service, it will become futile to try making major technology decisions without understanding the business—or major business decisions—without understanding technology. So while some technology experts certainly remain willfully ignorant of business concepts and concerns, theirs is the way of the past, and there will be fewer of them in the future.

2. GEEKS LOVE TECHNOLOGY FOR ITS OWN SAKE.

We've heard the same complaint again and again over the years from business managers who work with technology folk: "They want technology for its own sake." "They get fascinated with the latest gadget or the newest piece of software." "They constantly want the newest, most up-to-date hardware and software, whether or not it's what the company needs, and regardless of cost. They don't consider what's best for the company as a whole."

Anyone's who's ever watched a technology person with a new gadget or piece of software knows how true it is that geeks love technology. If they didn't, they probably couldn't do their jobs, which often involve spending long hours struggling with buggy code or other tasks that would be too frustrating for civilians. Innovations proceed in large part because of geek fascination. Consider Bruce Miller's description of how he learned high-level macro programming for the word processing software WordPerfect: "I was one of about five people in Washington State who could write the advanced document assembly systems. There was no school to go to. I got smart—like the other four—by spending hours and hours hacking out code to make things work."[1]

After learning these skills, Miller discovered he could perform a valuable service for local law firms by setting up these systems. "My first consulting gig saved the lawyer so much that he pulled a $100 bill out of his wallet as a tip," he says. This is just one example of how geeks' obsession with technology can wind up benefiting the organizations that hire them.

Nevertheless, there's truth in the complaint that geeks often want the most sophisticated technology whether or not it best serves their employers' goals. We remember a technology person once trying to sell us on complex communications software to be used by a far-flung group of people who needed a means of communication when working together on occasional projects. First of all, the software was overkill— the occasional, short information exchanges required for these projects could easily be done by e-mail, or perhaps an e-mail list. Second, it was expensive—no doubt worthwhile for a large, sophisticated organization collaborating on a daily basis. But spending the required thousands of dollars for a license made no sense for our small group. Third, and worst of all, it would have been counterproductive. This work group included several members who were very technologically limited—they had mastered their e-mail software, but were easily intimidated by new systems or new ways of doing things. So asking them to learn to use an intricate new piece of Internet-based software would have hindered, not helped, communications.

Would it have been fair of suits to expect the geek in question to take all those issues into account? That's an essential question that suits don't always stop to ask. The fact is that, at least in this instance, it was the geek's job to understand the technology; it was our job to understand the people who were to use it, whether and how easily they would learn to use the software, and whether the benefit would outweigh the expense.

Ultimately, we believe, this complaint stems from laziness on both sides. Technologists may not bother to learn much about business, but business folk don't necessarily want to learn much about technology either. Instead, they want easy-to-follow recommendations about what would best serve the company's needs. Thus, the complaint that technology people love technology for its own sake may really mean: "We want the technology people to decide for us whether this expenditure is worth it or not for our business, but they aren't objective enough to do that."

Is it reasonable to expect that they would be? Technology people, generally speaking, are focused on technology and don't necessarily have a complete view of the organization's goals, priorities, and resources. So maybe some business decisions really do need to be made on "the business side."

3. GEEKS EXPECT—SOMETIMES DEMAND— THAT SUITS UNDERSTAND AS MUCH AS THEY DO ABOUT TECHNOLOGY.

A few years ago, Clyde Steiner, working for a software development company, was checking the user interface screens for a new product to see if all the prompts, entry boxes, and pop-up help texts made sense.[2] He found the software's "final version" was flashy, but disorganized and confusing. So he had a conference with the company's star programmer, who had created it.

"Your screens really pop up," Steiner said, "but it is going to be hard for users to find which fields are required and which are optional. In addition, some of the important entry fields are on different screens."

The programmer looked surprised. "I was up all last night cleaning up and debugging the software. It is twice as fast as before and does everything with four thousand fewer lines of code."

"Great," Steiner said. "But the users will spend more time at the keyboard trying to decide what to do."

"Hey, that's the users' problem, not mine!" the techie shot back.

This was an extreme example, and of course most programmers would not take—and certainly not voice—such an attitude. But frustrated suits often report that the geeks they work with take too much technical knowledge for granted. In part, this has to do with the fact that technologically oriented people often spend the bulk of their school and working lives in the company of others with a similar bent. If you've worked only with people who know the difference between a Linux kernel and NetBSD acorn, you may not be attuned to explaining things on a sufficiently nontechnical level.

There's another, more problematic reason, though, that some geeks seem unwilling to deal with users who aren't technologically expert: they *are* unwilling to deal with them. A classic example of this attitude came from the developer we described in chapter 1 who expected his clients to send their employees for extensive training before using his software. He feels, as many tech people do, that software has integrity and esthetic all its own, and to dumb it down to make it more user-friendly is to besmirch a thing of beauty. A suit who encounters this kind of thinking needs to be a gentle but firm agent of reality, making it clear to the techie just what amount of learning is reasonable to expect from a user, and what is not.

That said, in some cases, the geeks have a point. A certain baseline knowledge of how software works is needed for anyone who ever uses a computer, and depending on what one is doing, a little bit of training may be an appropriate requirement. The challenge is to figure out what's fair to expect and what's not. (For more on this issue, see chapter 7.)

4. GEEKS CAN NEVER SEEM TO MEET DEADLINES OR STAY WITHIN BUDGETS.

"The most common term I hear when executives describe their IT departments is 'a black hole,'" says Ian Hayes, president of Clarity Consulting in Beverly, Massachusetts.[3] "You throw in money and requests and once in a while something pops out, but you never know when that's going to be."

Unfortunately, there is a great deal of truth in this complaint. According to the most recent Chaos Report by the Standish Group, only 28 percent of technology projects are completed on time and within budget.[4] Fifty-one percent end up "challenged"—that is, substantially late, over budget, or failing to meet specifications. (The rest are uncompleted or canceled before completion.) This is not a record for anyone to be proud of.

Why do technologists have such a hard time getting their work done on schedule? For one thing, there's the geek tendency to rebel against externally imposed rules and deadlines. They seek to do things their own way and on their own schedule. But many techies would argue that unrealistic expectations by suits make up the larger part of the problem.

They may have a point. It's worth noting that IT's best success rate for completing projects on schedule and under budget came at the bottom of the economic downturn following the dot-com bust. At that time, IT departments were working with diminished budgets and reduced personnel. One would think it would be harder, not easier, to fulfill management's requirements under those circumstances. But the requirements themselves were also scaled down to meet leaner times. Businesses then were less concerned with keeping up with the latest technological innovation, and more concerned with simply keeping their systems working and secure. It was in fact easier to meet these simpler expectations, even with more limited resources.

As the economy improved, businesses have once again begun planning more ambitious technology projects, which may be why the Standish Group's Chaos numbers, after improving over several years, have turned down again in 2004.[5] It's not just that the projects themselves are bigger, or that the new technology is now expected to accomplish more. With growing IT budgets come growing demands that new technology satisfy a wider variety of user needs, some of which may be added to the list even after the project has begun. The geek phrase for this phenomenon is "scope creep," and it's a major source of frustration among IT staffers.

In its most extreme form, the mismatch between expectations and deadlines is called a "death march project" by technology author Ed Yourdon, who describes why they happen and how to survive them in his book *Death March: The Complete Software Developer's Guide to Surviving 'Mission Impossible' Projects.*[6] He defines these as projects where the allotted time, budget, or staffing is half or less than half of what a "rational estimating process" would suggest is necessary. Yourdon and others, who've spent time in the trenches, report that a surprising number of technology projects qualify as death march projects, and that in some organizations, death marching has become business as usual.

The whole death march concept in itself is revealing about the state of communication between technology and business professionals: only in the odd world of business technology do whole teams routinely take on projects that they know for sure cannot be completed on time. Why can't they get together with their business counterparts and negotiate more realistic deadlines and budgets? In part, because of the deep mistrust between these two groups.

Most techies worry that they'll be accused of working too slowly or holding back company progress, so they agree to the deadlines they're given. Most suits, on the other hand, have seen many tech projects go past their deadlines so they try to compensate by setting deadlines that are artificially early—which only increases the likelihood that the techies won't be able to finish on time.

Perhaps the biggest problem has to do with the nature of technology work itself. Because it involves numbers, machinery, and long lists of instructions from the programmer to the computer, many outsiders assume that technology work proceeds rationally and predictably from one task to the next. But anyone who's done it knows this is far from the truth. Most technology work requires creative problem solving and moves ahead by sudden leaps, not rational steps. So it's almost impossible to say for sure how long a given job might take.

We recently saw the 2001 movie *Enigma*, a fictionalized account of work at England's Bletchley Park. During World War II, mathematicians and technologists gathered there to work together at deciphering Germany's radio transmissions that had been encrypted using its Enigma machine. In the movie, the Germans change a key component of the code—thus blocking England's ability to intercept—just as a convoy of American ships is steaming its way across the Atlantic, carrying needed supplies for Europe.

A flustered British navy official confronts the code breakers and demands to know: Will they be able to break the new code in the four days remaining before the ships enter U-boat territory? "Can somebody give me a straight answer to a straight question?" he asks. "Yes or no? Yes or no?"

By this time, we were ready to shout back at the screen, "Of *course* they can't give you a straight answer! They don't *know* how long it will take." After all, it's hard to say how long it'll take to finish a crossword puzzle until you've solved it—let alone decipher what was then the world's most sophisticated encryption machine.

In ways that may not be as obvious, all technology projects are subject to the same uncertainties.

5. GEEKS THINK RULES SHOULDN'T APPLY TO THEM.

Nowhere is this more obvious than when it comes to corporate dress codes, whether implicit or explicit. At IBM in the 1970s, a time when promotions were given or withheld based on whether one wore a white or pastel shirt, author Bill Pfleging used to express his geek rebelliousness by bringing a gym bag rather than the usual briefcase to staff meetings. Years later he worked at a dot-com start-up named Tripod—like many companies in the late 1990s, a place that was started and largely run by geeks. We'll always remember an early visit when we were sitting in Tripod's common area, which featured vintage video games, a heavy bag for boxing, a pool table, and a kitchenette filled with assorted snacks surrounded by coffee shop–style booth seats. A tall man with spectacles wandered in, dressed in a T-shirt and jeans. He had waist-length hair and bare feet.

The man stuck a bag of popcorn in the microwave, and sat chatting with us while it popped. It was clear he had been with Tripod since near the beginning, and knew the company inside and out, as well as the technology that made it run. When the popcorn was done he wandered off again, with a cheerful good-bye. We would learn later that this was Ethan Zuckerman, an uber geek who is now a research fellow at Harvard's Berkman Center for Internet and Society. At the time, he was Tripod's vice president of research and development. We would also learn that staff's tendency to meander around barefoot was an ongoing cause of concern for the company's office manager, who told us how she fretted about the liability issues that could arise.

It makes perfect sense that dress codes are the first rule of the corporate world which technology folk jettison, given half a chance. *It goes back to the fundamental difference between technology skills and business skills: solving problems, as opposed to influencing people.* From a suit perspective, appropriate business dress gives the office a professional feel, makes a good impression on outside visitors, and helps reinforce the sense that serious people are doing serious work.

There's also an unstated sense of power many people draw from knowing they look their businesslike best, and that their appearance can have a subtle and compelling influence on those they interact with—whether those are subordinates they wish to manage, customers they wish to sell to, or superiors they wish to impress. Awareness of how clothes influence perception is what gave rise to concepts like dressing for success and power ties.

We know one executive who left a corporate job to become an independent consultant. Even on the days he spends working entirely at home, interacting with clients only by telephone and Internet, he starts the day by donning a freshly pressed shirt and business suit, and carefully tying his tie. "I just feel different when I'm wearing a suit," he explains.

"Dressing for work makes me feel more confident." He's certain that feeling comes across, even when talking on the phone. Though most business people wouldn't go that far, most would understand where he's coming from.

For most techies, the whole idea of dressing for success runs directly counter to one of the values they hold highest: substance over style. Geeks have nothing but disdain for people who think that the clothes they wear—or what time they arrive at work—have any importance compared with whether the technology they create functions or not.

In fact, most believe that the effort it takes to, say, conform to a corporate dress code is effort that could be better spent on code. In his essay "Why Nerds are Unpopular," Paul Graham, designer of the Arc computer language and Yahoo! Store, among other accomplishments, argues that when geeks are in high school, wearing the right clothes, picking the right activities, getting in with the right crowd—all the people-influencing tasks that lead to popularity—are simply too time-consuming to bother with if they want to spend their schooling years actually learning. "The main reason nerds are unpopular is that they have other things to think about," he writes.[7] The same holds true when they grow up: they have a profound resistance to any rule or requirement that does not directly help them do their jobs. To technology folk, serious people doing serious work are probably wearing T-shirts and jeans. Anyone dressed fancier than that has expended energy on something other than the task at hand.

Geek rebellion runs much deeper than just not wanting to waste time on matters they consider superfluous. Technologists have always seen themselves as outsiders, even outlaws, especially in the corporate world, just as many of them did in high school. One of the best reflections of this is the word *hacker*.

To most business people, a hacker is a nefarious individual bent on breaking into their systems—the reason they need things like firewalls. But among technology professionals, hacker is also a term of honor. Not that technologists approve of breaking into others' systems—most don't—but to them, a hacker is a person who might or might not be nasty enough to penetrate someone else's computer, but, more importantly, has the skills to do so. (According to the Webopedia, an online dictionary of technology terms, among hackers themselves, the term for one who uses such skills to invade others' systems is *cracker*.)

Hack can be used to denote either an extraordinarily creative and elegant way to achieve a programming goal, or, more commonly, a quick and dirty fix to an immediate problem. Sounds contradictory, but what these two things have in common is that they achieve their goals by taking an unexpected approach, or to put it another way, by thinking outside the box.

Thinking outside the box is essential to most technologists' success. So it should come as no surprise that this same group of people may not be completely attuned to following rules.

6. GEEKS ARE BAD WITH PEOPLE.

You're either good with technology or good with people, but not both. This durable stereotype has given us thousands of pop culture icons from *Star Trek's* Mr. Spock to Scott Adams' cartoon character Dilbert (who knows all the programming languages there are, but spends all his time alone, in the company of a rat). It helps that history has also provided many technological geniuses whose human relations left much to be desired, such as Charles Babbage and Nikola Tesla (see chapter 2). There are less famous examples as well. "I have one guy working for me who's the best database administrator imaginable, just superb," says David Harrison, CEO of Intuition, a professional education company headquartered in Dublin. "But you couldn't put him in front of one of our clients, unless the client could actually speak binary."

Most business people who work with techies have encountered someone similar at one time or another. But to conclude from there that geeks in general are not good at dealing with people is a mistake—a mistake which suits too often make. This betrays unfamiliarity both with how geeks work and how they relate to others.

Not good with people? In his Tripod days, R&D VP Ethan Zuckerman used to organize a regular outing for twenty or thirty people to local single-A league baseball games. Business people and techies would all go together and sit side by side, and cheer for the home team together, though Zuckerman would pause now and then to make meticulous entries in his scoring sheet, reveling in the mathematics of the game. Tripod also had regular bowling nights, poker evenings, and parties. It even had a special blue drink (something complex involving curacao) that the elegant bar up the street made for its staff, who regularly dropped by to socialize after work.

During the late 1990s, this sort of atmosphere was seen in hundreds of dot-com start-ups across the country—the houses that geeks built. Yes, they spent ridiculously long hours in front of their computer terminals, and some would return to the office after a hard day's work to spend half the night playing games on their networked computers. They were certainly obsessed with technology, but they were also the last people on earth one would call antisocial or introverted.

Technology people work together just as well as they play together. One of the best proofs of this is the rapid growth of the open source software movement.

"Open source" simply means that the actual programming code to run a piece of software is released along with the software itself. This means any programmer fluent in the computer language in which the software was written can rewrite the software to fix bugs, widen its functionality, or customize it to his or her particular purposes. All over the world, tens of thousands of programmers are doing just that all the time—an international "software development team" which even Microsoft can't match no matter how many coders it hires.

Growing open source software requires much more than simply writing code. It's a massive coordination effort for each individual set of programs (Linux is only one example). The people working on it must assemble all the patches and improvements submitted by coders, evaluate and test them for effectiveness, decide which should be permanently added to the software, keep track of all these additions and changes, provide public representation for the software and the open source software community, and keep the thousands of developers involved in these efforts as happy as possible, whether their code is chosen to be added to the official version or not. These are complex tasks, many of them performed by volunteers, often requiring diplomacy, political acumen, and excellent communication skills. Not the right job for anyone who's bad with people.

So why do so many suits think that geeks are socially inept? Part of the problem has to do with the difference in the fundamental skill sets of technologists as compared with business experts. As noted earlier, for most business people, learning to engage and influence others is a key element of career advancement. If you can't motivate a team of people who report to you to do good work and to meet the goals you lay out for them, you're unlikely to go very far in the world of management. As you climb the career ladder, these teams become larger and larger, and include those with wider diversity of backgrounds, skills, job functions, and demographics. Thus, for most business people, being able to relate well to a wide range of people is necessary if their careers are to bloom.

The same is increasingly true for technology people, but this is a relatively recent development. Even a decade ago, most techies, as noted earlier, were relegated to geeky ghettos, where they supplied code and support for corporate computer systems, but were rarely seen or heard from by their business colleagues. Some rose to management positions, but oversaw only groups of other geeks. In this insular world, technology folk evolved their own practices, dress codes, mores, and language, none of which bore much resemblance to "the business side," and most of which are still with us today. So there's no denying that many technology people are better at dealing with other technology people and not necessarily great with others.

Beyond that, though, is a mutual lack of respect that sours many geek-suit interactions from the start. Most technology people think little of the skills it takes to keep a business running—even if it is those same skills that keep their paychecks arriving on schedule. Anybody can do it, they figure. They believe that they could, if only they wanted to bother, though some have less confidence now that they've seen what happened to many geek-run companies during the dot-com bust of 2000.

Suits, for their part, know perfectly well they could never learn to do what techies do. But many still think of technology as an isolated, external, and expendable part of their organization, something that mostly serves to annoy the business executives who must keep the organization functioning and do the "real work." Of course, in these days of e-commerce, online collaboration, intranets for knowledge management, and virtual offices, technology is looking less and less expendable. Without working computers, paychecks wouldn't arrive on time, either.

Until both groups learn to properly respect and value the other's work, geeks will continue to see many suits as clueless and ineffectual. And suits will continue to believe that geeks just can't work with people.

CHAPTER 7

GRIPES ABOUT SUITS

A technologist whom we know was working as a consultant for a law firm, setting up its firm-wide computer system. The job entailed meeting with each of the firm's attorneys, to find out exactly what she wanted the system to do.

One of them said, "I want to be able to ask the computer how much money I'm owed by clients, how much I have billed, and how much I have in the bank."

"OK," the techie said. "We'll set the system up with financial reporting software that will generate a report for you every day."

"No, no," the lawyer said. "I want to ask the computer."

"OK . . . We'll set up the report so you can type in a query and get exactly the information you need."

"You don't understand," the lawyer insisted. "I want to be able to walk into my office and say, 'Computer! How much money do I have in the bank?' And the computer will tell me."

"What?? What are you talking about?"

"Yeah," the lawyer said calmly. "They do it that way on *Star Trek* all the time."

True story.

When geeks get together among themselves, these are the sorts of war stories they tell, tales of the strange, irrational, and perplexing things business people say and do and, especially, what they want from technology. Here are a few of their biggest complaints, balanced by a look at these issues from the business viewpoint.

1. *SUITS REFUSE TO LEARN ANYTHING ABOUT TECHNOLOGY.*

"I manage a guy's Web site," notes Bruce Miller of *Puget Sound Computer User*. "For two years, every time he needed to attach a file to an e-mail he would ask me how to do it, and I would explain it to him. After two years I said, 'I'm not telling you anymore.' I think this guy prides himself on not being a computer geek."[1]

It's certainly true that some business executives seem to take pride in the fact that they know nothing about computers. "I don't want to know how it works! I just want it to do what I need." How many times have you heard a computer user say something like this, often followed by a self-deprecating smile: "I'm not very computer literate, you know"?

This last comment is probably intended to disarm the geeks' frustration, but it often has the opposite effect. "Why don't you *get* literate," they want to snarl in response. "Or else, quit wasting my time."

At this point in the twenty-first century, it does seem fair to expect everyone working in business to have a basic idea of how to use a computer, in the same way that most people are assumed to know how to make a telephone call. Yet, sad to say, there's nothing exceptional about Miller's client. Nearly everyone who works with technology in business has encountered many just like him. Geeks have an acronym for this level of determined ignorance: PEBCAK, which stands for "Problem Exists Between Chair and Keyboard."

If PEBCAK creates problems when business people don't learn to understand the technology sitting on their desks, it creates exponential problems when suits with decision-making authority don't understand the technology running their businesses.

A few years ago, a geek friend of ours was charged with heading a team to evaluate software for a chemical manufacturing plant. The purpose of the software was to track maintenance schedules on the plant's machinery. Our friend's team spent a year reviewing several software packages, meeting with vendors' technical staff, and refining the company's requirements. After all the research was in, they were confident they had identified the right package for the job. They made their recommendation to management and prepared to start implementation.

At this point, the company's top management stepped in. They were grateful for the team's recommendation, but they had decided to go with a different software package, the team's number two choice.

It turned out there were business issues at play that the team was never told about. The second-choice package was actually sold not by a software company but by another chemical manufacturing firm that had developed the package for its own use. What's more, the two companies had recently agreed on a merger. From management's viewpoint, it seemed an obvious, logical step to use the software developed for their industry—software they would soon have access to in any case.

The problem was, the software didn't work, or at least not dependably enough for the company's purposes. Maintenance in a chemical plant is not a haphazard thing. If this work isn't done on schedule, there could be shutdowns, worker injuries, or worse. While it was a great idea to use software to keep maintenance on schedule, it made sense only if the software in question was 100 percent reliable. If not, the plant should stick with manual record keeping—it was simply too dangerous to do otherwise.

A second issue that came up was support. Because the vendor was not a software vendor, but a manufacturing firm for which software was only a sideline, it did not have the support system in place to properly address issues that might arise. Our friend and his team found themselves, in some cases, waiting days for responses to their questions and concerns. Once again, with worker lives at risk, this was not a chance they could afford to take.

After talking it over with his CIO, our friend decided to pull the plug on the project, and recommend that the plant stick with manual record keeping after all. He also began looking for a new place to work. He had wasted a year and now hated his job. The company had also wasted a year—of his and his teammates' salaries—and was now losing one of its technological leaders. Plant managers still had to record their machinery's maintenance manually. It was a situation where everyone lost—because top management considered only the business issues it knew best, and did not bother to learn the technological and support issues involved in their software purchase.

The fact that many suits refuse to learn even the basics of technology is the single most frustrating aspect of working in the corporate world for most technologists. At the same time, some suits feel almost as frustrated when geeks expect them to be technology experts.

Somewhere between the suit who could not learn in two years how to attach a file to an e-mail and the geek who considers an overwhelmingly complex interface to be "the user's problem" lies a reasonable balance. Business people need a baseline understanding of technology to function in the modern world, and technology folk need to learn that a baseline understanding is only that. That balance lies at a different point from company to company and industry to industry, but it's there in every case. Finding it is an important first step toward closing the Geek Gap.

2. SUITS WHO DON'T UNDERSTAND TECHNOLOGY NEVERTHELESS INSIST ON MAKING TECHNOLOGICAL PRONOUNCEMENTS.

About a year ago, we attended a talk on how to do book promotion. The speaker was an author who had used a variety of clever promotional gimmicks to sell her line of party books and cookbooks. She discussed a variety of low-tech ways to generate publicity and interest in a book, and also how to use a Web site to help find potential readers. She closed her talk by saying: "Meta tags are very important. I can't tell you too much about them, but you should make sure you know about them and that your Web site has the right ones."

Saying in the same sentence that you don't understand something yet that something is important should be enough of a contradiction to give most people pause. But even leaving that issue aside, she was just plain wrong. Meta tags, for anyone who doesn't know, are invisible words embedded in Web sites, unseen by anyone looking at them, but visible to "spiders"—search engine bot programs that examine and categorize Web pages by the millions in an attempt to sort them for ranking in searches. The original idea was that meta tags would help the spiders sort pages correctly: for instance, the now defunct e-business Big Red Chair sold clothing for tall and large men. Its Web site could have had "apparel" and "large" among its meta tags, making it likely to come up in a search for those words.

The use of meta tags was soon corrupted by crafty developers trying to gain higher placement in search engines through any means possible. For instance, instead of just "apparel," they might also use "apparel, men's apparel, large apparel, men's clothing," and so on, the idea being that the more times something is mentioned, the higher one's ranking became in a search engine. Then, some people took it one step further, by inserting words like *porn* and *sex* to their meta tags.

Why would they do that? Because search engines were designed to recognize not only how many meta tags matched the words in the search, but also to increase the ranking of Web sites whose meta tags contained words that were popular in general. For many years, sexual terms were among the most frequently searched, so adding these very popular terms to a meta tag, even for an unrelated Web site, was likely to increase its rankings.

As meta tags became more of a source of misinformation and more of a means to jockey for position than anything else, many search engine companies began rewriting their software to take less heed of them. Then Google revolutionized the industry with an entirely new way of ranking Web sites—according to how many other Web sites had links to them—which made meta tags even less relevant.

All this had happened years before the book promoter made her speech. Why did she insist on talking about meta tags when she really didn't know enough about them to comment? She probably thought she was being helpful, and that her audience would make good use of the information when they set out to create their own Web sites. Or, she was proud of her little bit of hard-won technical knowledge and couldn't resist the urge to flaunt it. Maybe it was a combination of both. Whatever the case, the tendency of nontechnological people to make blanket statements on technological subjects they barely know anything about makes many geeks go ballistic.

Technologists' frustration level is all the higher when they're faced with business people making decisions about technology based on the same sort of limited information. In his essay "Revenge of the Nerds,"[2] Paul Graham rails against a certain category of bosses who know nothing about technology while still having strong opinions about it. For instance, he says, if a geek needs to write a piece of software, the boss may know nothing about how the software has to work, and yet thinks he knows what language it should be written in: Java.

"What he's thinking is something like this," Graham writes. "Java is a standard. I know it must be, because I read about it in the press all the time. Since it is a standard, I won't get in trouble for using it. And that also means there will always be lots of Java programmers, so if those working for me now quit, as programmers working for me mysteriously always do, I can easily replace them."

This would be less of a problem if computer languages were all interchangeable, but they aren't. Java is right for some jobs, wrong for others. It seems obvious that a business executive who doesn't know enough to understand these complexities has no business deciding the right language for a project.

Still, the answer is not for business people to leave all technological decisions to technology people, because the business elements of the decision tend to get left behind. We once met a company manager who had asked her company's technology team to design a new way of handling its online business. The team came back with a detailed plan for completely overhauling the company's software and creating something much more elegant and efficient. The plan described how the new software would be deployed over the company's worldwide offices. Though techies thought it was an excellent plan, the manager saw one fatal flaw. According to the techies' own calculations, the project would take six years to complete. Considering that Internet commerce was likely to change dramatically in any six-year period, the manager feared the new e-business software might well be obsolete before it was even launched. So she nixed the plan.

Most technology folk would never be so foolish as to propose a six-year plan in the rapidly changing world of e-commerce. Yet this team's proposal is an extreme manifestation of something many business people have observed: IT people are more interested in the technology they work with than the business it's supposed to serve.

As discussed earlier, this is a good thing in many ways: geeks' unending curiosity about whether and how to expand computer capabilities is the reason technological innovation continues to skyrocket. But it does mean business people who take an I-don't-want-to-know-the-details approach to technology do so at their own peril. The best solution is for technology people to work with their business counterparts to make choices that are right for the business and, at the same time, make technological sense.

3. SUITS DON'T VALUE TECHNOLOGY.

If one of business people's common complaints is that technologists love technology for its own sake, one of technologists' biggest frustrations is that they believe business people don't value technology at all. They may appreciate what the technology can do for their business—after a kindly techie has carefully explained how it works. But they don't appreciate its beauty and power.

"Think of it this way," says one disgruntled geek we know. "Did the ancient Roman emperors value the slaves they owned? No, they valued what the slaves could do for them, but they didn't value the human lives at all. Modern day suits look at technology the same way." We think that this comment perfectly captures the technologists' dilemma. Business people value technology only because of what it can do for them. Technology people think of it as a living, breathing thing.

Beyond not valuing technology, some business people seem to see it as a necessary evil: they need it to do their jobs, but they would prefer to give it as little thought as possible and deal with it even less. These are the people who tend to make technology the scapegoat whenever anything goes wrong.

We recently encountered this phenomenon when a colleague e-mailed us a Microsoft Word document we needed to read before a team meeting. We dutifully downloaded the document and sent it to our printer.

The document was eighteen pages long, but the printer could print only the first two before it ran out of paper. Unfortunately, we were distracted with many other matters and either failed to notice or forgot that the printer needed reloading. Instead, we grabbed the two pages it had printed, assuming that was all there was, and thus arrived at the meeting missing sixteen pages of essential information.

When we realized our error, we felt terrible and apologized profusely. But our colleague who'd sent the material turned to us with a smile.

"It's not your fault," she said. "It's the fault of the e-mail software."

At first, we thought she was just trying to be nice, but as we talked about it, we realized this was what she genuinely had assumed to be true. Geeks in many workplaces face this kind of antitechnology prejudice on a daily basis.

On the other hand, there are a great many suits who feel the opposite: they love technology and seek to understand as much as they can about it. "I'm a prime example," notes Karin Albert of Granite Construction. "I'm an aging Baby Boomer who just happens to use technology to do my job. In some people's eyes, that makes me a technology employee, because I can help them use technology."

But even business people like Albert who value technology and enjoy working with it don't have the same view that technology people do. "I think there is a fundamental difference," she says. "Geeks see technology as an end in itself while suits are only interested in technology as a means to an end. Neither group is conscious of the difference."

4. ALL SUITS CARE ABOUT IS MONEY.

If business people see technology as a means to an end, the end in question is nearly always money, which means either increasing revenue or cutting costs. Even business managers who stress that their focus is customers do so as part of an overall strategy for long-term profitability. (Since studies show it's much less costly to sell something to someone who's already a satisfied customer than go out and find a new customer, keeping customers happy is sound fiscal practice.)

This attention to profitability has fostered many a miscommunication. "Suit says, 'Tell me what this machine will do for me,' and is thinking ROI, improved customer service, better data to support decision making. The geek is thinking gigaflops and terabytes," Albert notes.[3]

Though geeks aren't wrong to value technology, it's important for them to understand the suit point of view, because, well, the bottom line is the bottom line. The technology in use in companies is there to serve the business—and its moneymaking goals—not the other way around. No profitability, no business.

This distinction between technology-as-means-to-an-end and technology-as-end-in-itself becomes much blurrier when the technology is part or all of what the company sells. A technologist whose job is to help create his company's product might naturally suppose that the technical aspects of that product would be of paramount importance. But, though the distinction may be a subtle one, it's essential even for these technology workers to understand that what they're creating is valuable only insofar as it fulfills specific customer needs.

This is why one top executive we know says that it always annoys him to hear his staff talk about how they are creating "technology." He tries to get them to use the word "solution" instead. Unfortunately, stressing "solution" over "technology" is the kind of management-speak that can set geeks to playing Buzzword Bingo, in which geeks keep track of buzzwords used by suits during meetings and win when a particular set of terms is completed (for more on this game, see chapter 9). But the underlying message is still worth paying attention to. Even when technology is part or all of the product a company sells, it still must serve a greater business goal.

5. *SUITS RESIST INNOVATION.*

"Geeks = technology = evolution," declares Bruce Miller.[4] "Suits = policy = status quo. The suit people seem to be eternally stressed at learning and adopting new systems."

There is no question that many business people are resistant to change, particularly where technology is concerned, and this often makes technologists' jobs harder than they need to be. We once worked with an organization that had an ongoing and lively discussion among its members via an e-mail list serve. (In a list serve, e-mails sent to a central address are forwarded to an entire group, so all can join in the discussion.)

When the association upgraded and expanded its Web site a few years back, it added an elaborate online message board. Users could now follow threaded discussions, they could search for topics of interest to them, and, since messages were divided by category and topic, they were free to read only what would be of interest to them. This was clearly a huge improvement over the list serve, but some users had grown comfortable with their e-mail based discussion and were violently opposed to the idea that they'd have to open a browser and go to a Web site instead. Vitriolic e-mail complaints began arriving, directed at the group's IT director, some claiming the new message board was "a scam," intended to drag its unwilling victims out onto the World Wide Web.

After gnashing his teeth for a while, the IT director managed to adjust the message board software so that those group members who so chose could receive the postings as e-mails, and reply to them the same way. This made for somewhat cumbersome reading for the message board users, since postings that arrived by e-mail often did not fit properly into the site's topic threads, and sometimes came out with odd extra characters generated by the posters' e-mail software. And that's how matters have remained.

It may be true that many suits back away from technological innovations. But it's important to remember the major differences between how techies and their business counterparts spend their day. For technologists, innovation is a daily concern; if they weren't constantly experimenting with new technologies, they wouldn't be doing their jobs. Business people, though, often see time spent learning new technology as time taken away from their "real" work. Thus, every new piece of software or new device is subjected to a cost/benefit analysis: Is the money and/or effort this device will save for me worth the time and effort expended in learning how to use it? A business executive who suspects the answer may be no will be reluctant to spend any time on the new item.

Thus what may appear like resisting new technology may simply be the suits' uncertainty as to whether and to what degree the new technology will likely help them do their jobs. Geeks should keep this unspoken calculus in mind whenever they recommend adopting new technology.

6. SUITS VALUE IMAGE OVER SUBSTANCE.

A couple of years ago, we did some work for a start-up company that provided real-time reports on medicines and medical issues for a large and well-known health Web site. The reports were written from announcements of new medicines or medical discoveries, or the results of clinical trials. The goal was to get the information to doctors and patients as quickly as possible, so time was always of the essence.

The start-up was a virtual company, with each of its employees and managers working from a home office. Conversations took place by instant message, and occasionally by phone. Report writers, spread around the United States and Canada, would submit their work via its Web site to the company's editors, who would then pass it on to the editorial director for a final check before sending the report to the client.

This would have been a good system, except for one problem: the company's editorial director was clueless about using technology and, worse, seemed unable to learn. "I remember one day we were walking her through the process of publishing a report, trying to teach her how to use the Web site," recalls one of the start-up's IT staff. "I was on the phone with her, and she said, 'There's a button here that says "Delete." What does it do?'

"I said, 'You don't want to hit that. You'll delete the report you're working on.'

"'I already did,' she said.

"What? Why did you do that?'

"'It should have been more specific,' she complained.

"'It said *"Delete!"* How much more specific could it be?'"

The editorial director's technical inabilities created an ongoing series of tangles, the IT staffer recalls, and because her approval was the last, necessary step before each report could be published, the company found itself routinely missing deadlines. "The raw material was created on a computer and delivered to us through the Internet," the IT staffer recalls. "We delivered it to the client via computer, and kept track of our billing hours on the computer as well. The editorial director didn't understand any of the technical issues, or even how to use our Web site."

If working with this executive was frustrating for the company's IT staff, working with the company proved just as frustrating for the company's single client. After more than eight months of daily delays and reports routinely filed late, the client abruptly severed its relationship with the start-up company, effectively putting it out of business. The editorial director, the IT staff, and everyone else found themselves looking for new jobs.

The IT staffer we talked to blamed the start-up's demise on its CEO—the one who hired the editorial director in the first place. "He said we needed an editorial director who had cachet," the staffer explains. The editorial director provided plenty of cachet, having previously been an editor at one of the most prestigious medical journals in the country. But, the IT staffer says, "We wasted time, and wound up getting into arguments with the client. We should have hired someone with less management experience and more computer experience."

In other words, the CEO's big mistake was choosing image over substance—someone who looked good on paper instead of someone who could actually do the job. This kind of thinking leads geeks to believe that suits have their priorities out of order, and worse, that they care only for superficial things.

But there's another element to this story. The company was a start-up with no track record, and most of its top management did not have much of a track record (in fact, their previous attempt to launch a medical-reports company had ended in failure). In order to launch, they needed solid investment, and they got it by obtaining a loan from the very Web site that would also be their single client.

Keep in mind that a company purchasing medical reports—where bad information can cause injury, not to mention lawsuits—requires a great deal of trust in the people providing those reports. Having the editorial director on board with her unimpeachable health background made it possible for the client to trust those reports. The start-up may have failed because she was on staff, but without her, it might never have existed in the first place.

We'll never know whether the start-up's management could have solved this problem. Perhaps the editorial director could have been a fig-urehead "advisor" instead of a hands-on editor. Perhaps the company could have assigned someone to handle the technical parts of her job, leaving her to oversee only medical questions. Or maybe there was no good answer, and the company was doomed from the start.

Whatever the case, the moral of the story is this: from a business point of view, choosing between style and substance can be more com-plex than it first appears. Although their work is very difficult, the param-eters of most geeks' jobs are fairly straightforward: they must solve tech-nological problems.

Suits' jobs often have more varied requirements and include such ele-ments as building trust among both internal and external constituencies, selling customers on the organization, coming up with marketing strate-gies, and building motivation among other members of the team. All these tasks require suits' best influencing skills. Carefully managing image is one way suits exert influence. So it's important for geeks to remember that a suit who seems overly concerned with image may simply be doing his or her job.

CHAPTER 8

GEEKS "GREP," SUITS "POTENTIALIZE": WHY WE DON'T SPEAK THE SAME LANGUAGE

I n one of our favorite *Doonesbury* cartoons, Reverend Scott asks his friend Mike to accompany him to a store to buy a computer for his new pro-peace newsletter.[1] The reverend is afraid of computers, he explains.

At the store, the salesman asks, "What are your storage capacity requirements? What kind of retrieval speed? How many bytes per second data transfer?"

"I knew it," the reverend says, turning to leave. "He doesn't speak English."

Luckily, Mike has brought along an English-to-Geekish phrasebook. He opens it and reads out loud: "'Excuse me, sir. Do you have any user-friendly sales reps?'"

Many business people find themselves wishing for just such a phrasebook when discussing their technology needs, systems, and problems with technologists. On the other hand, many technologists are just as mystified when business people use words like "incentivize," or talk about gaining "traction."

Geeks and suits both use their own vocabularies to talk about how they do their jobs, but this is only one aspect of a much larger cultural clash. In fact, the overriding way in which these two groups use language itself is different, and is meant to achieve different goals. Both use jargon that sounds mysterious to outsiders, but the reasons behind the jargon are completely dissimilar, and lead to even more misunderstanding than the words themselves.

As we discussed earlier, technology careers are built primarily on problem-solving skills, whereas for business careers, the ability to influence others—for sales, motivation, management, or many other purposes—is at least equally important. These differences in skills and priorities are reflected in how geeks and suits use words.

DO YOU GROK GEEK?

Shopping around on orders.geekstuff.com, we came across a T-shirt that reads "grep this." Grep this? We pride ourselves on having a fair knowledge of geekspeak, but this was a new one for us. We turned to the catalog copy accompanying the shirt, and read: "Wear this shirt when you need to discern the like-minded in your environment. If they laugh, buy 'em a beer; if they ask you to explain it, LART 'em!"

This wasn't much help. Urban Dictionary[2] to the rescue: "grep" is a Unix or Linux command to search a file for a matching keyword or pattern. "LART" is an acronym for "Luser Attitude Readjustment Tool,"—such as a large wooden club appropriate for hitting the offender on the head. Like "club," LART can also be used as a verb, as in "I will LART you appropriately." "Luser," in case you were wondering, is a cross between "user" and "loser," geekish for a nonexpert, or clueless, technology user.

This kind of thing is not necessarily what people mean when they say that techies speak their own language. But, as it illustrates, most geeks know perfectly well that nongeeks don't understand what they're saying—and much of the time, that's exactly the way they want it.

Technologists usually work in a counterculture within their organizations, interacting mainly with each other. And that's fine with them. They like not having to explain that when they say "perl," they are referring to neither jewelry nor knitting, but to an open source programming language. Eventually, a sort of laziness sets in, and it can be difficult to resist. Geeks would rather spend their time talking to other geeks. And the quickest way to cut nongeeks out of the conversation is to use words they won't understand.

But there's more to geeks' tendency to cluster together. It's also a matter of a strong affinity, of shared passions that run a lot deeper than most laypeople realize, something that is reflected in the geekish word *grok*. *Grok* is a Martian word from Robert Heinlein's 1961 novel *Stranger in a Strange Land*,[3] and though its literal meaning is "to drink," its figurative meaning is to have such a complete understanding of something that one has completely absorbed it, and been absorbed by it. Geeks tend to say that they "grok Linux" or "grok perl," and that business managers do not "grok geek." Geeks do grok other geeks. Sometimes that makes them want to leave the rest of the world behind.

But sometimes they don't, and at those times, geeks often discover that most technological terminology does little to aid communication between techies and their business counterparts, especially since acronyms, bizarre spellings, and unexpected combinations of upper and lower case letters are their norm.

For instance, a marketing manager we know once asked her company's IT consultant how difficult it would be to offer clients an online community with chat rooms and a message board. She got the following cryptic reply:

"We could throw up a quick and dirty ASP DEv XM forum, but not sure whether to use LDAP for member recognition. Or, we can do a phpBB and customize the SS to our specs, since we already have PostgreSQL in place."

Huh? The marketing manager was mystified. What the IT consultant was saying was: "We could set up the chat and message board on an outside provider's server. This would be an inexpensive way to try it out, but it would give us less control, and we may not be able to use a directory of our clients to make the community private. As an alternative, we can do our own online bulletin board and host it here, since we already have database capability in place." Unfortunately, the language of technology almost seems deliberately designed to discourage clear communication.

THERE'S NO PLACE LIKE 127.0.0.1

When they talk about technology, geeks and suits are not just speaking different languages, they are often speaking about two different things, or at least two different aspects of the same thing. In chapter 5, we discussed the difference between process and product or use, and the idea that technology people are mainly interested in how to make a piece of technology work, while business people are mainly interested in how that technology can help them do their jobs after the techies have gotten it working. Those differences materialize not only in how the two groups approach technology, but also what they say about it.

A computer consultant friend of ours is on the board of his hometown library. Like many other libraries, for the last few years, this one has been providing patrons the use of computers with Internet access. Recently, it added Wi-Fi to its offerings. As a board member, our geek friend was forbidden from doing business with the library, so another local computer expert installed the wireless instead.

Our friend happened to be on site when the other computer expert arrived for a final check of the new system and the two stood around and chatted.

"What IP are you using? 192.168.1.1, or 0.1?" our friend inquired. "And are you using static IPs or letting the router do it?"

"No, 169.172.123.1 with auto DHCP set," said the techie. "Splash is at 169.172.123.9 if you need to load any changes. You have admin access already set up."

Two librarians who'd been listening to this exchange turned to each other. "It's another language," one sighed.

In this instance, that isn't entirely true. A lot of things geeks discuss are deeply mysterious, but IP numbers are not among them. An IP number or "address" is a unique number assigned by a computer system to every computer that interfaces with a network, such as a LAN (Local Area Network), WAN (Wide Area Network), or the Internet itself. It's like a Social Security number for a computer, although much less permanent. The IP number lets all other systems recognize and grant or deny access to individual computers or computer devices that request connections. This is not a concept that requires an engineering degree to grasp.

In essence, then, these two geeks were deep in discussion over what numbers one of them had chosen to assign to the various elements in a computer network, an important question in the intricate world of computer networking, and thus a subject of limitless fascination for many tech folk. All computers' self-referring "loopback" IP number is 127.0.0.1 (used for testing network settings without actually using a network)—a fact that has spawned the Geekish saying, "There's no place like 127.0.0.1."

None of this is unimportant, but we still suspect that when faced with this type of concern, most suits would think, "Who cares?" For the techies, the question of how, precisely, the wireless network was linking to the Internet, and what protocols it used to do so were important. For the librarians and their patrons, the essential fact was that anyone with a wireless-enabled laptop or PDA could now surf the Net. No wonder the two conversations sounded so different—what they were discussing was not at all the same thing.

TECHNOLOGY WITH INTERESTING NAMES

Underlying the differences in how geeks and suits talk about technology is another basic distinction in how they view their work lives. When they're doing their jobs, most technology people tend to see themselves at play, rather than at work.

A few years ago, a programmer we know stopped in the middle of a long coding job, turned to his colleague at the next station and exclaimed,

"I don't believe we get paid to do this stuff!" before diving back into his work. The company he worked for, however, sounded like one of the least pleasant working environments we've heard of. It was a large corporation with draconian rules about such issues as dress and, especially, tardiness. During one of the harshest winters in the snow-laden region where we live, this particular geek risked driving through blizzard after blizzard to make it to work on time, aware that he faced dire consequences if he was late, no matter what the cause. In spite of all that, he still saw his work as play.

Even technologists forced to work long hours trying to meet impossible deadlines on "death march" projects (see chapter 6) may become resentful of the managers or business pressures they face, but this resentment likely will not carry over to the technology itself (unless they also dislike it on a technical basis). However hard they may be working, they still fundamentally view technology as a game.

There's no better proof than the names geeks choose for the products they create. Programs from Apache to Java are simply named after people or things their creators like or admire. This is nothing, however, compared to the fun technologists have when naming products by acronym. For instance, we spent many a fun hour playing with a digital recording device called MOTU. What does MOTU stand for? The company's name, Mark of the Unicorn. The operating system Linux contains much that comes from GNU, an organization devoted to open source software. The acronym GNU stands for "GNU's Not Unix." (The circular logic of this ought to be enough to make most non-techies' heads spin.)

Some time after that we installed a scanner on our computer. We found that we needed TWAIN software to make it work. We got the scanner going eventually, but kept wondering what the heck TWAIN could be an acronym for. After a little digging, we found the answer: TWAIN was an acronym for "Technology Without an Interesting Name!"

We found that amusing, but what may be funniest about it is—it isn't true. TWAIN, in its original form, was not an acronym at all, but simply a name. After inventing it, its creators thought it would give the TWAIN name more cachet to be written all in upper case, and so they sponsored a contest to come up with words that would fit that acronym. "Technology Without an Interesting Name" won the contest, and a techie urban legend was born.

The original name was just as whimsical as the contest-winning acronym. It came from the first line of Rudyard Kipling's poem "The Ballad of East and West":[4]

"Oh, East is East, and West is West, and never the twain shall meet," and was intended as a wry comment on the difficulty of making image devices like scanners connect with computers.

We could go on, for the list of technology with interesting, witty, or downright funny, names is virtually endless. Clearly, many technology folk don't take the names for the products they create all that seriously. This can be a real problem for suits, because most of them do.

"CHALLENGES" NOT "PROBLEMS"

Excuse us—what we meant to say is, the fact that geeks don't take words seriously can be a real *challenge* for suits. Most suits learn early in their careers: never call something a "problem," call it a "challenge" or—if it really seems insurmountable—an "issue." We don't suffer "defeats" but "setbacks." Instead of saying something we haven't done right is a failure, we say it requires a "laserlike focus" or a "paradigm shift."

This kind of verbal recasting can seem silly, but the logic underlying it is very serious. It goes back to the importance of being able to influence and persuade other people. This is an essential skill for most business people, and they're smart enough to recognize the awesome power that words have to alter perceptions and thus influence behavior.

A popular political example of this phenomenon occurred when estate tax opponents began referring to it as the "death tax." An estate tax sounds like it would only affect the landed gentry, while death, of course, will eventually happen to everyone. The word "death" has a far more powerful impact than "estate." The new name caught on, and soon estate tax levels were heavily curtailed.

The same effect can be seen throughout the world of business. In the examples we just gave, negative events are recast not only in a more positive light but also with a call to action. We're more likely to try to rise to a challenge than we might be to struggle with a problem, and more likely to move on after experiencing a setback than we would be if we suffered a defeat. And knowing some part of our business is failing miserably might only invite despair, whereas knowing that an area needs our "laser-sharp focus" might impel us to try harder.

Suits are so keenly aware of the importance of words that there's a whole industry of books, seminars, consultants, and Web sites devoted to helping them with "business communications." (Ironically, the only communications books we've found aimed at technology folk are intended to help them communicate specifically with business folk. The implication is that only in the strange world of suits do such things matter.)

In the *Harvard Business Review on Effective Communication*,[5] Michael McCaskey describes a disagreement between two aerospace executives whose project's funding was about to run out. Both agreed they should ask management to renew funding for what they knew to be important research. Their conflict arose over which words to use when asking. The project's research director wanted to offer their bosses a "menu of options."

"By using the word *menu*, he was saying, in effect, 'After all, everybody has to eat something—the question is what,'" McCaskey explains.

The project manager wanted to ask top management to "bite the bullet" and fund the research. "His phrasing depicts a situation in which a big step—even though painful or risky—was necessary for the long-term health of the project," McCaskey notes. This had the added benefit of evoking the Wild West and cowboy bravery, but could also be seen as too negative an approach.

We don't know which won out in the end. But it's a good illustration of the enormous importance most business managers place on words and the power those words have to subtly change the listener's perceptions and bring about a desired result.

"SOMETIMES YOU MANAGE DOWN"

There's an essential distinction between using words honestly, if obliquely, to influence listeners' behavior and using them to try to obscure the truth. Nowhere is this more obvious than in the words business managers use when they lay off people. The term *layoffs* gave way in the 1980s to *downsizing*, a euphemism that was briefly mocked, but soon became standard.

Then, in 1988, a vice president of personnel administration for General Motors Corp. said in an interview that he preferred the term *rightsizing* to describe the company's layoffs.[6] To us, this appears to be a perfect example of a suit attempting to use a word change to shift perceptions. GM wasn't just having minor cutbacks—it fired 25 percent of its salaried staff, a move that devastated entire Michigan communities (chronicled in the 1989 film *Roger & Me*). It left the entire cities of Flint and Saginaw feeling definitely down. While it's doubtful the GM vice president believed changing the word for what had happened could make those laid off feel better, he was trying to send a message to the company's stockholders that it was the correct step for the industrial giant, and it would help guarantee its future financial health in the face of growing competition from Japan.

Rightsizing never really caught on, but there was another, better, euphemism on the way. In more recent years, suits faced with the unpleasantness of layoffs have tended to use the term *restructuring* to describe the event. The meaning is not precisely the same—a restructuring does not necessarily involve layoffs. But these days, when most companies announce "restructuring" plans, most listeners understand it means fewer people on the payroll.

As subtle verbal changes go, *restructuring* does a better job than *rightsizing*, because it more clearly indicates that the company is reinventing itself as a means to achieve future success. Also, it suggests that having too many people on staff is not the only thing wrong, and that the company will change its way of doing things from top to bottom. Of course, either of these might or might not be true—just as they might or might not be true for a company having *layoffs* or *downsizing*. But executives know that if investors and the remaining employees believe, once restructured, the company will be stronger and better, the chances of these becoming true are greatly improved.

Sometimes suits who try rephrasing layoffs to sound more positive go too far, however. In one egregious example, a company that was terminating five hundred employees in order to reduce staff size denied it was having layoffs at all. "We don't characterize it as a layoff," the company spokesman purportedly explained. "We're managing our staff resources. Sometimes you manage them up, and sometimes you manage them down."

That reported comment has been ridiculed on Web sites and articles ever since.[7] The moral of the story is clear: only use the power of verbal manipulation with a very light touch, or risk the consequences.

Calling a layoff of five hundred people "managing staff resources down" clearly crossed the line between inspiring people to feel more confident and getting them to laugh at you. But sometimes it can be hard to tell exactly where that line is. Is *restructuring* an acceptable replacement for *layoff*? Is *rightsizing*? And is the answer to these questions the same for everyone? Or does doublespeak depend on the ear of the listener?

"BINGO, SIR!"

To most geeks, these questions seem just as ridiculous as any doublespeak itself. Why, most wonder, would anyone even try to manipulate language this way? Just say what you mean, and leave it at that.

This is not only a matter of temperament for many geeks, but also a requirement of their profession. The problem-solving world of technology leaves little room for obfuscation, verbal manipulation, or ambiguity. This is particularly true for programmers: writing effective code demands the exact opposite skill. When it comes to a computer, the way to achieve the desired results is to tell it as plainly as possible exactly what you want it to do. Leaving room for interpretation always leads to trouble. Geeks' use of language tends to follow the same rules—it may seem confusing and impenetrable to suits, but is actually specific to their work, and very much the opposite of doublespeak.

Most geeks feel nothing but scorn for anything they see as double-speak. Since they tend to view their work, to begin with, as a game, it's hardly surprising that the collision of geek sensibilities and the suit vocabulary has led to the creation of Buzzword Bingo. As mentioned earlier, Buzzword Bingo works like real bingo, except that instead of letters with numbers, the cards carry such words and phrases as *potentialize* or *outside the box*. Participants bring them to workplace meetings and mark off buzzwords as they're used. Of course, the lucky winner doesn't usually leap to his or her feet and shout "Bingo!" Instead, a win may be signaled with an innocuous-sounding cough.

Or, a carefully camouflaged phrase. In Scott Adams's *Dilbert* comic series, Dilbert and his friends arrive at a staff meeting armed with their Buzzword Bingo cards, and their pointy-haired boss observes them hanging on his every word.[8] He notes how attentive they are, and says "My proactive leadership must be working!"

"Bingo, sir!" one of the staffers replies.

Both the game and the name were invented in 1993 by Tom Davis, cofounder of Silicon Graphics in Mountain View, California.[9] In a *Wall Street Journal* interview, Davis disclosed that he got the idea while in the office of a friend who had such phrases written on his blackboard. The game spread so quickly that three years later, when then Vice President Al Gore gave the commencement speech at the Massachusetts Institute of Technology, the students came equipped with bingo cards.[10] The instructions for the cards are a perfect illustration of how geeks often see suit speakers. "You are surely familiar with the tendency of nontechnical people to use buzzwords when discussing technical issues," they read. The instructions further noted that the game was "designed to gently remind him that he is at MIT, where we can see right through his strategy." The veep had been tipped off, however. When his audience cheered at "paradigm," he paused to ask good-naturedly, "Did I hit a buzzword?"[11]

CAN WE TALK?

It's easy for geeks to dismiss buzzword-infested corporatespeak, just as it is for suits to dismiss phrases like "quick and dirty ASP DEv XM forum." The problem, though, is that members of each group may be trying to say something to members of the other, and the messages aren't getting through. We have no hope of bridging the Geek Gap until we at least learn to talk to each other. Here are a few suggestions that may serve as a starting point.

If you're a suit:

1. Always keep in mind that—whether they're packing a bingo card or not—technology folk have no patience whatsoever for anything that smacks of hype. Say something like, "This effort is ramping up and building momentum," you'll lose your listener, possibly forever. Think about how geeks say things: without sugar coating or ambiguity. Speak to them that way, and you're likelier to get your point across and achieve your goal.

2. You are responsible for speaking up when you don't understand something. There are very few things in the technological world that a layperson can't understand—at least as a basic idea—if they're explained clearly and with a minimum of technical jargon. So if a techie says something you don't understand, ask for an explanation.

   This runs against the grain of many business people, because the culture of the corporate world discourages its executives from admitting ignorance. However, pretending to know more than you do is unwise when dealing with technology. There's no shame in not knowing what MySQL is, but if you don't ask, you won't know next time either.

3. Because technology folk master machines and processes that are incredibly complex, it's easy to focus on their grasp of things that you don't understand. But the reverse also holds true: you likely

have a better grasp than they do of both business priorities and business terminology.

"This move should become accretive within six months," said the text on a financial Web site where a technologist friend of ours considered applying for a job. The reason we know this is that he came to us in despair. "I can't understand a word of it," he lamented. Not every geek would have this problem, since some are almost as smart about business as they are about technology. But they are the exceptions. Chances are, you may be talking to someone who needs to have business concepts explained.

If you're a geek:

1. Don't assume your audience knows computer terminology or the names of products. Explain things as you go—both the words themselves and the underlying technical concepts. Better yet, ask your listeners how much they know about the system you're discussing and then tailor what you say accordingly.

2. Talk use, not process. Remember that just because you're fascinated with figuring out how a new piece of software or a new system works doesn't mean your business colleagues will be. Suits tend to want to know the bottom line: Is it working now? How soon can I start using it? What will it allow me to do that I couldn't do before?

3. Remember that suits really are trying to convey a point. It can be hard to believe that there's any actual content to some of the things business people say, we know—but they usually are trying to tell you something. Once in a while, they're trying to avoid telling you something, as in the example of a large company whose quarterly report we heard. "Unit price has gone up 3 percent," the CEO said proudly of one of his divisions. Sounded good, but in fact he was reporting unit price because both revenues and volumes in that business were on the decline. Unit price had gone up simply because they raised the price on a few prod-

ucts. So listen carefully to both what suits say, and what they neg-lect to say. There's always a message there, for those who are smart enough to hear it.

CHAPTER 9

CYBERCRIME: WHEN GEEKS SEEK REVENGE

I n March 2000, Internet Trading Technologies, Inc. (ITTI), a New York City provider of Internet trading for securities companies, suffered a devastating series of computer attacks. ITTI staff learned of the first one when they arrived for work one Friday morning to find that their system had gone down during the night.[1] It took them more than two hours to get it back up again. But it wouldn't stay up. The system continued to crash intermittently throughout the day, including a half hour before the market closed. Since ITTI carried a significant portion of NASDAQ trades,[2] these outages were disruptive, to say the least.

The company traced the attacks to its test accounts—dummy accounts that allowed customers to test the trading software without actually making trades. Over the weekend, IT staff cut off access to the test accounts, but come Monday morning the hacking continued, keeping the system down for a total of four and a half hours.[3]

At that point, ITTI's desperate managers called in the Secret Service, whose agents were on site the next day, taking down the company's complaint, when yet another attack began.[4] Knowing the attacker must be online at that moment, the agents spent the next couple of hours on the phone, obtaining subpoenas and contacting Internet service providers. Using IP numbers (see chapter 8) they tracked the hacker's whereabouts to a computer at Queens College, and he was arrested the same day.

The culprit turned out to be Abdelkader Smires, an ITTI employee who lent new meaning to the term "disgruntled." He had helped design ITTI's computer systems, and knew exactly how to break into them. The day before the attacks began, he'd walked off the job after negotiating for a salary increase and stock options. The odd thing was he had gotten both.

"Programmer Rejects $70k Bonus, Is Charged With Online Attack," read a *Computerworld* headline at the time.[5] The *Geek News*[6] headline was less tactful: "Man Goes Berserk."

Why would someone respond to an offer of much more money with a cybercrime attack that would bring his employer to its knees and land him in jail? It's easy to assume Smires must have gone whacko, but there's more to the story than that.

The trouble really began well before Smires demanded his pay increase. It dated back to a conflict between ITTI and someone else entirely, purportedly the company's chief development officer, who remained unnamed in court documents and news accounts. This officer had hired Smires, selected him to help design the company's new system, and trained him in its intricacies. Then ITTI hired a new chief operating officer, who decided to let the chief development officer go.

The two negotiated terms for this departure, but the talks apparently failed, and the chief development officer gave two weeks' notice and left the office. With its IT department in disarray, ITTI hired outside consultants to keep its systems up and running, and called on Smires and another programmer to train these newcomers on how to use the systems.

Both programmers were reluctant. Under the circumstances, teaching the software to others seemed like disloyalty to their former boss. So they went to ITTI management and informed them that they would continue their work only if given a $70,000 bonus, $50,000 in stock options, and a more substantial salary increase in the future.

The company had little choice: its product depended on technology; without working systems it had nothing to sell. And so, management negotiated with the two programmers and reached a tentative agreement the evening before the attacks.

The next morning, the programmers arrived at the office and informed their bosses that they'd changed their minds. They now had a whole new list of demands. Then they left, reportedly saying the bosses should call them—but only if the company would meet the new ultimatums. At that point, ITTI's managers decided they could live without the two programmers after all, so they did not call. A few hours later, the first attack started.[7]

WHY NERDS WANT REVENGE

The length and severity of Smires's assault on ITTI might have been unusual, but he was not the only IT employee who has allegedly turned techie skills against a former or even current employer. In a 2004 survey of five hundred security and law enforcement professionals, 41 percent reported attacks that were known or suspected to have come from past or present employees.[8]

A more recent government study, "Inside Threat Study: Computer System Sabotage in Critical Infrastructure Sectors,"[9] closely examined forty-nine such insider incidents over a period of six years and found that 86 percent[10] of employees-turned-cybercriminals worked in technical positions, the majority as systems administrators or programmers. It might be easy for some suits to conclude from these statistics that geeks just can't be trusted. Indeed the study's recommendations all focused on creating better IT security, for instance, by changing passwords and revoking access for technology experts who are fired or quit, as well as creating redundancies in case primary systems are hacked.

These may be worthwhile measures. First off, this is not to say that the many hundreds of thousands of firms that have IT employees are being attacked by them. It's saying that if and when there are attacks from inside, they will likely be from IT people. But even in those situations, a simpler solution is often available: deal with technology people fairly in the first place, before they get to the point of attacking.

"In almost every case, the act which occurs in information systems area is the reflection of unmet personal needs," explains Jerrold Post, MD, president of Political Psychology Associates, Ltd. in Bethesda, Maryland, and psychiatry professor at George Washington University in Washington, DC. "Almost all of these people are loyal at the time of hiring."[11] The "Insider Threat" study bears him out: according to its findings, 92 percent[12] of attacks were reactions to workplace events that amounted to a real or perceived slight. (This explains such actions, but of course does not excuse them.)

What would make a technology person want to turn to crime? "A great deal of the movement from a once loyal employee to a disaffected one is due to the culture gap between business and technology," he notes.[13] He also blames inflated expectations of some in the technology world, where, as he puts it, "Everyone should be a millionaire by 25."

Another reason is geeks' very real fear that they will be taken advantage of by their business colleagues. "Techies constantly worry about suits 'stealing' their ideas and code, or that their work will help found business that they won't have a say in or profit from," comments one prominent geek we know. He notes that the relationship between Nikola Tesla and George Westinghouse (discussed in chapter 2) is just one real-world example of the treatment technologists fear will happen to them. From this point of view, geek anger can seem well founded.

Then there's the changing world of employment and its effect on employee loyalty. "It used to be that if someone got a job at General Electric or IBM, the job was for life," Post says. "Nowadays, companies are quick to lay people off. Many IT workers are now long-term temporary employees, working side by side with regular staff, but without benefits or stock options. Is there any reason to think someone like that would be loyal to an employer?"

Instead, many technology workers think of themselves as "knowledge entrepreneurs for rent," he says. "They see themselves as there to be used by the employer, and when the employer is done using them, they'll be laid off. So they believe they have to take care of themselves in advance."

This type of job insecurity and lack of benefits makes it likelier that technology workers will feel little loyalty to their employers. But even without this, the Geek Gap means that most technology folk tend to feel disconnected from the companies they work for, or at least less connected than suits do. This is the logic underlying the term *the business side*, first mentioned in chapter 6—technology people make up their own group, and everyone else is on some other side.

With this in mind, it seems easy to foresee that ITTI's negotiations with Smires would end badly, whether he did or did not commit the alleged acts. For while he and his colleague may have demanded more cash, the bonuses failed to address the real problem, which had nothing to do with money and everything to do with the company's perceived mistreatment of their mentor. If helping his replacements seemed like disloyalty before the negotiation, now it became merely better paid disloyalty. Nothing had really changed.

It should have occurred to anyone who knew anything about working with technology folk that they would likely be loyal to the person who hired and trained them. When they first asked for the bonuses, the situation could have been saved before it got completely out of hand, by understanding the demand for what it was, not a real request, but an expression of discomfort at what felt like a betrayal. (Again, the intent here is not to excuse what Smires and his colleague did, but to explore how the incident might have been avoided.) Addressing, or at least discussing, their boss's dismissal, might have helped—maybe. We'll never know, because no one tried it.

"BUT ARE YOU WORTHY?"

Sometimes, in addition to being loyal to one another, geeks want to protect the technology they've created. "A hotshot programmer for a bank had earned something like $550,000 in 18 months creating one of the systems the company depended on," Post recalls. "Then a new supervisor came in. 'Gee,' she said, 'we're awfully dependent on this one programmer. What if something happens to him?' so she asked him to train a backup person who would also be able to work with the system, just in case."

The programmer responded with an irate e-mail. "He said, 'This is my system, and I won't turn over the source code until I'm convinced it won't be turned to trash by someone else. You have to prove to me this other person is worthy,'" Post recalls.

The supervisor wrote back that, no, it wasn't in fact the programmer's system. The system belonged to the bank, which had paid him good money to build it. Soon thereafter, she informed him that the bank would no longer require his services as a full-time employee, but only instead as a consultant.

"He wrote back a charming e-mail, saying the bank could always count on him for anything it needed," Post says. This in itself should probably have aroused suspicions among the programmer's former managers, but they thought matters were resolved. Sure enough, a few months later, both the bank's main server and its backup server were mysteriously disabled, costing the bank an estimated $10 million. The attack was eventually traced back to the angry programmer. Given the complexity of what he'd done and the time it must have taken, investigators concluded he had begun his nefarious work when he sent his conciliatory message. This was, of course, a criminal act, whose perpetrator was rightly punished, but it's also a good illustration of how technologists view their work.

ARTISTS OR PLUMBERS?

In his essay "Hackers and Painters," the master programmer Paul Graham writes:

> When I finished grad school in computer science, I went to art school to study painting. A lot of people seemed surprised that someone interested in computers would also be interested in painting. They seemed to think that hacking [programming] and painting were very different kinds of work—that hacking was cold, precise, and methodical, and that painting was the frenzied expression of some primal urge.
>
> Both of these images are wrong. Hacking and painting have a lot in common. In fact of all the different people I've known, hackers and painters are among the most alike.[14]

Try looking at the hotshot programmer's actions in this light, and you gain a whole new perspective. Imagine a painter being told that another artist is to take over any desired changes or restoration to a mural he has created. When he asks about this other painter's qualifications, he is told he has been paid for the mural and it does not belong to him. From this point of view, is it really surprising that the programmer reacted as he did?

"Creating software is the same as creating an art work," said one geek we know. "But suits don't understand this. They see the software as something more like plumbing, and us as maintenance people, and they deal with us accordingly. A lot of insider cybercrime could be avoided if they thought of us more as artists."

OK, we answered, but in this case, the work of art is also something that the bank depended on for its business, and it had a legitimate need to have more than one person able to work on it. So what should management have done?

"They should have treated the programmer with respect," the geek answered. "They should have explained, 'We've come to be very dependent on your system, and in case something happens to you, for our company's safety, we need you to train a backup person who will also be able to work on it. Here's a list of names. Please choose the one who is best qualified.'"

It's possible, of course, that the bank's need to spread the risk over more than one coder was in direct opposition to the programmer's need to protect what he had created, and perhaps the two parties were locked in to an escalating conflict no one could have prevented. But it's just as possible that a respectful, sensitive approach like the one above could have saved the bank $10 million and the programmer from going to jail.

GEEKS HAVE BIGGER GUNS

Unfortunately, thanks to the Geek Gap, sensitive treatment of technologists is the exception rather than the rule. The vast majority of insider cybercrimes result from real or imagined slights by the employers. In some cases the cause may be unrealistic demands from the technologist, but in many others, it's simply management's ignoring employees' legitimate complaints. And geeks have the knowledge and power to get revenge.

In one of the "Insider Threat" case studies,[15] a female employee filed a series of complaints about her male supervisor and coworkers, claiming they had both sexually harassed her and undermined her work by overriding her decisions and contacting her clients behind her back. This woman had been a stellar performer for more than four years, but now began to receive negative reviews and even a demotion.

The situation cried out for some intervention or at least investigation by the company's human resources department, but they took no action. After a year of waiting, the woman gave up and took a job elsewhere. A couple of months later, she learned that her former employer had only forwarded her more recent—and bad—performance reviews to her new company. She was frustrated and enraged.

This is the kind of thing that happens all the time, and most often, the story ends there. An employee whose legitimate concerns have been ignored for too long leaves in disgust and rails helplessly against her former bosses. But this time was different, because the woman in question was a database expert. Using one of her old company's shared accounts, she hacked into its database and deleted table spaces, rendering critical information completely useless. One hundred and fifteen of her former colleagues had to spend eighteen hundred hours recovering the lost data and putting it back in.

It was an expensive lesson in the dangers of allowing sexual harassment and discrimination to go unchallenged. But for employers, the moral of the story is also this: technically trained people have more power to exact revenge than most run-of-the-mill employees, and employers ignore geeks' legitimate concerns at their own peril.

JUST A "WEIRD TECH GUY"

Still, many managers do exactly that. One unhappy network manager made a habit of leaving work without notice and spying on colleagues from home via a Web cam he'd installed on one of the company's computers.[16] On at least one occasion, he showed a coworker an item he intended to steal from the company. Eventually, the company fired him. It further put a stop on his severance check after management learned he had company equipment that he had not returned.

In what seems almost a logical progression from his earlier behavior, the network manager responded by using a "back door" to gain access to the system at his former employer. (A back door is a shortcut for remote access to a computer, usually used by programmers for benign purposes such as maintenance.) Once in, he disabled a server, cutting his old company off from interstate and foreign communications—and disabling that portion of its business—for two and a half days.

The network manager couldn't have given a better warning that he was likely to attempt sabotage if he'd come out and said so. And, as a matter of fact, he did say so. In a phone conversation with a former coworker, he announced that he had back doors into the company's systems and planned to use them for revenge.

Why didn't anyone do anything to intervene? It seems his managers just didn't take him that seriously. They later told researchers from the "Insider Threat" study that his strange behavior was no more than to be expected from a "weird tech guy."

Their response, or lack thereof, is hardly uncommon. One tends to think of insider saboteurs as stealthy, working away in apparent contentment while secretly plotting mayhem. But that image is completely wrong. In fact, most insider hackers give ample warning of their attacks, for anyone who chooses to pay attention. Eighty-five percent of saboteurs in the "Insider Threat" study had a grievance well before the attack, and 57 percent were considered disgruntled by coworkers.[17] Not only that, 80 percent displayed some sort of hostile behavior well before they struck.[18]

For instance, another technician expressed the hope that his company's owner wouldn't show up at lunch that day, adding, "I might wind up pummeling [him]."[19] That same systems administrator, when asked to complete a task he didn't agree with replied, "If you insist, so be it, but I can assure you the job will be completed with very little effort and no attention to detail." Eventually, he resigned of his own volition, but asked if he could pay to keep his old e-mail address at the company. Management saw no reason why not, so they agreed. A few weeks later, he used this continuing access to change all the company's administrative passwords, change the computer's registry, and delete its entire billing system. He also deleted two internal databases for good measure.

It should have been obvious to anyone with even the slightest management experience that an employee bragging about stealing and threatening to pummel his boss was someone in need of intervention—indeed, the man's actions seemed like the proverbial cry for help. Possibly, he had a legitimate grievance that could have been addressed, defusing the situation. Or maybe he was simply troubled and would never fit into that workplace. Either way, to ignore him was obviously courting danger, as was granting him continued access to the company's system. But no one at his workplace was particularly concerned.

Why not? We believe the answer harks back to the Geek Gap: Suits tend to assume that geeks are oddballs who are prone to erratic behavior. Therefore, weird or hostile behavior is nothing to worry about—it's just geeks being geeks. As the network manager's colleagues put it, he wasn't a normal human being; he was a weird tech guy.

"ONLY AN IDIOT"

Unfortunately, technologists can pose something of a conundrum for their business counterparts. In some cases, what would seem like horrendously rude behavior in the more formal and cordial world of business interactions may be geeks just being geeks. We went for drinks and dinner recently with a technologist friend. He brought along a laptop, which he had propped open in front of him throughout the evening, first in the bar, then in the restaurant, then at a second bar where we went for after-dinner drinks. He's a good enough friend that we understood he was not trying to tell us he didn't value our company or our conversation. He was simply relaxed enough with us to be his geeky self, and we were happy that he was.

Imagine this same behavior at a business dinner, however, and it would be easy to see how a suit who didn't know our friend might think he was being intentionally hostile. Indeed, in *Leading Geeks*, Paul Glen describes a meeting where a similar misunderstanding actually occurred.[20] A technology expert went along on a consultant's visit to a potential client and spent the day examining the company's systems. Then, the consultants' group sat down with their potential client's top executives to discuss the possible job.

Among the managers in the room was the client company's chief technology officer, who had just overseen installation of a new network system. During the meeting, he turned to the technologist and asked his opinion of the system.

"Well, you've got Windows NT 3.51 installed on a number of your systems," the geek responded. "Only an idiot would put that in."

No one said anything for a few moments, as the rest of the visiting consultants looked at each other in consternation. Needless to say, they would never get the job now, and the CTO's feelings were deeply hurt.

The only unperturbed person in the room was the consulting technologist. He'd had no intention of insulting anybody; he had merely responded to a direct question with a direct answer, stating the facts, as he saw them, about Windows NT 3.51. What's more, he later said that he thought the meeting went well. He hadn't the slightest idea that he'd said anything wrong.

"Almost every manager of geeks has a story something like this one," Glen observes. No wonder some business people find it simplest to ignore unexpected behavior from their technology counterparts. And no wonder many try to keep technologists away from their companies' customers—although this only serves to worsen the Geek Gap.

But while ignoring what seems like odd geek behavior may be the easiest approach, it's also the most dangerous. Technology is integral to most companies' operations. The IT staff who manage that technology can either help a business tremendously by keeping the systems running smooth and up-to-date with the latest developments, or hurt it just as easily by disabling those systems.

The best strategy for learning what technology folk think is to spend some time with them, preferably in their own environment. This would give interested suits a chance to learn why they say the things they do, and also to ascertain whether techies are happy or unhappy in their jobs.

It would also help prevent suits from making blunders like those described in the "Insider Threat Study," or worse, the stupid move by the supervisor described above who fired the hotshot programmer. Remember the sequence of events: the programmer expressed outrage at having his system taken from him, was fired for his attitude, and then sent a very friendly e-mail. Does this sound like logical behavior? Shouldn't it have dawned on the supervisor that the ingratiating message might be less than sincere?

After all, it would be human nature to be even more furious at a former employer after being let go than one was before. But that's the whole problem: because geeks often seem so eccentric, some managers don't expect them to have normal human reactions—but they do. And so, this man's supervisor was so blinded that when she first learned that the servers weren't working, she contacted the attacker himself to ask him to fix them.[21]

THE ROOT OF THE PROBLEM

Spending enough time with technologists to understand them better is one important step toward reducing the likelihood of cybercrime. It would also help to learn about the technology itself. In case after case in the "Insider Threat" study, management opened the door to sabotage by allowing disgruntled technologists continued access to their companies' systems. In some cases, as those described above, this was a matter of misplaced trust. But in others, the problem was ignorance of how the technology worked.

One company that fired its systems administrator cut off his user account promptly at the time of termination.[22] Unfortunately, management neglected to also cut off his remote access to the system through the company's firewall, and also failed to change the root password on its system. Either one of these moves would have denied the former systems administrator access. As it was, he was able to get on the system after hours, shutting it down for three days.

In another case, a manufacturing company that was about to fire a software engineer cut off his access just before informing him of the termination. From then on, the engineer would no longer be able to open a connection to the company's network. However, at the time of the firing, he already had a connection open from his home computer, and he arrived home after the dismissal to find it was still connected. Faced with what some might consider a great temptation, the engineer used this last access to delete several critical files, thus shutting down the factory for four days. If someone at the company had thought to check for an open connection, the sabotage could have been prevented.

But if getting to know geeks well enough to understand the reasoning behind their behavior is a daunting task for most suits, learning enough about technology to cut off access to would-be cybercriminals is even more challenging. It's one thing to know enough about technology to, say, install new software or create an e-mail account. But understanding both how and why to change the root password, to use just one example, is likely to be beyond many business people's capabilities.

Even if they did learn, it wouldn't help them for long. Technology is changing at a staggering pace. And this rapid advance is why most technology professionals spend a large portion of their working lives studying new systems and programs, running in place to stay as current as they can. It's also why many techies actually choose professional development opportunities, such as the chance to go for training or to work with the latest software or language, over promotions and even raises. Staying current with technology is a survival skill for geeks that can also become a full-time occupation.

The growth of technology is especially swift when it comes to things like networks and remote access; keeping security systems safe; and the newfound ways to circumvent those systems. It's unrealistic to think that any business manager could keep up well enough to outsmart a geek. The only option, then, is for business people to rely on their technology colleagues to help them keep their systems safe and unwanted entrants out.

This brings us full circle to Abdelkader Smires. ITTI learned the hard way that techie coworkers of a dismissed technologist may have greater loyalty to their former colleague than they do to their employer. So it seems paradoxical to have to depend on these same techies to block unauthorized access. Yet most managers have no other choice.

What's the best approach? In an ideal world, a wise manager would keep all technologists happy—and everyone else, for that matter—by never firing or angering anyone. In the real world, there is no simple solution, but here are some ideas that may help:

If you're a suit:

1. Get to know and understand the technologists who work with you. Learning their motivation, what they value, and what makes them angry will help you spot a bad situation in time to deal with it, before it escalates into all-out war. The relationships you build now will also stand you in good stead if you ever find yourself faced with an insider attack, by providing you with allies who may be willing to give their best effort to help protect your job.

   Keep in mind that most technologists are very loyal to their colleagues and also to the technology itself. They might or might not feel the same way about your organization, especially if it has not demonstrated great loyalty to its technology staff. If you want to win their allegiance, get to know who they are and what most inspires them. Try to have your organization's interests aligned with theirs.

2. Technologists can seem odd, we know, but it's dangerous simply to dismiss erratic and overtly hostile behavior as normal for geeks. If a technology expert seems rude or angry, it's important to understand why.

   It's especially vital to explore any situation in which a technologist appears to have stopped caring about his or her job. Most techies love technology and tend to stay at their desks way beyond the point of reason. It's not abnormal to see geeks come in late or miss scheduled meetings. But someone who's actually working fewer hours may be getting dangerously disaffected. You need to understand why.

3. Make sure there's backup—but be sensitive to how it's presented. It's unsafe for any organization to be completely dependent on a single technologist who's the only one who understands its sys-

tems. However, bringing someone in unexpectedly after an individual technologist has worked long and hard on a project is a bad idea. Instead, it's smarter to have more than one person participate from the very beginning, and to make sure programmers and others know before they begin their technological creations that they are required to provide clear and detailed documentation for their work, as well as training for other staff members.

4. Don't underestimate geek power. We hope your organization never has to face an attack from an insider. By building strong relationships with your IT staff you will likely prevent it. If this fails, though, it's helpful to understand as much as you can about the technology you depend on, as well as to have other IT staff members ready to help you out. It's also common sense that when IT specialists leave, whether on good terms or bad, to make sure that their access to company systems is completely disabled.

5. Remember that, to geeks, technology is the same as art. Whether or not you're convinced by Paul Graham's observations about the similarity between painting and programming, you should know that technologists see their work this way. So treat these technological creations, and their creators, with the same respect you'd accord to an artist commissioned to paint a portrait.

If you're a geek:

1. Make sure your grievances are heard. Most technologists are not good at corporate politics, but sometimes you need these skills for survival in the business world. This means that if a business colleague or manager is treating you disrespectfully, you need to look for powerful allies and/or other venues within your organization to make your position known. Voice your concerns in quiet discussions—venting your feelings of rage to coworkers might make you feel better but won't change a difficult situation. Requesting a lateral transfer to a different department, for instance, might be more constructive.

2. Make as many friends as you can. This is always a good idea in any workplace setting. The more suits you can count among your

allies, the better positioned you'll be if you find yourself embroiled in a workplace conflict.

3. What's art to you is survival to them. We understand why Graham likens programming to painting, and why many technologists have great creative pride in the software they write and the systems they build. We agree with our angry geek friend that too many suits view technological achievements as plumbing rather than art.

   At the same time, it's important for technologists to understand that, from a business point of view, these systems are tools that keep the business alive. As with plumbing, business people have little interest in admiring their intricacies but know that they must be kept working at all costs. Try to understand this limited point of view.

4. Find legal ways to get even for unfair or demeaning treatment. In most situations, there are many ways to strike back at your employer without breaking the law. For instance, while we don't know the details, on the face of it, the woman who was demoted after complaining of sexual harassment had the makings of a heck of a good lawsuit. That would have been an effective way of striking back at her former employer.

5. Here are a few sobering statistics on cybercrime from the "Insider Threat" study:

   Ninety percent of the perpetrators faced criminal charges, and of those, 83 percent were found guilty. Most (59 percent) were ordered to pay restitution, in amounts of up to $2 million. Forty-two percent went to prison for their acts, and spent an average of twelve months behind bars. According the researchers, 85 percent of these insiders did not consider how severe the consequences of their acts might be.

   The message is clear: hacking into the system at a company that's slighted you might yield some temporary satisfaction, but has the potential to badly disrupt your life—by bankrupting you, sending you to prison, or both. It isn't worth it.

CHAPTER 10

PING-PONG VERSUS POWERPOINT

Afriend of ours, who had spent several years working from home at various Internet jobs, went to interview for a full-time on-site position at an Internet start-up company. We fretted that if he got the job, he'd have to spend his first couple of paychecks on acceptable office clothes. But upon returning from the interview, he assured us: "I already have the perfect wardrobe to work in this place." He went to his second interview in his jeans, denim jacket, and favorite shoes, a pair of bright red high-top sneakers. He credits the shoes with helping him land the job.

The company was in a small town, on the upper floor of an old warehouse. It had fifteen-foot ceilings and open girders. One wing was filled with cubicles and workstations, and the break room was a small wing of its own, complete with an endless supply of sodas, a Ping-Pong table, and a dartboard. We dropped by to visit him there once, and couldn't shake the feeling that we'd wandered onto a movie set—this was precisely what an edgy new Internet start-up company was supposed to look like.

But it wasn't that way for show; the company's management had genuinely created the working environment that they liked best. Most employees were geeks, and many were recent college graduates. And the break room was only part of the fun.

For many months, a second large wing stood mostly empty, with a few boxes and pieces of old equipment stored in the corners, in anticipation of the growing staff that—it was hoped—would eventually fill the space. To many of the geeks on staff, it seemed like the perfect playground. There were radio-operated cars racing around one day, roller hockey another day, skateboarding yet another. The company eventually installed cubicles, but the geeks just played around them. When dignitaries came for tours, they were steered clear of that section.

Around the time our friend began working there, the Internet start-up was acquired by a larger company, and, after a few months, he was offered the chance to move to the parent firm. The offer came with a promotion and potential for advancement, so our friend accepted.

When he got to his new workplace, he was astounded at how different the two companies were. The parent company occupied a glass cube building in a corporate suburb of a big city. Called to the upper—executive—floor for meetings, he realized he was entering an area created by and for suits. The colors were muted, with plush carpeting underfoot, and few personal items on display. The only art works were either tastefully abstract or motivational (for instance: a mountain climber clinging to a cliff with the caption "Perseverance"). The offices up there were much larger than on the other floors. Nearly all the executives had assistants seated outside their offices who would offer to fetch our friend coffee, once they knew he was there for an appointment.

The lower floors were not as plush, but still very different from the start-up he'd left behind. Where the start-up had hardwood floors, there was wall-to-wall carpeting in a neutral shade of gray. The outside walls were all glass, with windows that didn't open, and the gray fabric cubicles were neatly arranged around the perimeter. The colors here, too, were muted and tasteful, and there were certainly no toys in evidence. The start-up had been an environment created by and for geeks; and the parent company had been created by and for suits. The difference was evident wherever he looked. Where the geek-created environment he'd left behind had been imaginative and playful, and focused on fun, the suit-created environment was serious and professional, and very much a place for grown-ups.

The Geek Gap is a deep-rooted cultural divide that affects every aspect of technologists' and business people's work lives. But nowhere is it quite as noticeable as in the clothes they wear, the hours they keep, and the workspaces they favor. To geeks, the neutral, inoffensive décor and relative neatness of most business-oriented offices intended for business tends to feel sterile, perhaps artificial—and conspicuously lacking in fun. Geeks can find such an atmosphere stifling.

To suits, technology workplaces can seem chaotic, with computer equipment, toys, and posters everywhere, and what appears to be little regard for orderliness. Business executives can be just as uncomfortable amid this disorder as geeks may be in the orderly world of the suits. Left to their own devices, many business people and technology people tend to reinforce the Geek Gap by preferring to stay out of each other's territory.

BEHIND THE LOCKED DOOR

At least, that's what happened at our friend's new company. Visitors who entered the lobby, he told us, would naturally proceed to the reception desk, and then up the open center stairway or elevators that led to the corporate offices above. Most never even noticed the side door they passed on the left, or assumed it led only to a storage area. If they did happen to try the door, they'd find it was locked; one needed a special key card to enter. Behind this door, the company's coders and other technologists were hard at work, creating and constantly updating its products.

Although our friend worked in a business area, his expertise—and inclinations—were mostly technological, so he often had good reason to head down to this area. What he found there was an environment far more similar to what he'd left behind at the Internet start-up. Sock monkeys and Japanese anime posters adorned the cubicles. The walls of the conference rooms were graced with 1950s sci-fi movie posters and large white flip chart pad sheets covered with lines and lines of code.

Why was this area locked? Initially, our friend believes, it was a management decision, based on concerns over corporate espionage. The company was among the leaders in its field and was worried that corporate spies would try to get their hands on the latest software that its programmers were developing. The thing was, though, the geeks liked the locked door, too. It may have kept their proprietary code locked safe inside, but it also kept the rest of the company safely outside. "The only way to get inside, if you didn't actually work there, was to have somebody let you in," our friend says. "Marketing people couldn't go there."

Over time, he recalls, this geek area that was off-limits to suits became zanier and zanier. "It got to be like *Animal House* down there," he says. Computer parts and other technological bits would be strewn all over the place. Once, as he walked in, a radio-controlled robot rolled up to his feet, stopped then turned, and rolled away again. He never did find out to whom it belonged.

Not surprisingly, the company's business-oriented employees found the area less than appealing. Even our friend's boss, who seemed comfortable with all the latest technology and who was open to new experiences, once asked our friend to represent their department at a meeting in the technology staff area.

"Sure," said our friend, who had been planning to attend this meeting.

"Good," said the boss. "Then I won't have to. I don't like going down there, it's so . . . strange."

Over time, our friend believes, management came to regret its decision to put the programmers behind a locked door. In any case, the techies were informed one day that their department would be switching offices with the administrative workers who occupied the other side of the ground floor. That area did not have locks. The geek enclave was now open to all comers.

Meanwhile, our friend accepted a higher-paying job at yet another Internet start-up. On one of his last days in the office, he headed downstairs to the technology area to say good-bye.

"It's not the same as it used to be," one of them told him. The geeks had been instructed to take down their posters, clean up their computer parts, and stop using the hallways to play with their toys. "This is a public area now," they were informed. The space was now much less of an embarrassment—not to mention less of an accident hazard. But the geeks who worked there were a lot less happy than they had been before.

From the technologists' point of view, being told that the area had to conform to business norms seemed to prove that the business managers were killjoys, people incapable of having fun, and quick to quash anyone else's attempt to do so. But, whether or not this was the right move, the suits did have legitimate reasons for wanting the techies to change their environment. Aside from the concern that someone could trip over a piece of computer equipment—or a stray robot—get hurt and file a lawsuit, there was also the issue that many people find clutter and constant play not conducive to their working environment.

In the end, it goes back to the issue of influencing people versus problem solving—the fundamental difference between business and technology people. For geeks, the issue seems simple: the focus is on solving problems and anything that helps them do so (such as the lines of code posted on the wall) or helps them unwind between bouts of intense work (such as playing with sock monkeys) is well worth it. Anything that does neither of these—such as having a neatly laid out desk—is a waste of time.

For suits, the question of a working environment is a complex one; it involves keeping with their goal of influencing people—whether company insiders or outsiders. "The design of a firm's office reflects the firm's attitude toward budgets, goals, and plans, as well as its attitudes toward its employees, customers, visitors, and vendors. All of these reflect the image of the company," write Christine Piotrowski and Elizabeth A. Rogers in their book *Designing Commercial Interiors*.[1] "The company image is an expression of the company itself." From that perspective, a corporate insistence on, say, muted colors, which could convey calm and serenity doesn't seem so trivial.

GOING WITH THE FLOW?

Some businesses take the idea of design as a way of influencing business success a step further, by using the ancient Chinese art of *feng shui* (pronounced "fung shway") to help plan office décor and furniture placement. Though many regard feng shui as superstition, it is considered highly important by many Chinese and other Asians who value it; it is therefore a worthwhile consideration for any company that does business with Asians and plans to have many of them visit the office. But many companies where this is not a consideration still take an interest in feng shui, less in terms of spirituality than in setting up spaces with intrinsic appeal.

The principles of feng shui might seem odd to those not steeped in Eastern philosophies. "On a very subtle level, beyond our ability to see, lies an ocean of energy that ebbs and flows in and around us," writes Darrin Zeer in *Office Feng Shui: Creating Harmony in Your Work Space.*[2] "The Chinese refer to this energy as *chi* (pronounced 'chee'). In the world of business we need to pay attention to the chi in our workplace."

To those who practice feng shui, managing chi in the workplace can mean things like placing a red cloth beneath a telephone (red is supposedly an auspicious color) or installing a fish tank since fish symbolize wealth and good luck. But many other rules are just plain good design advice. For instance, Zeer recommends keeping the entrance area well lit, free of packages, and open "to invite good fortune to your door." But with or without good fortune, a well-lit and inviting entryway, with air circulating freely and natural elements such as plants or fish does create a welcoming environment for customers, business partners, and employees— and that has to be good for business.

Feng shui ideas seem intrinsically at odds with the way most technologists function and the workspaces they create. For one thing, the biggest taboo in feng shui is clutter: removing clutter to create a clean, calming, and orderly environment is integral to most feng shui makeovers. But few geeks we know can successfully banish clutter from their work areas. For one thing, they tend to accumulate bits and pieces of information— books, notes, CDs, and so on. And they especially tend to collect technological devices of all kinds, large and small, most of which wind up crowded into their workspaces.

From a feng shui perspective, with its emphasis on living things, natural materials, and uncluttered spaces, technological devices are to be hidden away or disguised as much as possible. In *Feng Shui Goes to the*

Office: How to Thrive from 9 to 5, Nanciee Wydra writes, "High-tech surroundings often exude feelings of strain and tension, isolation, and obsession."[3] In fact, these comments appear under the heading "Curing the Technological Workplace"—and in case it's not clear what the cure might involve, she adds: "Moving, reflective surfaces are particularly hypnotic. Therefore, in many workspaces, computer screens compete for our attention. Mesmerizing, stimulating surfaces, like thorns piercing the skin, should be removed or minimized."[4] While this may or may not make sense for, say, a marketing manager or other "high-touch" executive, it obviously is an unworkable office style for anyone whose job revolves around technology.

The austere principles of aesthetic office design clearly won't work well for the average geek. But neither does a workplace in which the techies work in their own gloriously chaotic atmosphere while everyone else works in an orderly, corporate setting. For one thing, it's a good way to encourage the tendency that geeks and suits already have—to stay as far apart as possible from each other.

It may not have bothered our friend that his boss was reluctant to head down to the tech department, but if we were managing the company, we would consider that cause for alarm—and would want to do something about it. In this particular case, however, where management ultimately moved the department and made it clean up its act, there were gains and losses. Yes, they now had an area where visitors—not to mention their own staff—could more comfortably go. On the other hand, they broke up some of the camaraderie and fun of their technology department, and may have instilled deep resentment among their coders in doing so. Was the trade-off worth it? It's hard to know for sure.

EARLY OR LATE?

Geek and suit differences are evident not only in the appearance of their offices, but also in their working styles and even preferred schedules. Many of the most successful business people we know love to rise early, beat the traffic to the office, take some time alone with the morning paper, and answer e-mails before launching into their day. The technologists we admire like beating rush hour, too—but by coming in late rather than early. But once at work, they stay and stay, often till late into the evening—and once they're home, they are often still at work. We heard a rumor once that in a large software company, developers, working at home far into the night, would send a 3 am e-mail with a question to a colleague, only to have an answer arrive a few minutes later. No wonder these people don't arrive at the crack of dawn.

Since the bulk of the workday for most suits is dedicated to influencing people, it makes a lot of sense for them to come in early, get informed about the day's issues and events, and center themselves before launching into meetings and phone calls with others. On the other hand, once geeks get to work on a problem, they're like a dog with a bone: reluctant to let go until they've finished it off, no matter how long it takes. As always, the trick for suits and geeks is to find a middle ground—a time of day to meet, for instance, that is comfortable for both.

HUNTING FOR PORN

Meanwhile, back at our friend's employer (before he left it), efforts were made to combine the geek culture of the small start-up with the suit culture of the new parent company. This well-meaning effort unfortunately led to frustration more often than not. One example was how the start-up dealt with pornography.

The small start-up company was designed to allow the public to create its own Web sites on its servers. As is always the case in the untamed world of the Internet, a certain percentage of these sites showed pornography, promoted hate, or encouraged illegal activity. This violated the company's terms of service, which dictated that such material would be removed. The trouble was that a vast number of pages were posted each day, and finding the offending items among all the others was tedious work.

The geeks, who viewed their work as play, found a way to make even this fun. Every few weeks, they would schedule an evening for porn hunting and many employees would volunteer their evening well into the wee hours to help search through the sites to seek out terms-of-service violations. Quantities of Chinese food were delivered from the restaurant up the street, and the employees would form teams and compete to see who could find the largest number of bad pages, as well as the most disgusting ones. It turned an otherwise deadly boring job into fun and a social occasion, and helped the start-up stay current with the content on its site.

Some time after the purchase, though, the parent company announced it was putting an end to the practice. Management had become concerned that if word got out that the (mostly male) employees were sitting around the office late into the night, munching egg rolls while looking at pornography, the company would have a public relations problem on its hands—which it probably would have. Further, they noted that there was a privacy issue: in order to find porn, the start-up's staff was looking not only at publicly posted Web pages, but also at private, password-protected files. Yes, these private files had to be reviewed so as to ensure that their content stayed within the rules. But that job should have been done only by the company abuse department, which had direct responsibility for enforcing those rules.

With the porn-hunting evenings now ended, the start-up's two-person abuse department had no choice but to review all the Web pages by themselves. One would find them at their desks, looking through thousands of pages, one after another in rapid succession. They looked miserable and bored, and their colleagues both felt bad for them and missed the fun of the porn-hunting evenings.

The parent company's concern about both public relations and privacy issues was a legitimate one, but simply pulling the plug on an event that had become part of the start-up's culture seemed heavy-handed to the techies who worked there. Resentment grew among the start-up's staff.

POINTS FOR PING-PONG?

Next, the parent company tried bringing one of the start-up's ideas to corporate headquarters. Management at the larger company was impressed by the smaller company's spirit, and thought providing some fun activity within its own workplace might boost both teamwork and morale. The company had a gym room with weight machines and treadmills, but nothing on-site was purely recreational. So the parent company installed a Ping-Pong table in its lunchroom.

The Ping-Pong table proved wildly popular, which meant there was always a huge line to play. This came to be a worry for managers in the larger company's departments, who feared their employees were spending too much time either waiting or playing, and not enough time at their actual jobs. At the start-up, with its small and dedicated staff, everyone had so much work and stayed in the office for so many hours that managers rarely worried about how much break time they took. But this was not the case at the larger, more established firm. So, one by one, the corporate department heads issued a point system, in which employees had to earn points to trade for Ping-Pong time.

"That missed the idea completely," our friend recalls. Having to earn points for Ping-Pong took all the fun out of the concept, and employees quickly forgot about the game and turned their attention to other things. "It became mostly a utility table for the regular PowerPoint pep-rally sessions they held there," our friend says.

SUITS IN FAT SUITS?

The acute difference between work styles, and the difficulty in blending them, became particularly evident when the combined company reached a business milestone—surpassing its main competitor in page views (the number of times someone had viewed their Web site). It was time to celebrate, and the start-up threw its own party and invited the other company's staff to attend.

The small start-up's event was a giant barbecue at the country home of one of the founders. There was swimming, volleyball, and other assorted games, as well as dancing to a local band and fireworks after dark. As at all of its events, the party's only agenda was for the people there to relax, have fun, and spend time together away from the intensity of their workplace.

The geeks at the start-up had rented a set of huge foam rubber fat suits in which to simulate sumo wrestling for anyone who wanted to try it, as well as a "human gyroscope" that would spin the person strapped into it in three different directions at once, and a carnival dunking booth. The dunking booth proved especially popular when the CEO of the small company and then—dared into it—the CEO of the parent corporation took turns as targets.

Many executives from the parent company attended the smaller company's party, and most looked almost as uncomfortable as their boss had in the dunking booth. Told that this was an informal event, they'd arrived wearing "business casual" dress—button-down shirts and Dockers, or summery dresses—while their counterparts at the start-up were frankly dressed for fun and sports in T-shirts, shorts, and bathing suits. The corporate employees liked fun, but they'd never seen anything like the giant sumo suits or the human gyroscope. They were perplexed by it all.

"THEY DON'T SHARE WITH *US*."

The start-up's employees were just as uncomfortable when they attended the parent company's celebration. The party had a lavish buffet, volleyball, and a DJ, but it was also combined with a business meeting. This meant, among other things, that while the parent company's executives were merely invited to attend the start-up's barbecue, staff of the start-up was actually *required* to show up for the parent company's party.

The parent company rented a convention hall where its executives gave presentations from the stage (the CEO arrived dressed in a giant bird suit, a nod to the company's logo of an eagle in flight). One of the event's goals was for staff at its various subsidiaries to learn about one another's operations, so executives from each of these smaller companies got up on stage to talk about what they did and how their business was going.

Our friend and his pals sat in the back row and sneered. "It was all corporate rah-rah," he told us later, in a dismissive tone. "It was all about how well these sub-companies were doing for *them*. Of course, they never shared the benefits with *us*."

We were so surprised by his statement that for a moment we didn't know how to respond. The parent company had a generous stock-options program and had provided our friend a block of options from the day he joined the company. As discussed in chapter 4, stock options proved a disappointing form of compensation for some Internet employees. But in this case, the company's stock price rose solidly during the time he was employed there, and when he left—after only two years—he cashed them in for nearly $20,000.

In short, financially speaking, the company's management had done what it could to align his goals with theirs, and made sure that their success would indeed directly benefit every employee. But this had done nothing to change his view: "Of course they never shared the benefits with *us*."

What went wrong? We think the answer has everything to do with the Geek Gap, with styles of working rather than actual work, with how things were communicated, rather than what was being said or done. The fact that the stock options program let our friend share in the parent company's success was meaningless in the face of the alienation he felt when confronted with its gray cubicles, dress codes, and countless PowerPoint presentations. All these trappings of the traditional business world made him and the other techies feel like outsiders.

The suits from the parent company felt just as alienated when faced with sumo wrestling fat suits or robots roaming the hallways. They knew they'd encountered a world where they could never fit in—whether or not they ever learned to fathom the complex technologies that enabled them to do their jobs. And so both groups remained wary and aloof.

What could they have done differently? We believe the underlying problem was arrogance on both sides. Just as geeks and suits each tend to assume that their work is the only factor that matters in a company's failure or success, the geeks and suits in these two companies each believed that only their way of running an office, meeting, or party was the right way.

In fact, what was right for one could never be right for both. The freewheeling geeks could never be fully at home, or fully creative, in what seemed to them the dulling atmosphere of the corporate firm. And strictly business-oriented types were never comfortable in the chaotic, constantly distracting atmosphere of the start-up. Indeed, one of its business managers complained that her job amounted to being a den mother.

Then there was the start-up's elevator—or lack thereof. The one elevator in the place was for freight, usable only by special arrangement. The only other way in was to climb three flights of stairs. This was no problem for the company's mostly twenty-something staff, but it effectively meant that no one with a physical disability could work there—leaving the start-up vulnerable to lawsuits under the Americans with Disabilities Act. Even our friend, who loved the little company in every other way, was disturbed by this and he gave some thought to deliberately recruiting a staff member in a wheelchair just to force his employers to deal with this issue. But, given the warehouse's physical limitations, any solution would have been awkward at best.

FROM A BUNCH OF STUDENTS TO AN ORGANIZATION

In the few years since its inception, the small start-up had evolved from a bunch of college students trying out an idea for a company, to a real organization with more than sixty employees. But its work schedule, working style, and physical plant had not kept up with that transition. In an atmosphere of mutual trust and respect, executives from the parent company could have helped the smaller firm make some adjustments that would have preserved its fun and creative atmosphere but allowed for wider diversity in its employees, and a workplace where more traditional business executives could still feel comfortable. Meanwhile executives from the start-up could have helped the bigger firm inject some of their creativity and fun into the staid proceedings at the parent company, and helped foster some of the technical innovations that it needed to continue to prosper.

But none of that happened, and in the long run, everybody lost. With little meeting of minds between the geeks and the suits, relations between the two remained strained. Each pursued its own strategies independently. This meant that the suits at the parent company lost the benefit of input from some of the most talented and innovative technologists around in the design of their new products and services—and it showed. Over the next few years, the parent company was increasingly left in the dust by its more technologically advanced competitors.

Meanwhile, the start-up lost the benefit of the business acumen available among the parent company's executives. Its products were cutting-edge and intensely popular, but its geeky staff never quite learned to translate that popularity into a healthy return on investment. It began making clumsy changes to its products in order to try to transform them into moneymakers but without much success.

A few months after our friend left, the parent company announced, as noted earlier, that it was moving the small start-up's offices into its own headquarters. This news was greeted with dismay at the start-up, of course. Its founders, and most of the top executives, quit rather than make the move.

Today, the start-up still exists, but in name only. In fact, it's a small division of the corporate parent, with its staff, offices, and personality fully absorbed into the larger entity. The parent company has itself been purchased and is now part of an international conglomerate. The founders of both the large and small firms have moved on, but to nothing as promising as the companies they once headed. They, and the firms they created, have fallen victim to the Geek Gap.

This needn't happen to all firms. Here are some ideas for overcoming work style differences:

If you're a suit:

1. One person's chaos is another person's creative atmosphere. As discussed earlier, most geeks see themselves as artists rather than technicians. Whether you agree with this view or not, the fact is that most technological problems do take creativity to solve. If you think of geek areas in terms of artists' studios, the clutter—not to mention the time off to shoot each other with rubber-band guns—take on a different meaning.

   Yes, it's fair to expect geek workspaces to be free of safety hazards and reasonably pleasant for their business colleagues to visit. On the other hand, expecting technologists to conform to strict workplace standards might actually cut their effectiveness, just as it might for other creative types. Try to find a reasonable balance.

2. How you communicate is as important as what you say. The normal trappings of business communications—reports using words like "proactive," PowerPoint presentations, and motivational meetings—all tend to be off-putting to many geeks, some of whom have a deep distrust of anything "corporate." Recall our friend who was so alienated by company boosterism that he actually forgot that his stock options made him a beneficiary of his employer's success. His case may be an extreme example, but there are many others out there like his. Whenever possible, it's best to communicate with geeks in their own language—in a straightforward manner, without boasting about management's successes.

3. When it comes to control, less is sometimes more. It's possible to motivate technology people so that they'll happily spend time working long hours on projects that will help your company succeed. It's also possible to control people's work lives and carefully monitor their time so that you know you're getting your money's worth out of their paycheck. But it isn't possible to do the two things at once. Remember our friend's company where management installed a Ping-Pong table but then couldn't trust employees with the free time to go use it? That's the kind of nonsense that happens when employers try to have it both ways.

In the typical high-tech start-up, people work very long hours, come in on weekends, or even sleep in their workplace on sofas or cots, and no one asks them to earn points toward break time. It is possible to harness some of that energy among tech people in a more established workplace, but it requires a great deal of trust. You have to believe tech employees care about getting the job done, even if it looks like they're standing in line to play Ping-Pong.

Do you have that kind of trust in your tech workers? Do they care enough about their company to knock themselves out making its technology work? Maybe, or maybe not. But if you don't show them trust, no quantity of Ping-Pong tables will help foster the motivation you're looking for.

If you're a geek:

1. One person's creative atmosphere is another person's chaos. Some geeks work well in offices where old computer parts are piled up and there are sci-fi movie posters on the walls. If it makes their business colleagues uncomfortable, they reason, so much the better. After all, the more the business people stay away, the fewer interruptions technologists will face as they're trying to concentrate on solving complex problems.

   This kind of thinking, however, leads to trouble. All technologists accomplish by making suits want to leave them alone is marginalize themselves from the business workings of the company that employs them. After all, management might reason, if we never see them or talk to them or go into their workspace, why do we need them here at all? Couldn't someone at an outside vendor do that job instead?

   Geeks who like having suits stay out of their offices invite the Geek Gap in instead. So make sure your workspace is one your business colleagues can feel comfortable working in, too.

2. Focus on content, not form. To many geeks, PowerPoint presentations seem as inconsequential as motivational posters or a carefully selected "power briefcase." And while these things are indeed pointless in the technology world, most suits are schooled in the world of business, in which formalities abound and much is always left unsaid. In that world, the trappings of business—from which briefcase you carry to how your office is decorated—all carry coded messages about status and power, and the nature of one's work. Suits ignore these messages at their peril, and those

who do will never be taken seriously by their business colleagues or customers.

Try to keep this in mind when looking at or listening to business presentations. Our friend and his colleagues who sat in the back snickering during their company's presentations by subsidiaries took an opportunity to feel superior, but missed one to learn about the rest of their organization. That knowledge might have come in handy when it came time to look for career opportunities. Along with the corporate-speak and boasting about business successes, there is almost always useful information in business presentations. Make sure you're open to hearing it.

3. Learning to adapt to a business work style is a good investment in your future. Like it or not, it's pretty clear that the technologists who'll be most successful in the years to come will be those who have business acumen as well as technical smarts. If you're uncomfortable in business-oriented meetings or dislike business presentations, that will likely wind up working against you at some point in the future. In fact, many geeks are working to acquire business communication skills, so they can create their own presentations and speak to business folk in their own language. They think those skills will serve them well down the line, and we think they're right.

CHAPTER 11

OUTSOURCING THE GEEK GAP

A tech consultant for a major outsourcer was hired to set up a call center for a company. The new center would feed customer information and all kinds of data back to the computer system of the client company. After the consultant had been working on the project for some time, the company's CEO resigned. While the board sought a replacement, the CFO decided to pull the plug on the project.

"We were told on a Wednesday that he wanted us out by Friday," the consultant recalls.

The consultant vigorously protested, pointing out all the benefits the new system would bring, noting that it was nearly finished, and begging the CFO for the chance at least to show him what it could do. The CFO relented a little, and a compromise was reached: the consultant and his team would have a month to finish their work and they would be allowed to demonstrate it for the CFO.

The demo couldn't have gone better. "We had a great project review," the consultant says. "Everything worked perfectly. All the benefits we promised were in place." Given this resounding success, he was sure the client would want the system completed. Instead, the client informed him that the project was canceled.

Why? The client offered no explanation, but the consultant thought he knew. This was a very large company with a long history of computerization, and a legacy mainframe system that had been in place for many years. "There was a very clear divide in the culture of the technology team," the consultant explained.

"One side said, 'We can code this for the mainframe, it can do it.'

"The other side said, 'You're crazy! You need more modern tools to stay competitive!'"

Unfortunately for the consultant, the mainframe's proponents were mostly long-time executives with the tenure to make their preferences stick. Those lobbying for an up-to-date system were newer employees with less clout. And so, he believes, his project was doomed from the start, no matter how good it was.

The Geek Gap can be enough of a problem when business people and technology people work together for a company. It takes on a whole new complexion when suits are clients and geeks are vendors. Worse, the two may be working on the same project, but report to different employers. Business people find getting information to and from technologists is harder than it would have been in house. And technologists may not get the support they need to do their jobs effectively.

One geek we know is a freelance development manager at a company that provides detailed online reports on real estate nationwide. He works off-site, overseeing a team of content providers who work in different locations and converse via online chat and instant message. The team creates, edits, and updates thousands of listings of real estate offered for sale.

Though the company depends on our friend and his freelancers to create the product it sells, he is always aware of his status as an outsider. "I am definitely 'out of the loop,'" he says. "Stuff comes from on high without much input from me. Even changes in software are just announced to me, many times after the fact, rather than before. Of course, if I make any changes without telling someone, I hear about it, and not in a nice way."

He and the freelancers who report to him use specially developed interface software to input complex information on real estate offerings and deals. Since they're the ones who have to use this software, it would seem logical for our friend to have a say in—or at least be kept informed of—feature changes or upgrades for it. But this never happens, he says. "I'm not even told what changes were made, just that I need to download the latest version."

Eventually he concluded that the only way to make sure that he knew about changes affecting his work was to make contact himself. "I have gotten into the habit of scheduling conference calls with my boss and a couple of other people at the company on a semi-regular basis. Many times the calls are more like bull sessions than work related, but it helps to make me feel more connected. If I expect to stay in touch, I have to make the effort."

56 PERCENT BY 2007

A growing number of geeks will find themselves in a similar position over the next few years. According to the IT research company, Gartner Inc., outsourcing will grow to 56 percent of the world IT service market by 2007. "Outsourcing is becoming the dominant way that enterprises buy IT services," noted Allie Young, research vice president for Gartner's sourcing group.[1]

This trend has infuriated many in-house IT workers who've either lost jobs to, or believe their jobs are threatened by, the move to outsourcing. And some have retained their jobs but have lost benefits. Many large corporations have weighed the advantages of having experienced talent in house against the savings they can get by outsourcing—and decided they want both. Their solution is to move in-house IT functions to outsourcing companies. Under these circumstances, technologists who worked for them suddenly find they're getting their paychecks from a vendor instead. This may be a win for the employer, which gets to retain its talent at what is usually a lower cost, but it's a loss for the employees, who nearly always find themselves receiving fewer benefits than they did before.

This practice led to a lawsuit against Honeywell when it allegedly outsourced its facilities and utilities engineering function to a vendor who retained most of the group's former staff members.[2] Nine of them sued, claiming Honeywell had engaged in outsourcing solely to rid itself of their pensions. They lost. Apparently, some of the group's senior managers were also let go as part of this process. Honeywell had purportedly been dissatisfied with the group's performance under these managers, so the company could reasonably assert legitimate business reasons for switching to outsourcing. In order to win, the former employees would have had to prove that ending their pensions was Honeywell's one and only reason for outsourcing.

Whatever the legalities, it's easy to see why geeks who've been moved to outsourcing companies are often bitter, especially if they later wind up out of a job altogether. One technologist reported he'd spent many years working for a large company, which then transferred his department to an outsourcer.[3]

"The CEO addressed all of us taken over in the deal, and said we were all highly valued," he recalls. A year later, the technologist was out of a job, a victim of layoffs that totaled some 25 percent of the outsourced department's work force. As if to add insult to injury, his boss gave him the news by phone, adding, "This is a great chance for you to advance your career."

Many months later, and still unemployed, he says his only consolation is hearing friends report on the current disarray at his onetime employer. "I have spoken with several people who say that after the deal, things are much worse than when my former company operated with the IT organization in house."

HIDDEN COSTS

Indeed many IT staff argue that the drawbacks of outsourcing outweigh its financial advantages. "From what I have observed at my employer, outsourcing software development projects resulted in products that had lower quality and missed deadlines, sometimes by more than a year," notes one programmer. "We had a big multi-year project that was out-sourced to an outside vendor and they were a year behind schedule, so my company ended up taking the project back in-house to fix the mess they gave us. The software system developed in-house has been cheaper, better, and on time. Management learned the lesson the hard way."[4]

"Outsourcing makes submanagers look like they are saving money by reducing head count," comments another disgruntled geek. "This makes them look good, even if the overall cost to the company is greater in downtime, costs, and time for training contractors, and other soft costs that are difficult to quantify."[5]

Or maybe not all that difficult. In a recent Deloitte Touche survey of executives at twenty-five large companies, 70 percent said they'd had bad experiences with outsourcing and would be more cautious in the future.[6] And 25 percent said they were so unhappy they were actually reversing course, bringing formerly outsourced functions back in-house.

According to 62 percent of respondents, outsourcing required more management than expected. Eighty-one percent were frustrated not to know more about vendor costs and 57 percent wound up paying for services they'd thought would be included in the service. Perhaps for reasons like these, nearly half—44 percent—said the cost savings supposed to be associated with outsourcing had not materialized.

But whatever its drawbacks, outsourcing is clearly here to stay, as the arguments in its favor are too powerful for most business managers to ignore. First there's the issue of "core competencies"—the notion that the best way to run a company is to focus attention on those tasks that are essential to its operation. That is, if your company makes widgets, you should focus your attention on producing and selling those widgets. It's probably a bad idea to expend energy and attention on tasks that are not directly related to this effort.

Many upper executives view technology in the same light, as some-thing they need but is not directly related to what they do. They also believe they can never attract and keep the best in-house IT expertise. And so, they prefer to choose contracting with an outside vendor over hiring an in-house IT staff. For some, this is a legacy of the high-tech boom of the late 1990s, when hiring competent geeks was a struggle, and employers found themselves turning to outside vendors out of necessity rather than choice. For others, it seems like common sense, as technology becomes ever more complex and intimidating, and they seek to streamline and simplify their operations.

The second issue is flexibility: a company may need twenty-five programmers while it's creating a new system, but only two or three to maintain it once it's done—at least until the next project comes along. Being able to add and subtract programmers without actually having to hire and fire full-time employees can be a great advantage in situations like these.

Third, the Deloitte study notwithstanding, outsourcing does create significant cost savings for many companies that try it. On average, according to the Meta Group, moving a technology function from in-house to an outsource solution reduces IT expenses by 30 percent.[7] This is a powerful motivator that will lead most companies at least to explore outsourcing IT functions.

SHIPPING JOBS OVERSEAS

The biggest generator of cost savings—and controversy—is the growing practice of "offshoring," that is, using the Internet to send jobs overseas to countries where pay scales are dramatically lower than in the United States and other developed nations. Outsourcing to underdeveloped nations is such a huge national issue that many people assume this is what "outsourcing" always means.

With the high-speed Internet and voice-over IP technology, outsourcing technology jobs to developing nations has never been easier or made more economic sense. An anonymous post to the online community Slashdot.org illustrates the economics at play: "About a year ago I hired a developer in India to do my job. I pay him $12,000 out of the $67,000 I get. He's happy to have the work. I'm happy that I have to work only 90 minutes a day just supervising the code. My employer thinks I'm telecommuting. Now I'm considering getting a second job and doing the same thing."[8]

Whether or not this post is actually true, the numbers in it are probably accurate enough. This huge discrepancy in pay adds up to an opportunity most companies can't ignore. And indeed, offshoring is growing fast. In a 2004 survey, Cutter Consortium found 45 percent of responding companies had begun offshoring IT in the previous four years.[9]

Work is being outsourced to a wide variety of low-wage countries, including the Philippines, China, and various eastern European nations. But India, with its English-speaking workforce, stable electrical and Internet infrastructure, and large cadre of technology workers, is dominating the offshore market for the moment.

That market consists of much more than just IT jobs. Offshoring call centers and back-office functions have become ubiquitous. Recently, an Indian back-office employee working in Chennai had to check on insurance coverage for an American employee. He phoned the employee's (US) insurer—and found himself talking to someone else who was also in Chennai.[10]

More high-skilled jobs are ripe for offshoring as well. Clerical work, such as medical and legal transcription is routinely sent overseas. Even the doctors and lawyers who employ the transcriptionists are not immune from offshore competition. A small but growing number of US hospitals are sending digital x-ray images to India to be read by radiologists there.[11] And companies such as Microsoft, General Electric, and Cisco systems are having lawyers or paralegals in India to conduct legal research or draft documents to be used in the United States because of the cost advantages.[12]

How bad is all this for US workers, whether radiologists, programmers, or customer service reps? It depends on whom you ask. Lobbying groups point to the hundreds of thousands of jobs that have moved offshore in an attempt to prompt the federal government to intervene.

"Forrester Research estimates that $151.2 billion in wages will be shifted from the United States to lower-wage countries by 2015," writes Lou Dobbs in his 2004 book *Exporting America.* "Interestingly, the sector leading the way will be the information technology industry. There's a cruel irony at work here: No one batted an eye when we moved manufacturing jobs out of the country, because we were sure those jobs would be absorbed in the services sector—specifically the information technology industry."[13]

On the other hand, some pundits argue that while offshoring might certainly disrupt individual lives and careers, the overall economic effect is good, not bad. "We would argue that not only is the United States fully able to withstand these changes, as it will be able to create jobs faster than offshoring eliminates them, but that the current debate misses the point entirely," notes a McKinsey & Co. study. "Offshoring creates wealth for U.S. companies and consumers and therefore for the United States as a whole." Moreover, the study asserts, "Offshoring is just one more example of the innovation that that keeps U.S. companies at the leading edge of competitiveness across multiple sectors."[14] That study also postulates that IT workers who lose their job to outsourcing are freed up for redeployment into more interesting and higher-level jobs.

This sounds suspiciously similar to the boss described earlier who told the techie he was laying off that it was "a great opportunity to advance your career." But even if it's true that geeks who lose their jobs to lower-paid foreigners wind up with even better positions—which has yet to be proved—offshoring is a surefire way to worsen the Geek Gap.

It also stands to reason that if culture clash is a problem between geeks and suits who are working in the same company, at the same location, on the same workday schedule, and are able to speak face-to-face whenever they like, it's likely to be a much worse problem where none of the above is true, and geeks and suits are not only in different locations but different continents, living their lives in societies with completely different norms and values.

IT'S NOT THE SHOW, IT'S THE PROCESS

A wonderful example of these differences is Karma Yatra, a program put in place in the Indian divisions of US-based companies, as well as in outsourcing firms. The inspiration for Karma Yatra came about because of high attrition at Indian outsourcing companies, according to its inventor, Ayush Maheshwari, an employee relationship management (ERM) specialist and motivational singer who also goes by the name Big Indian.[15]

The reason for the high attrition was in part that with the offshoring industry booming, Indian employees with IT skills were in something of a seller's market. When the Internet boom caused a similar skilled labor shortage in the United States a few years ago, employers responded by offering lavish salaries, stock options, and performance bonuses. But Karma Yatra derives from a whole different philosophy.

"Companies were trying to retain them with a little more money, and then a little more, and the whole sense of the Eastern values of connection and family bonding was missing," Maheshwari says. "So I said, what are companies doing today to emotionally connect with the lives of people?"

This is especially true for those who work in call centers, he adds, where they're required to take on American sounding names and disguise their Indian accents—in essence being forced to put on a different identity. "If I want to switch from call center A to call center B because I was offered $50 more, I might not do it if I and my family feel connected to my current employer and the people there know what's going on in my life," he says.

This is the basic idea behind Karma Yatra, which roughly translated means "my journey of destiny," and is intended to connect both the employee and his or her family members to their coworkers and employer. Everyone in the company is divided into randomly combined teams, in which the CEO might be side by side with a receptionist or quality assurance worker. Each team then has two weeks to prepare a performance, which will be presented at a gala, celebratory evening. Family members, from spouses to children, to parents and grandparents, are expected to attend.

"The show is not the only thing, it's the process to get there," Maheshwari explains. "It breaks inhibitions and gets people to look at their own and each other's talents, and come up with something that makes sense." By the time it's all put together, it can make for an emotional evening, he reports, with grandparents weeping at the sight of their grandchildren onstage—or joining in the dancing themselves.

Perhaps most surprising, from an American perspective, is how effective this is. "When they return to the workplace, everybody knows everybody," Maheshwari says. "They are all connected."

"Karma Yatra is the means by which the participant (Yatri) can extend the limits of his own capabilities," is how one participant put it. "After the journey he feels his Organization (his Karma Bhoomi) is just an extension of his own family."[16]

Maheshwari says he's been asked to do Karma Yatra events in the United States, and he believes they would work here. Whether or not they would, this is as far as you can get from the compensation packages most US firms come up with to try to boost retention. And therein lies the challenge: there are significant cultural differences between the United States and India. Executives on both sides of the equation need to be aware of these differences—and take steps to address them. Having a Karma Yatra event is a good way to start.

"American companies are putting a lot of effort into getting Indians to blend with the U.S.," Maheshwari says. "And some are now starting to connect with our core values as well. They've got to continue the process—they have to blend with India."

"YOU'RE IN A BIND"

This is sound advice, but not a step most US offshoring customers will likely pursue. Thus, thanks to the distance and culture clash, many American companies are finding offshoring to be more challenging than they'd imagined. A 2005 DiamondCluster study of offshoring trends found 62 percent of IT offshoring buyers were satisfied with the service, down from 79 percent in 2004.[17] And 51 percent reported ending an offshoring arrangement before the contract was up in the previous year, up from 21 percent in 2004. The downturn in satisfaction is in large part due to the complexity of managing offshore relationships, the study added.[18]

"If you don't have resources available to you locally and that expertise—and that work gets sent offshore—you're in a bind because you're dependent on somebody else that's 3,000 or 4,000 miles away," noted Larry Mana'o, CEO of Detto Technologies.[19]

But distance and international culture clash are not the only Geek Gap issues that go with offshoring. Companies that engage in offshoring are likely to see a negative impact on the techies they have working for them at home—especially if they believe some of their former colleagues lost their jobs as a result of the move.

It's no secret that feelings about offshoring run very strong throughout our society. And though technology workers are not necessarily a politically active or outgoing bunch, some have taken to the streets in organized protests outside of high-level business conferences.

"Last year, a large throng of these people showed up on Park Avenue outside the Waldorf-Astoria to get their message across to executives attending a Conference Board meeting about outsourcing," writes Ellsworth Quarrels in *Across the Board*.[20] They were technology workers who had recently lost their jobs to offshoring, or current employees who feared that they soon would. From an employer's point of view, it may make little difference: an employee who believes he or she will be a likely victim of offshoring is not one who's likely to feel aligned with company goals. If geeks are threatened by the fact that their jobs are viewed as more expendable at home than those of others, more distrust and resentment will set in.

Signs at the Conference Board protest said things like "Outsource the Outsourcers," and "Has Money Become Everything to You?"[21] At another 2004 protest outside a meeting of the Washington Software Association, one protester's sign reportedly spoofed Microsoft's slogan "Where do you want to go today?" with "Where do you want your job to go today?"[22]

The message from on-site geeks is clear: offshoring makes suits their enemy. And suits have heard the message: 88 percent of respondents in the DiamondCluster study said they were concerned about anti-offshoring backlash from employees at home.[23]

OFFSHORING IS HERE TO STAY

Whatever its drawbacks, offshoring isn't going away any time soon. Despite the negative effects they reported, 74 percent of the executives in the DiamondCluster study said they planned to increase offshoring in the coming year, up from 64 percent in 2004.[24] As Mana'o said, "It's definitely coming down to costs. The problem is that when they're going through a contracting firm, they're billing us at $100 an hour, whereas we can get it outside for $15 to $20 an hour." This is why, despite his reservations, his company uses offshoring for its customer support and for about 10 percent of its software development.[25]

The fact is, offshoring IT is one more step in a long-standing tradition. Check the labels on the clothes you're wearing right now. Do they say "Made in the USA?" More than likely they don't—because textile manufacturing is pretty much dead in this country. Were your car, your cell phone, your television all made domestically? Chances are the answer is no.

For the better part of a century, Americans have routinely taken advantage of the fact that people in many other countries draw lower wages than we do. This has enabled Americans to purchase everything from SUVs to American flags for less because they were made abroad. A wide variety of US industries have suffered as a result. (The same is true, by the way, for residents of other wealthy, developed nations: several European nations, as well as Australia, are currently seeing their own waves of offshoring.)

Many members of the service sector thought we were immune to such overseas competition because it seemed services could not be shipped across oceans. They further believed that people in third world countries could never acquire the skills to do such work as writing code. It turns out that they were wrong on both counts.

Whether or not this is fair to American technology workers, and whether or not it's the best way to get IT work done, offshoring will continue to grow and be used for a wider variety of jobs. Whatever their sympathies, most employers, especially large and midsized companies, will be forced at least to consider offshoring at some point because of cost competition from other companies who have done so.

With that in mind, our only choice is to accept offshoring as a fact of modern life and find the best ways to survive its effects. Here are some steps that may help:

If you're a suit:

1. Weigh *all* the costs of offshoring. There's no question that off-shoring can save your company money. But many managers who've done it report that the cost savings were less than expected, and managing the complexity of offshoring is more difficult than it at first appears. Not only that, there is likely to be a major morale drain among your in-house IT staff, the brightest and best of whom may well start updating their resumes. It's wise to take all these factors into account when making an offshoring decision.

2. If you do it, make sure it's for the right reasons. Increasingly, conventional wisdom among managers is that cost savings alone is an insufficient reason to enter an offshoring relationship. Whatever the reduction in expense, it is almost never worth the disruption that offshoring inevitably causes among remaining employees, and within an organization in general.

   "Over the last several years there has been a gradual shift away from cost as the dominant driver for outsourcing decisions," note the authors of the DiamondCluster study.[26] Though "Reduce or Control Costs" is still the number-one reason for outsourcing, "Better Manage Variable Capacity Needs" is a close second. ("Variable Capacity Needs" refers to the fact, discussed earlier in this chapter, that companies need more IT help at certain times—for instance, when creating and implementing a new system, than they do at other times, for instance when only maintenance of existing systems is needed.) "Free Up Internal Resources for More Critical Purposes" is a close third. One reason, they note, is that companies who outsourced have found that the cost savings were not as great as they had imagined.

3. Do it the right way. If offshoring in your organization means freeing up IT staff for more critical tasks, you'll be a step ahead of the game, because IT staff will recognize this rationale, and you can avoid the morale downturn that often goes with offshoring decisions.

But even if your rationale is to cut costs, and you plan to reduce your IT staff, there's a right way and a wrong way to do it. Many laid-off IT workers whose jobs went abroad report with rancor that they were forced to train their replacements before departing. This may have resulted from a well-intentioned desire to keep them at their jobs a bit longer, but for most, it felt like insult was being added to injury. On the other hand, if you're genuinely in need of training for offshore workers, consider making training a permanent position. Given the huge turnover rates in offshore IT providers, chances are there'll be new people to train on a regular basis.

4. Consider insuring IT workers. It sounds like a radical idea, but it comes from McKinsey Global Institute: provide insurance for IT staff who lose their jobs to overseas competition and must take lower-paying positions. The insurance would cover workers only once they were reemployed full time and last for only two years, and would refund 70 percent of the wage difference as well as replace lost health benefits.[27] This would allow a displaced IT employee, for instance, to hold a "day job" while retraining in new technologies, and still enable him or her to make the mortgage payments. (We believe, if a company were to offer such insurance, it should also cover displaced IT workers who work 35 hours a week or more as independent contractors, since such contracting has become commonplace in the IT world, and amounts to full-time work without benefits.)

   We realize most employers will probably not consider this option—especially if they turned to offshoring in the first place out of a desperate need to cut costs. But we should note that Mc-Kinsey estimates employers could pay for this insurance with as little as 4 to 5 percent of the money they save by offshoring. Given the strong resentments that the threat of offshoring raises among IT staff, it might be a worthwhile investment.

5. Cross the Geek Gap. Many technologists view business people as heartless and greedy, believing they care only about the bottom line. They think they see IT staff as nothing more than a resource to be tapped, not human beings with families and needs.

   Offshoring, if done for the wrong reason or handled in the

wrong way, is a very good way to confirm those beliefs. That's an issue worth considering, given most organizations' growing dependence on technology and, therefore, on the people who understand and can manage it.

The world of IT is a close-knit one, with most technologists more loyal to each other than they are to their employers, and equipped with the latest communications technology with which to trade information across geographic borders and industries. An employer that lays off large numbers of people to replace them with offshored workers risks gaining a reputation that could make hiring geeks very difficult in the future.

If offshoring is a necessary step for your firm, the best way to avoid bad feelings is by handling the move as sensitively as possible. Transfer as many displaced IT workers as possible into other jobs, and deal generously with those who must be let go to give them the best chance of landing on their feet.

A second key is communication: make sure the techies understand exactly why the move is necessary, whose jobs will—and won't—be affected, and how the company and its employees as a whole will benefit.

When it comes to offshoring, it's extremely easy to turn the Geek Gap into a wide chasm. Once that happens, it can be almost impossible to reach across it.

If you're a geek:

1. Be indispensable. There is, unfortunately, no such thing as an off-shore-proof job. The best bet is to be ready with a wide variety of skills, so that if one job vanishes, you'll be well positioned to step into another. Adding new certifications and taking ongoing training in new technologies is one way to help prepare in case your job is affected. It's also important to form close connections with people outside your area, both within your company and within your profession as a whole. This way, if the need arises, you'll have more avenues to help you find a new position.

2. Be competitive. "System administrators can become cranky and unresponsive because they're not directly exposed to competitive pressure," notes Paul Graham. "A salesman has to deal with customers, and a developer has to deal with competitors' software, but a system administrator, like an old bachelor, has few external forces to keep him in line."[28] This is why he suggests outsourcing any function not directly facing competition, and why many business experts recommend managing IT departments (and others as well) as though they were independent entities, which invoice other departments for their services.

"We aim to improve 'departmental' 'efficiency' and 'effectiveness,'" Tom Peters writes in his most recent book, *Re-Imagine!* "But 'improvement,' no matter how dramatic, misses the point. In fact, it is deeply misleading. We must *destroy* 'departments,'—and create aggressive, imaginative, entrepreneurial Professional Service Firms (PSFs) in their stead."[29] After all, as he notes, "Every job (every!) done in White-Collar World is also done 'outside' . . . for profit!"

3. Be a liaison. In an organization using offshoring, one of the most difficult jobs will be maintaining clear communication between overseas IT workers and the company employing them. Management may not realize at first how big a job this is, but they'll learn over time as the inevitable problems of communication and distance occur. If you're ready, willing, and able to step in and ease communications, you may find yourself with a whole new career.

4. Cross the Geek Gap. If you've been wondering why you should bother learning anything about running a business, consider this: a job is only offshorable if it is completely separate from a company's business functions. If your job is to develop software based on a wish list your business colleagues have given you, that can be done from anywhere. If your job includes learning the business processes inside out, so that you can suggest features that would help the business run most efficiently, you'll be tough to replace with someone thousands of miles away.

CHAPTER 12

SAME BED, DIFFERENT DREAMS

I n 1998 the Internet start-up Tripod.com was acquired by Lycos for $58 million, leaving its mostly twenty-something top executives with a fabulous track record and a handsome net worth. A few would make the move to Lycos's boxy corporate offices in the Boston suburb Waltham. But most would choose to remain in elegant, rural Williamstown, in the Berkshire Mountains of Western Massachusetts. With Tripod on their resumes and plenty of money in the bank, they could pretty much do whatever they wanted. What would each of them choose?

Tripod cofounder and former business student Bo Peabody chose venture capital as his next step. After all, a venture-capital company originally gave Tripod its start. So Peabody cofounded Village Ventures in offices across the street from Tripod's former headquarters. Created to invest in high-tech start-ups, Village Ventures now manages funds totaling more than $250 million. More recently, he authored a book, *Lucky or Smart? Secrets to an Entrepreneurial Life.*[1]

Ethan Zuckerman, Tripod's former vice president of research and development took a different path entirely. He cofounded the Geek

Corps, a nonprofit organization that sends groups of technology professionals to countries in Africa and Southeast Asia, trying to close the information gap by providing both infrastructure and high-tech training to people who really need it. More recently, he became a fellow at the Berkman Center for Internet and Technology at Harvard Law School, where he is working on the impact of technology in the developing world.

Zuckerman and Peabody are a geek and a suit who, each in his own way, pursued a similar path: they turned their backs on high-paying and powerful corporate roles to remain in a community they loved. They both also work at passing on what they learned at Tripod to others who could benefit from the knowledge. Even so, their post-Tripod careers took them in somewhat different directions. When geeks and suits follow their dreams, they don't often lead to the same place.

We first encountered the idea of "same bed, different dreams" as a way to describe Western ambitions when working with the Chinese in a joint venture. But it applies to the career paths and priorities of geeks and suits as well. They may work in the same company, on the same project, even on the same cross-functional team. And yet, their ideas about success may differ in ways that may or may not be obvious at first glance.

"LOOK BEYOND YOUR NAVEL"

We recently spent some time perusing books about achieving business success. One piece of advice was repeated over and over in various forms: to be successful at business, you must look beyond yourself. In the book *Career Warfare: 10 Rules for Building a Successful Personal Brand and Fighting to Keep It* by John Hancock's CEO David F. D'Alessandro, the first chapter is titled "Rule One: Try to Look beyond Your Own Navel." It notes: "'I' is certainly the first consideration in organizational life. Most people's reaction to anything that happens in the outfit they work for is, 'What about me? Will this be good for me?' For example, the company is suddenly engulfed in scandal. Your first thought is probably not, 'How will we get out of this mess?' It's, 'Am *I* in trouble?'"

This is just human nature, he writes. "However, to build the kind of personal brand that will help you be successful, you will have to add another filter to the lens. . . . In other words, you have to view your own actions in the same way that the people judging you will view them."[2]

There's an extension of this thinking in Jim Collins's management bestseller *Good to Great: Why Some Companies Make the Leap . . . and Others Don't*. Collins studied a small set of companies that, for over fifteen years, consistently outperformed the stock market, their competitors, and their industry. He identified something he calls "Level 5 leaders" at the top. "Level 5 leaders channel their ego needs away from themselves and into the larger goal of building a great company," he notes. "It's not that the Level 5 leaders have no ego or self-interest. Indeed, they are incredibly ambitious—*but their ambition is first and foremost for the institution, not themselves.*"[3]

All of this is strikingly dissimilar from the career advice offered to techies, which encourages them to indeed focus on their own navels, or at least their own certifications and abilities. Here's one example from *Get Your IT Career in Gear! Practical Advice for Building a Career in Information Technology*: "Depending on your skills, the options for a career in IT are essentially boundless and can be shaped as much by your interests and work style as by your prior experience."[4]

These days any set of suggestions for techies who want career advancement emphasizes their need for ample business skills. "To succeed, an IT professional—from the lowest rungs of the rank-and-file up to the executive suite—should be as much M.B.A. candidate as technical guru," author Leslie Jaye Goff writes.[5] But if the stress is on business, the instruction is still to build one's own skills, not to concern oneself with corporate goals or coworker perceptions.

We think that this makes sense, in view of geeks' and suits' differing focus on problem solving as opposed to influencing people. That difference carries over into how the two groups approach their work lives and how they dream those lives will turn out.

"WE GET TOGETHER AND WRITE CODE"

For most geeks, success seems to revolve around technological innovation, either by creating new technology, or, as Zuckerman is doing, bringing technology to new places. As we mentioned in chapter 9, technologists tend to view themselves as painters, not plumbers, and they value technology for its own sake, the same way that a painter values art. However they may feel about their current jobs, love of technology is what originally inspired them to seek technology careers, and many thus spend their free time on . . . yet more technology.

This was driven home to us recently at a party attended by several geeks. One was talking to an acquaintance about a mutual friend. "We almost never see each other," he was saying. "But every once in a while we get together and write some code." Chances are, even if they weren't paid for it, most technologists would spend a lot of their time creating some kind of technology.

Technologists may aspire to management positions, but often in a different spirit from their business colleagues. Where suits tend to like the idea of becoming leaders and influencing and inspiring others, for many geeks, the appeal of management is the opportunity to climb the corporate ladder, have more responsibility and decision-making power, and be more in control of their own destinies.

Not long ago we came across a tech employee who'd been offered a promotion. The new position was a leadership role that involved mentoring other employees and helping them learn the company's new systems, but not directly supervising anyone.

Without any actual staff to manage, the techie wasn't sure that accepting the new job would be a good career move, and put the question to other IT managers via an online discussion group, asking, "Would this be a help or a hindrance if my goal is to position myself for management at some point?"

Several managers responded. Most recommended taking the job. And, they added, far from being a detriment, the absence of subordinates was probably a benefit. "I've had most of the available roles throughout my career, and I have to say that direct management of staff and budgeting were not among my favorites," noted one longtime IT professional. "Like everyone else I wanted to become a manager because that was the definition of 'success.' But it's not for everybody."

Indeed, this responding techie had actually chosen to leave a management role and focus on technology instead. "I haven't done any real 'managing' in ten years and I'll tell you, I don't miss it a bit. The pay for staff work is pretty similar, there's less stress, the hours are more regular, and sometimes people even appreciate what you're doing."[6]

ORGANIZATIONAL PRIDE

That attitude toward management is the polar opposite of most suits'. Business executives are usually attracted to the power and prestige that goes with management positions. "I've come up through the business units of the organization and have management as a career aspiration," says David S. Fry, business analyst at a major insurance firm. "I typically equate my desire for management to my father's career. I admire and greatly respect my Dad's business acumen and he went into management (actually rose to VP ranks, which I will never achieve)."[7]

For many business people, desire to take on a leadership role goes hand-in-hand with organizational pride. They enjoy and value being part of an organization, and take pride in the work they are helping it to accomplish. This is the kind of team spirit many companies seek to develop through motivational meetings (what one disaffected geek we know calls "pep rallies"). While such efforts are likely lost on most techies, many suits find that such things as company-wide meetings and mission statements help them feel connected to a larger purpose. The ones who are most successful and happiest in their jobs will often take the company's mission deeply to heart.

This is why Peabody notes in *Lucky or Smart?* that a carefully crafted mission statement—something to do with the greater good—delivered with charisma and passion has a near magical ability to inspire employees to great efforts for their company. At Tripod, which provided the means for ordinary people to publish Web pages and thus get their opinions and interests out onto the Net, the mission was "to fight the most important battle on the frontier of the First Amendment!" he wrote. As he points out, "No matter what anyone might tell you, all but the most hardened human beings want to believe that they get up in the morning to pursue a goal greater than simply padding their pockets."[8]

This is what Jim Collins was getting at when he reported that the top executives in the best-run companies were ambitious for their organizations rather than for themselves. He notes that executives who run the most successful companies are very passionate about what they do, even when that passion might seem unexpected. "When we interviewed the Philip Morris executives, we encountered an intensity and passion that surprised us," he notes, adding that most top executives were passionate consumers of the company's products. "In 1979, Ross Millhiser, then vice chairman of Philip Morris and a dedicated smoker, said, 'I love cigarettes. It's one of the things that makes life really worth living.'"[9]

Organizational pride tends to be less of a factor in how techies see their jobs. A study of more than three hundred techies at nineteen companies conducted by the consulting firm BlessingWhite and Stanford University showed six key differences in what motivates IT employees, compared with other types of employees. Among them is something that most people who work with technologists already know: IT people tend to identify themselves by their professional skills, rather than by where they work. "First and foremost they are engineers, analysts or programmers—the company comes second," according to BlessingWhite director Juliet Killen.[10]

This is consistent with geeks' natural orientation: they tend to see themselves as loners who feel more affinity for others in the same profession than their corporate colleagues. To some degree, this is a dynamic that corporate leaders themselves have augmented, by employing techies on an indefinite contractual basis, rather than making a commitment to them by investing in their careers (see chapter 9) and by readily shipping their jobs overseas as a less costly alternative (see chapter 11). Policies like these can give tech folk the impression that they are commodities, not valued individuals, which reinforces their own views of their position within the larger company.

The notable exception to this trend is within high-tech start-up companies. In this high-wire world, the success of the company, not to mention its very existence, rests squarely on the innovations the technologists bring to the table. In situations like these, geeks will not only knock themselves out at their jobs (they tend to do this anyway) but also take enormous pride in what they are helping to build.

And still, we believe these geeks are taking pride in the technology they're working to create, not necessarily in the organization that sells it. This is a subtle distinction, easier to see in situations where the technology and the company become separate. One good example is the story of Handspring, a company founded in 1999 by Jeff Hawkins and Donna Dubinsky, creators of the Palm Pilot.

Three years earlier, before they started Palm Inc., handheld computers were considered poison in most conventional biz/tech wisdom, and no investor would take a chance on the idea. Lacking other options, the pair showed their prototype to U.S. Robotics. Execs there loved the concept, and allowed Hawkins and Dubinsky to launch Palm as an autonomous unit within their firm. "They let us run Palm independently, with our own sales force and marketing people, and we were able to forge our own manufacturing relationships," said Donna Dubinsky. "They were more like our bank than our boss."[11]

Things changed the following year when U.S. Robotics was acquired by 3Com. The new corporate owner purportedly insisted on integrating Palm's operations into the company at large. "We had to negotiate a lot about the destiny of our product and company, which suddenly became a division of a global, multibillion-dollar company," Dubinsky recalled.

That arrangement was never what either of Palm's founders had had in mind, they said. So, after working out an amicable departure that let them license the Palm operating system, they left to start anew, without a backward glance at the company-within-a-company they'd created. They had taken the technology with them, and that was what mattered.

The two then founded Handspring. Its first product, the Visor, was an immediate success, not surprisingly, since it was designed by the same technical minds that had come up with the Palm. Ironically, that early success may have been Handspring's undoing. Faced with a powerful, lower-priced competitor, Palm lowered prices on its own devices, driving both companies into a price war that was great for consumers but not great for their bottom lines. Facing losses on their products, the only logical solution was for the two companies to merge again, which they wisely did, in 2003.[12]

"AN EXCUSE FOR BEING TOGETHER"

Another motivation for many business people is the chance to be part of a group for which they feel affection or affinity. Some years ago, a friend of ours worked for an advertising agency. She was part of a ten-person copywriting group for business travelers. It was a hard-driving work environment where working late into the evening and on weekends was the norm.

One day, she had a job evaluation with the group's director, who ended her comments by saying ". . . and I know we all get very stressed out over deadlines here, but I always think that if we weren't working on these ads, we'd have to come up with another excuse for all coming here and being together every day."

Our friend was completely taken aback by this, particularly because she didn't much like the director, and neither did most of her coworkers. The director had put off many people with her high-handed management style, though she always remained smiling and pleasant as she issued orders or criticisms.

"It seemed ironic that someone whose behavior made it seem she didn't care about people's feelings would say something like that," our friend says now. "The funny thing is, she was right. It really was a fun group of people to work with. And they were all very talented, so it felt great be part of this brilliant group."

In fact, our friend had never set out to be a copywriter in the first place; she'd taken the position in the hopes she could use it as a stepping-stone to a career in book or magazine publishing. "I stayed for years because I was having too much fun with the job," she says. "And what was most fun about it was being in that group of people."

For techies, coworkers can also make or break job satisfaction, but in a subtly different way. Another key distinction between technical and nontechnical motivations which turned up in the BlessingWhite study was that IT folk could be stimulated by the chance to share ideas with colleagues whom they respect.[13] This is not quite the same as the pleasure business people feel in being part of a group they enjoy. While suits take pleasure in belonging to the group, geeks take pleasure in exchanging thoughts and ideas that can help them specifically deepen their own learning.

It helps to remember that however the outside world sees them, most technologists view themselves as artists. Keep this in mind, and it's easy to understand their thinking. After all, what would most painters prefer to be able to say, "Gee, I belong to this great artists' group!" or "Gee, the other day, I got to discuss oil painting techniques with Georgia O'Keeffe!"?

WALTON OR TORVALDS?

Which brings us to an interesting question: Whom do suits and geeks idolize? If they could be like anyone they wanted to be, whom would they choose? For many suits the pinnacle of success might mean climbing the corporate ladder to become the head of a large, successful enterprise. Or, they might dream about striking out on their own, starting their own companies and hitting it big. Their heroes are people like Dave Thomas and Sam Walton, people who started with little and built their companies into empires.

When geeks imagine success, it has less to do with power and profits, and more to do with technological ability, maverick innovation, appreciation from users, and recognition from peers. Microsoft founder Bill Gates may be an idol for business people, but geeks are more likely to dream of emulating Linus Torvalds, the enigmatic Finn who developed the operating system Linux.

Torvalds's software is in widespread use and giving Windows its only serious competition. So since Gates is supposedly the wealthiest person on the planet, one might logically assume Torvalds would be up there, too. But he isn't, because the operating system he created and devotes his days to improving doesn't belong to him. Having created it, he promptly gave it away for free and so is now an employee of Transmeta Corp.

Of course, it is precisely its "copyleft" provisions—the opposite of a traditional copyright in that no one can ever own it—that make Linux such a powerhouse in the world of software. Moreover, Torvalds has called his decision to give it away "the single best decision I've ever made."[14] That decision is what made him a legend in the techie world. The principles of open-source programming, Linux itself, and even "Tux," Torvalds's penguin logo which has been adopted as Linux's symbol, are beloved by geeks the world over.

THE GO-BETWEENS

While many geeks and suits seek success at the top of their respective professions, some are seeking a third way, forging a new career path that is somewhere in between. Their backgrounds may be in technology or business. Their titles may be "business analyst" or "product manager"—or pretty much anything else—and their salaries and responsibilities vary widely. But their core skills are always the same: they have the ability to talk to both suits and geeks and understand the needs and priorities of both.

"I've made a career out of stepping across the gap," reports Mitchell Abramson, technology architect, Customer Training & Information Products for the Depository Trust & Clearing Corp. in New York City. He did not originally set out to be a go-between. Abramson started out as a writing school graduate who needed a paying job, and went to work for Dean Witter reading and answering managed-account customer inquiries and compiling compliance reports.

"I was irked by the fact that the information I needed for those reports was only available on one text based black and green mainframe screen at a time," he says. "I couldn't even copy and paste what was in it. Here I was looking at information that was only there because someone else had typed it in, and I had no choice but to type it all over again."

Determined to find a way to solve the problem through technology,

Abramson embarked on a project that turned out to be part research and part development work. He was lucky enough to connect with a colleague, a network engineer, with a diverse body of knowledge in a wide array of software, and the generosity to share what he knew. Abramson soon learned how to reengineer the system he worked on and removed the need to input the same data more than once.

Along the way, he also discovered he had an affinity for technological matters in general, and software and code-driven solutions in particular. With his writing/communication background, he had the perfect aptitudes to become a successful go-between.

He also learned what he now says is an essential skill for anyone bridging the gap between IT and business: "Don't be afraid to ask stupid questions. When I was first starting out, I would walk down to the people who knew SQL and ask them the dumbest question possible to get them to put the answer into my language. If I wasn't sure if I 'got it yet,' I would feed back to them what they had just told me, but in my own words, and then let them correct me when I got some detail wrong."

With the most tedious part of his job now automated, Abramson found he could complete his assigned tasks in a fraction of the allotted time, leaving him with extra hours during the workday. He spent those hours learning more and more about the technology that ran his company. His expertise soon came to the attention of another manager who needed to generate financial reports more quickly.

Abramson got input from the people preparing the reports, learned how it was done, and then, in consultation with some of the company's tech folk, found ways to automate parts of the process. With Abramson's new system, a report that had previously taken six weeks for six people to compile could be completed by one person in a day and a half. A new go-between career was born.

"No one knew what to call me," Abramson says now. "I thought I was a technical liaison." But when he asked his new boss for a promotion, the boss wrote him up as a "technical analyst." "Human Resources would never have paid what I was asking to a 'technical liaison,' because HR departments see a liaison as a low-paying position," he explains.

Today, Abramson has eleven years' experience working in the no-man's-land between business and IT, and his technological skills are growing. Ironically, despite an ever-growing list of successfully completed tech projects, he's concerned that on paper, his credentials don't match what HR departments would look for in attempting to hire people to do the very things he has already done.

"I'm a 'jack of all trades and master of none,' and my talents have more to do with solving problems than being an 'expert' in a particular technology" he says. "I don't think I'm unique. There are a lot of people like me whose jobs aren't advertised and you never hear about them.

"From what I've seen, in a large-scale organization, you almost need some kind of technical liaison to help the business side and the IT world understand each other. And yet I've never seen a company have that as a clearly defined role."[15]

NEVER HEARD THE TERM "CEO"

Barbara Finer came to the go-between role from the other side of the Geek Gap, having started out as a technologist rather than a business person. She began her career as a software engineer in a large technology company. Over time, she says, "I learned that I was a good engineer, but not a great one. I also figured out that I was a people person. So I looked at myself and said, 'Now what?'"

The answer was to become a product manager in a start-up computer hardware company—a job that demanded precisely her combination of engineering know-how and people skills. This is a relatively common role in technology companies, for while these companies may be no more attuned to the Geek Gap among employees than other types of companies are, most are keenly aware of the need to close the gap between the engineers who design the hardware, and the customers who buy and use it.

Finer says she came into her new job with very little knowledge about the workings of the business world. "I had no business background, I had never heard the term *CEO*," she says. Nor did she have any idea what a product manager was. "The company explained that it was someone who had to be good at talking to both customers and engineers."

Further, now that she was working for the marketing department, she encountered unexpected resistance from her engineering colleagues. "Even though I was fresh from being an engineer, the engineers looked at me as a marketing person," she recalls. "It was hard to figure out how to be successful."

Over time, however, she learned. "The major lesson, one that has served me well, was that to be a good marketing person in a technology company really means collecting data about what the customer wants," she says. "If you are very data driven, engineers respect that."

Just as important, she learned what not to do. "I had to not tell them how to solve the problem," she says. It's tempting, she adds, for anyone in that role. "A lot of people in product management and product marketing in tech companies came over from engineering. Even though you understand the technology, you have to resist getting involved in designing actual solutions."

It can be a delicate balance, she notes. "You do have to stay aware. When people tell you something is impossible, and they're pulling your leg, you have to be able to challenge delicately." That's when it helps, she adds, to back up one's requests with a lot of customer data.

Today, Finer heads QuiVivity, a technology marketing company in Marlborough, Massachusetts, is also adjunct professor of entrepreneurship at Babson College in nearby Wellesley, and is entrepreneur in residence at Olin College of Engineering in Needham, which has cooperative programs with Babson. Much of her work still revolves around helping engineers understand business needs. A lot of it consists of helping them understand the big picture, and how their work will fit in with what the company wants to do. "We're trying to reach this goal, process this many thats," she says. "Very often, if you can give that context, you can get someone excited."[16]

"YOU NEED THE BUSINESS PERSON"

Positions like Finer's may be the wave of the future for go-between careers. Recently, we spent some time chatting with Cameron Herold, chief operating officer of a Vancouver company that recently hired a product manager with similar responsibilities and skills to Finer. What's surprising about it is his company is not a technology company at all, but a trash removal franchise business, 1-800-GOT-JUNK?

The move makes sense, though, because GOT-JUNK? depends heavily on JunkNet—software developed by its in-house IT staff—to distribute nationwide jobs to its network of franchises and handle their accounts. Franchisees can also use it to figure revenues, calculate the size of the average pickup, pinpoint which neighborhoods produce the most junk, and provide a host of other types of information. In short, JunkNet is an important part of what franchisees pay for. "In some aspects we're a software house, we're building software for people who are buying it," Herold explains.

In the past, he adds, software decisions all fell to the vice president of IT, which sometimes caused problems. "The IT team tends not to be marketing centric," he says. "So you need the business person."[17]

1-800-GOT-JUNK? might be the trailblazer. Other nontech companies may follow suit, bringing in a go-between, because technology is an important element of delivering their products or services. And those who can make themselves understood on both sides of the Geek Gap may find that their skills are very much in demand.

Whether their long-term goals lie entirely in the world of business, entirely in the world of technology, or somewhere in between, both business people and technologists need to keep in mind that these goals may not make sense to everyone they work with, and that with differing long-term goals come differing assumptions about the best way to tackle problems of the present.

If you're a suit:

1. Keep in mind that your IT colleagues may have different goals from your own, and that they may be more interested in compiling new technology and technological knowledge than obtaining money. This is a good thing: their passion for technology serves your company's needs in many ways.

2. It's important to recognize that IT folk identify themselves more with their professions than their employers, which is one reason they sometimes seem more loyal to the technology itself than to the company that pays for it. In the current atmosphere of restructuring, offshoring, and permanent contract employment, that attitude makes sense. Don't expect that you will necessarily be able to change it.

3. Are you good at analytical tasks, and do you have an aptitude for technology? If so, a move into the new career of business/technology liaison might make sense. It's an opportunity to learn firsthand how your geek colleagues work and think, and work directly with the technological innovations that can change how your company does business. Even if your long-term goals have nothing to do with technology, a temporary move into a go-between post will give you powerful insights on how to bring technology and business together, and avoid getting stuck in the Geek Gap.

If you're a geek:

1. Keep in mind that your business colleagues may have different goals from yours. If, for instance, it seems as if they are obsessed with money for its own sake, remember that this is the scorecard for all businesses—and many business executives use it to define success. Moreover, solid earnings will ensure the organization's survival.

2. Understand that your business colleagues may value your organization itself in ways that you don't, and that working there may be an important part of their identities. This does not mean, of course, that you can't be critical of the company or that you should pretend greater loyalty than you feel. But if you have negative things to say about the company as a whole or its policies, they'll be better received and understood if you express them in the spirit that "we're all in this together."

3. Are you a good communicator? Do you like working with different types of people and getting a look at the big picture? If so,

consider a career path in the field of liaison between technology and business. This career path is growing and gaining recognition. Better yet, the more you serve as a conduit for IT and business folk to work together, the more indispensable you will become.

CHAPTER 13

CLOSING THE GEEK GAP

The Geek Gap is a deeply rooted, seemingly intractable problem that goes all the way back to the days of Galileo. Is there anything that can be done about it? Are any companies getting it right?

The answer is yes. No firm we've ever encountered has been able to completely eliminate the business/technology culture clash, but some are taking effective steps to improve communications. Throughout this book, we've offered suggestions for how geeks and suits themselves can take steps to narrow the gap and learn to work effectively with their business or technology counterparts. Here we take a look at how a few companies have created a working atmosphere that encourages them to do just that.

All workplaces and workplace cultures are different. But the companies we've seen that improve cooperation across the business/technology divide offer valuable lessons, which could be applied to nearly all organizations:

1. *First, do no harm: Avoid or mitigate policies that actually separate geeks and suits.* This sounds hopelessly obvious, yet we are frequently amazed at how many organizations seem to intention-

ally *prevent* technologists and business people from effectively interacting with each other—or interacting with each other at all.

In most companies, geeks work away from everyone else, on a separate floor, or in a different building, far from anywhere a customer might venture. They appear in the company's corporate offices only when they are needed to solve an immediate technological problem, or to receive an assignment for a technological task. When business executives meet to discuss such issues as strategy or marketing, the technologists are not invited to attend. It's as if the two groups work in separate organizations.

Some companies are deliberately structured with just such a separation in mind. In many large and even medium-sized companies, IT is managed as a separate entity, a company-within-a-company that actually bills other corporate departments for technologists' work time and also for use of resources, such as server space. Some technologists spend most of their time working with complex software to track which resources the IT department's "customers" have used; they then generate invoices and collect payment accordingly.

As we discussed earlier, treating IT as a separate department, and even billing other departments for its resources, offers many advantages, especially in these days when nearly every internal technology function must compete against outsourcers who will almost always do the same job for less. Even in the absence of such competition, billing other departments for their IT work is an effective means of demonstrating their ROI (return on investment)—something technology departments are under increasing pressure to do.

Even without being treated as employees of a separate entity, though, geeks tend to think of their work and their departments as disconnected from the rest of the organization, with completely different priorities and goals. Creating IT departments as separate entities within a company will tend only to reinforce that mentality—unless management takes specific steps to bring technologists and business people together.

Unfortunately, in most companies there's a natural tendency to do just the opposite. It's human nature to do what's easiest, and, from a management perspective, it's hugely easier to keep IT and business separate than try to bring them together. First, as we've seen, most members of both groups would just as soon not have to deal with the other. Second, any conversation that includes both geeks and suits will necessarily proceed much more slowly than separate conversations would. Even if all are careful to avoid terminology that their counterparts won't know, they will still need to pause and explain the concepts and presumptions underlying, say, the design of a database or a financial plan.

Beyond all that, much of today's corporate structure revolves around teams, and it may seem clever to pit these teams against each other as a motivational tool. "A lot of managers create this internal competition, sometimes consciously, because they believe competition will strengthen the company," notes Jordan Chanofsky, CEO of Fusion Public Relations.[1] This may be an effective motivator, but it could also widen the Geek Gap. Fusion PR intentionally works in the reverse direction, he adds, with events designed to increase interaction between business and technology experts.

We're not suggesting that companies must rearrange their offices, change their IT departments' billing policies, or stop treating departments as teams. We do think, though, these decisions should be weighed against the cost of misunderstandings between business and IT which will likely result. Possibly, the best solution is to counteract some of this effect through policies specifically designed to bring geeks and suits together, such as those described below.

2. *Create multiple points of contact.* At a company we visited not long ago, we talked to some suits about the Geek Gap. They proudly told us, "There are no misunderstandings between business and technology at our company. We have found the solution. All communication between us and IT goes through one single person. She's the only one allowed to talk to them on our behalf. That way, there are no mixed messages, no competing priorities, and no confusion about who wants what."

Intrigued, we sought out this person and asked her about her role as the communication pipeline between her company's technologists and their business colleagues. "Yes, it's true," she told us ruefully. "No one can talk to them unless it goes through me. So I'm the bottleneck. If I'm out of the office or backed up with too many projects, nothing can go forward."

While it may be a good thing to have someone on the team whose main role is as liaison between business executives and their technology colleagues, it's a bad idea to make this the only point of contact between the two groups. You risk having all work grind to a halt if that one person is unavailable. Worse, opportunities for professional development, creative brainstorming, and greater understanding of how to serve the organization's needs are lost when members of the two groups are kept from communicating fruitfully.

"I think the hierarchical organization where the only point of contact is at the top of the pyramid is a real shaky project structure. It needs to be hands clasped together with all fingers intertwined," says Doug LaBoda, recently retired from St. Paul Travelers, who for fifteen years, was a CIO of several different lines of business including Claim Services and Personal Lines.

"In our projects, the relationship is deeper and more intricate than just the business project leader and the IS [information systems] team that works with him or her," he explains. "It goes down many levels and involves many people."

As a Line of Business CIO, he says, he not only had a relationship with the head of the of the department where he worked, but also with all that person's direct subordinates, and many of those in the next level down as well. Similarly, the technologists who reported to him would have multiple relationships with business colleagues up and down the chain of command. "The success you have in IT is directly related to the strength of those partnerships," he says.[2]

3. *Get geeks involved in projects from the start.* ECI in Glenwood, Iowa, provides software for banks and credit unions to help manage loans. Company founder Gary Kruse started out helping farmers process loans on paper in the 1980s, then turned to his brother, a computer expert, figuring there must be a way to auto-

mate some of the work. Banks soon asked if they could use Kruse's systems as well, and things grew from there, with the result that Kruse, who said he had no technical training whatsoever, found himself at the head of a software company. The only way to make it work would be for Kruse to build very solid partnerships with the geeks at the company.

One important way he does this, he says, is from the very beginning involving technologists up and down the line in projects they will work on. "I and the sales people on the business side have an idea of what we want," Kruse explains. "But two or three weeks into the design, not only the program manager is involved, but also the programmer who is going to lead actually writing the code. And when we tell them what we think would be good, they always come up with additional features and nice-to-have things they think of as they're going through. While we may think the software needs to work a certain way, they may see that a different way would work better." The end result, he says, is that 30 to 40 percent of the new features and capabilities in ECI's new products or upgrades come directly from programmer suggestions.[3]

A further advantage is buy-in: geeks who've been privy to all discussions about a new product or upgrade tend to better understand the decisions made along the way and are likelier to put their best effort into making the project work. "If we only had the program director in on the planning, then when they got the specs for the project, the geeks might say, 'This is stupid,' and meanwhile, she might have spent the whole previous week in meetings, learning why it had to be done that way," Kruse explains. "All the way through the release and support process, the technical people have buy-in because they thought of a lot of the things that are included in the final product."

Getting geeks involved from the beginning also means bringing them into contact not only with their business counterparts in-house, but also with outside customers who will ultimately use the systems they create. "When we get into design, and customers ask for customization, I absolutely get the programmer directly involved," Kruse says. "It's easy for me to say, 'The customer wants you to do this,' but it's totally different when you take the middle person away, and if there's a problem, we'll send that customer directly to the programmer."

In fact, even before the bank has ordered a product, ECI's techies are already involved. "They'll be in on the conference calls and the meetings, ready to respond to any technical questions. That's part of the sales process."[4]

Some managers may be hesitant to put programmers or engineers in direct contact with customers, on the theory that sales and marketing employees are best trained to handle these communications. But while it may be tempting to let salespeople be the ones to do what they do best, it's also a good way to worsen the Geek Gap. If any part of a company's technology will be used by outside customers, it's important to create some opportunity for those customers and the geeks who created the product to work directly together. Says Barbara Finer, whose consulting company QuiVivity helps technology companies design marketing plans, "If a company says it won't let its engineers out the door, I run the other way."[5]

> 4. *Keep geeks in the business loop.* At 1-800-GOT-JUNK? a junk removal franchise based in Vancouver, frequent meetings of the entire 110-person headquarters staff are part of the corporate culture. There's the "Huddle," a daily meeting that takes seven minutes and is conducted standing up, Weekly Action Review, or "WAR" meetings, monthly Strategic Operational Review Meetings (or "STORM" meetings), and more.

None of these meetings is particularly geared for the company's IT staff, but, like all departments, they are invited to participate, share their opinions and ideas about what other departments are doing, and sometimes make presentations to the rest of the company. "IT is always involved in those discussions, and we play a big role," reports Jay Heffernan, desktop support analyst at GOT-JUNK? This is true even when the subject at hand may have nothing to do with IT.

"Our former network administrator was on the social committee," Heffernan recalls. "He was touring other offices to see how the social climate worked and to see if there was anything that would be applicable to us here."[6]

"One thing that's really helped us is, from the top down, we don't believe we have any of the answers," says Cameron Herold, chief operating officer. As a result, he says, management is happy to listen to anyone on any subject. "We'll turn to IT people for advice on marketing. They feel like they're a part of something rather than just writing lines of code."

In keeping with this philosophy of building something together, GOT-JUNK? has a profit-sharing program for all employees. Not only that, there's a special monthly meeting where top managers share detailed financial information with the company at large.

"They see the financial statements every month," Herold says. "We actually walk through reporting of different areas of the business, how the balance sheet works, the cash flow statement, and talk about each of the different line items. That way they know what they're building."

And, just as important, they see what they can do about it. "We believe employees tend to think you're making more money than you actually are," he says. A typical reaction when they see an actual financial statement is, "Oh my God, I didn't realize it cost so much!" he reports. "So the more they know, the more they can help."[7]

"We don't only talk about the general ledger, but also possibilities and opportunities," notes Roman Azbel, vice president of IT at GOT-JUNK? This kind of knowledge, along with updates, allows IT employees to correctly prioritize their efforts. "Understanding where help is most needed right now is crucial, because if that area runs better, the whole company will be better off," Azbel says.[8]

5. *"Federalize" IT.* Of course, company-wide meetings to discuss general problems and financial details work well in part for 1-800-GOT-JUNK? because of its size: it's relatively easy to bring 110 people together. But how do you better integrate geeks with suits when there are thousands of employees at a company spread over the United States, or around the world?

The answer has partially to do with a company's organizational structure, LaBoda says. At St. Paul Travelers, "We have what I call a federalized IT organization," he says. In other words, although there's a centralized IT department, each of the company's lines of business has its own IT organization which provides application development and support (though not such services as telecommunications or infrastructure). The two functions operate jointly, with the "local" line of business IT integrated into the business units.

Thus, LaBoda explains, "When I was leading the IT organization for the Personal Lines business, I had two reporting relationships, one to the head of the Personal Lines business, and one to the corporate CIO."

LaBoda says this model works much better than a single IT department in a large company. "You start fostering some partnerships by showing the business people that the technology resources are part of their business." IT staff benefit, too, he says, since they're not sequestered in a centralized location getting all their input from the technology organization. "Their responsibility is to take direction from the business," he says. "It also fosters some accountability on the part of the business executives, if they feel like those IT people are part of their own organization."

Federalized IT also helps reduce the size of individual IT departments, and that's a good thing. "I see in the smaller organizations, the technical people seem more integrated with the business," LaBoda notes. "So maybe the solution in a large organization is to deploy as many IT people as possible within the lines of business."[9]

6. *Get everyone sitting together.* "Along with the organizational model, the physical placement of IT people is important," LaBoda notes. At his company, IT managers make a point of locating IT staff near business staff so that, if possible, they work on the same floor. Sometimes this is impractical for reasons of size—even the "local" IT operations can number four hundred to five hundred people—in which case they're placed on adjacent floors. "We would work very hard to get our IT folk to be with their business counterparts," he says. "When you have to make an appointment

and walk a long distance to see someone, spontaneous conversation never happens."[10]

1-800-GOT-JUNK? takes sitting together a step further with a completely open environment in which no one, not even top management, has a separate office. "If you need to talk to someone privately, you can go to a meeting room and close the door, but if you're doing your normal work, you're out on the floor with everyone else," Herold says. "IT people are walking past everyone else every day."[11]

"It helps," Azbel reports. "You're tapping someone on the shoulder, you know him personally—you may not be buddies, but you know how he would react to things, potentially some of his interests outside work."[12]

7. *Encourage geeks and suits to trade jobs, even if temporarily.* An acquaintance of ours, who had been working as a pure technologist in a large company, decided to take an IT-related business management job several years ago. "It was a big decision," he says. "I saw it as an opportunity to broaden my perspective on American business. I'd been on the IT side for ten years. I didn't always understand what people in our business unit were talking about."

Today, our friend is back in a strictly IT role, having learned a lot and gained career momentum from his sojourn among the suits. "Being on the other side has broadened my perspective," he says. "I would encourage many more in technology to take jobs in a technology-related business field."

In some companies, rising IT managers are formally encouraged to take business jobs for a while. "We have had a leadership development program in IT since 1982," LaBoda reports. "In this program, exceptional IT people spend about five years doing various assignments through the organization, and one is in a business role, in an accounting operation or claim operation or whatever. They are given real business responsibilities—they're not just the local programmer assigned to the business group. We feel very strongly about our leaders in IT having that kind of experience."

Of course, the reverse is much more challenging: it's easier for an intelligent and well-rounded technologist to take on business responsibilities than it is for a business person to learn, say, Unix. But LaBoda notes that business people who have good project management skills, or have overseen an operation such as a call center may be able to use those skills to take on management positions in IT.

In general, he adds, "I think the people who would want to change jobs this way are lifelong learners. You think, 'I've learned everything I want to learn in this position and I want to learn something totally new.' And as long as they have enough transferable skills to start out with some chance at success, you give them that chance."

It can be well worth the effort, he notes. "I think it can work in both directions," he says. "And I've seen some people just do marvelously well with their careers after one of these swaps."[13]

8. *Find ways to build respect.* The more we look at business and technology, the more it seems to us that most of the problems really come down to the Geek Gap. And the more we see that the Geek Gap itself comes down to a basic lack of respect, on the part of both geeks and suits, for the skills, experience, and wisdom of their counterparts.

Whatever else we may do to try to improve communications or help business people and technologists work better together, the only way to truly bridge the gap is to help those on both sides of the divide change these basic attitudes.

One way to start is to impress on both geeks and suits why they need to absorb at least a rudimentary understanding of each other's disciplines. "This is something I often preach to IT folk who want to become managers," LaBoda says. "I tell them they are expected to be masters of their technology—and to understand quite a lot about the business they're in as well. So they have a dual responsibility. I don't know if that's what they signed up for when they went into IT, but that's what's expected."

On the business side, executives who lack at least some understanding of the technology they're working with are likely to underestimate its complexity, he adds. "We have the big software companies to thank for this, because they like to make it appear easy to make these systems run, and of course there are technical complexities the business user never sees."

The result, he says, is that business executives who know little about the workings of computer systems are likely to respond with a blank stare when a technologist explains, for instance, that the company's two versions of the same software are incompatible, despite vendor assurances to the contrary. That's the kind of thing that can lead to frustration on both sides.

"If you're looking for a piece of wisdom to help address the Geek Gap, that's one," LaBoda notes. "Business and technical folk need to understand the work of the other person, have some empathy, spend some time learning about the management or technical responsibilities of their counterparts. At the end of the day, it's important to be able to converse in both languages."[14]

FROM *GLAMOUR* TO *EWEEK*: CLOSING THE GAP AT FUSION PUBLIC RELATIONS

Public relations is an odd industry. It's based on the subtle art of influencing the supposedly unbiased media to portray a given organization, product, or service in the best possible light, or gain the widest possible attention for an unknown. PR professionals speak of "clients"—the companies that pay to have their names and products promoted in the press, and "customers"—the journalists who actually decide whether and how to feature these clients. It's a process whose ultimate effect can be hard to predict: even several press mentions can make little difference to a company's well-being or all the difference in the world if readers take an interest and rush out to buy the client's products or stock.

For technology companies in particular, PR is an essential issue, as publicity provides both visibility and credibility for new innovations. It can influence investors or corporate executives looking for a high-tech investment. For start-ups in need of funding, good PR can bring rising stock prices or acquisition offers—and thus can make the difference between staying in business and closing up shop.

This is also an industry badly plagued by business/technology communications breakdowns. Most high-tech firms are headed by expert technologists who not only know little—or nothing—about marketing, but are resistant to the simplification needed to quickly describe a product's benefits to lay consumers. Meanwhile, most public relations professionals come from marketing or journalism backgrounds, and have little understanding of how the high-tech products they represent actually work.

It was in this landscape that Jordan Chanofsky founded Fusion Public Relations seven years ago. With a BA in electronics and engineering, as well as an MBA in marketing, Chanofsky's idea was to bring together PR smarts with technical expertise.

"The usual MO in public relations is to call up a journalist and say, 'Did you get the press release and are you going to run it?'" Chanofsky says. "I thought public relations could be taken to a higher level, where it would become a counsel to the client. In order to do that, we needed people who came from technology so as to be able to have a rational conversation about a base band semiconductor chipset for the mobile industry or a fast router lookup table, or a business-based rules management product being integrated into middleware."

While the client can teach a nontechie something about these kinds of products, "It never has the same meaning," he says. Worse, even PR professionals with rudimentary knowledge of technological products can find themselves in over their heads when faced with detailed technological questions or discussions. "What we needed was a way to integrate—or 'fuse'—people who come from public relations or marketing with people who come from technology," he explains. In short, the company's fortunes would rise or fall on its ability to overcome the Geek Gap.

Chanofsky began by seeking out engineers from the telecommunications and mobile industries. He then created teams of these tech industry experts, coupled with public relations professionals. "The technology person would spend time with the PR person, barreling through the technology and getting that person as smart as possible. Then the PR person would talk to the tech person about strategies and methodologies for going after the media," he says.

Each would be warned before hiring that continuous learning would be a job requirement. "I would tell the PR people, 'Your bathroom reading is going to go from *Glamour* to *eWeek*. Are you prepared for that?'"[15]

Today, Fusion has about forty-five employees—mostly in its New York City headquarters, plus smaller offices in Los Angeles and Washington, DC—and many of them spend their time both teaching their business/technology counterparts and learning from them.

Much of this learning takes place through informal mentoring, but Fusion has formal learning programs, too. For instance, every Wednesday, the company holds "ed sessions" on different topics—some covering technology, others on public relations. Recent tech topics have included an overview of the mobile phone industry and storage technology. Most often, the session leaders are Fusion's top management. But any employee with good knowledge to share can lead a session, such as the recent one by a fairly junior account executive on client management.

"I've done one on how to go into an organization and ask the right questions of the very technologically oriented people running it," notes Joseph Dans, director of accounts. He gives an example: He recently visited a mobile technology company that had been testing its product for two years but had nothing to sell yet. While touring the facility, he noticed the head of a dummy sitting in a corner—not the usual item for a high-tech concern. He inquired, and learned that the dummy head was filled with fluid and was used to test whether the client's mobile phones would heat up with prolonged use next to a human head. The clients were actually attaching the phones to the head, and then driving around town through various levels of signal to test it out. In Dans's mind, the idea soon became a headline: "Cell Phone Dummies Cruise New York City Looking for Good Connection," and the wandering dummies did indeed garner television coverage. "That's the kind of thing geeks who are very focused on what the technology is doing might not pick up on," he says.[16]

In addition to the ed sessions, Fusion staff—both techies and non— must spend a great deal of time reading to keep up on the technologies they represent. "One of the biggest challenges is to keep up with the reading," says vice president Michael Lane, who came to Fusion from the telecommunications industry. To help, the company instituted reading groups, similar to book clubs, but which focused on topics like optical networking.[17]

Part of Fusion's credo is having fun at work (there are magnetic dart boards on the walls, and the conference room is well stocked with jelly beans and peanut M&M's), so one of the company's favorite education tools is an in-house game called Tech Jeopardy. Players compete in teams of two, and categories are posted on the conference room wall, complete with covers that pull off to reveal the answers for which contestants must find the corresponding questions, much like the TV show of the same name. The answers focus on technological topics, but also promotional subjects, such as which trade shows are most prominent in different technological industries. In each case, one Fusion staff member or another takes on the responsibility for the answers and questions in a given category. Typical prizes for winners are gift certificates to places like Best Buy.

"Last time I was responsible for the History of Technology Category," Dans recalls. His answers included one about the original use of the word "bug" in relation to programming—going back to 1947, when an actual insect caused a malfunction by getting caught in one of the switches. (Dr. Grace Murray Hopper, the first woman to be involved in modern computers, is perhaps best known for her discovery of the first computer bug in the Harvard Mark II computer. The bug now resides at the Smithsonian's National Museum of American History in Washington, DC.)

"Some of the answers are funny; they're not all hard technology, so it's almost impossible to study for them," he notes. "Every now and then, Jordan sneaks in a really targeted technology question."

The result of all this education is that working with Fusion would likely be completely different for technology clients than working with many other PR firms. "Everyone here is brought up to think like an engineer, with a thirst to understand how things work," Chanofsky says. "So when we sit down with a client who says, 'This is the product, and this is how it works,' instead of responding with 'OK, how do we sell it?' we ask questions like, 'Why did you design it this way?'"

CHAPTER 14

THE FUTURE OF THE
GEEK GAP

Ⱨ ow will the Geek Gap look two years from now? Five years? Ten? Prognostication is always a risky business: any forward-looking statement, as the corporate financial reports put it, is fraught with "risks and uncertainties." With that caveat out of the way, let's take a look at some of the developments on the technology horizon, and how some of these are likely to affect the business/technology culture clash.

1. *The Internet is in its infancy.* This may be an unsettling concept for those who are already sick of seeing "www" in front of everything imaginable, but it's a fact. Today, the sense of the Internet as a current fad or obsession is already giving way to the calm recognition that the Web is a normal communications conduit for everything, as ubiquitous and unremarkable as the telephone. If it's not surprising that nearly every business has a telephone number, it should be no more so that nearly every one also has (or will have) a Web site. And the concept of "Internet addiction," popularized in the late 1990s, will become as quaint as the concerns raised by the

Knights of Columbus that introduction of the telephone would make people lazy, break up family life, and might put an end to the practice of visiting friends.[1]

The future development of Internet technology is hard to predict because the only thing we can know for certain is that these future uses will include some items that none of us today can easily imagine. But it's possible to get a glimpse of the coming power of the Internet by taking note of the industries it is already on its way to displacing—beginning with the above-mentioned telephone service. Voice over Internet Protocol (VoIP)—in which voice conversations travel over the Internet rather than traditional phone lines—has already taken hold in the corporate world. According to a recent survey of one thousand companies by Forrester Research, Inc., 36 percent were either using or considering installing VoIP systems, and 48 percent believed their companies would eventually switch to all-VoIP.[2]

VoIP, with providers such as Vonage, is making inroads into household use as well. The market research firm eMarketer.com predicts 32.6 million Americans would subscribe to a VoIP service. According to eMarketer, in the next two years, using VoIP at home will become "mainstream."[3] Even in rural areas, some of our friends have jettisoned their landline phones in favor of VoIP and mobile cells.

Then there's radio. This displacement is already in process, as most radio stations these days simultaneously broadcast over both traditional radio waves and streaming audio from their Web sites, making it just as easy to play over a computer as over a traditional receiver. Thousands more "radio" stations already exist only in cyberspace. It's only a matter of time before the old-fashioned signals fall by the wayside.

Less obviously, television will also lose ground to the Internet. This applies not only to competition for the leisure time of the typical home computer users who spend their free time surfing the Web instead of watching the tube. A growing number of Internet users are actually using their computers for some version of television watching. For instance, a friend of ours who's a long-time fan of the old *Mystery Science Theater 3000* show, which aired through most of the 1990s on the Comedy and

Sci-Fi cable channels, was ecstatic to discover recently that old episodes were being Webcast (broadcast over the Internet) and has since pretty much abandoned his television in favor of his computer. Other acquaintances of ours watch Internet-only video sources such as RantTV.net and WebRanger.net, and, after last year's disastrous flooding in New Orleans, one friend sent us the URL of a local Louisiana TV station so we could watch the local hurricane coverage online.

For most viewers, one big impediment to switching from traditional television to Internet stream is that their televisions and computers are located in different spaces in their homes, with the computers not necessarily set up where they relax. But technology is solving this problem, too. Today, wireless networking devices can send streaming audio/video that comes in over the Web to a television; modern sets are also built to accommodate Internet input.

We're not predicting when or how exactly this will happen, what the financial implications will be, or who will come to dominate this market. But right now, radio, telephone lines, and broadcast/cable/satellite television all exist as different ways to bring communications to consumers and all can be carried more easily and efficiently over an Internet connection. Odds are that the logic of eliminating unneeded duplication will eventually prevail.

2. *Everyone will use the Internet.* A few years ago, we visited my very sophisticated cousin in France. A banker who loves fine wines, Cuban cigars, jazz concerts, and the good life in general, he had an elegantly modern home that boasted every convenience one could wish for—except a computer. Technological crusaders that we are, we spent hours trying to persuade him that wonders could be found on the Internet. Cigar reviews! News of distant lands! A world of online shopping! All to no avail. He spent enough time using his computer at work, he told us. He didn't want one in his house as well.

Two years later we visited again, and everything had changed. Not only had my cousin acquired a computer, but it had a place of honor on a large desk in the center of a new home office (formerly a guest bedroom) where my cousin and his wife now spent quite a bit of their time. On weekends, we watched the men in the family gather around, reading detailed wine reviews over my cousin's shoulder, as they selected which ones to buy. At holiday time, we began receiving family photos by e-mails from our formerly computer-rejecting cousin. The Internet had won another convert.

Here in the United States, the last demographic group to adopt Internet technology is the oldest segment of society—people who, as one of them put it to us recently, are very much *not* digital natives. So it's interesting to observe that Internet use is climbing in this last group of holdouts. According to eMarketer, less than 25 percent of Americans over sixty-five used the Internet in 2003, but by 2008, more than a third will do so. And among fifty-to-sixty-four-year-olds, use will have climbed to more than 73 percent.[4] In part, this reflects the fact that those born in the era of silent films and party line phones are aging out of the population. But it also reflects the coming reality that not knowing how to use the Internet will soon be like not knowing how to drive a car: a semi-crippling inability that makes those who live in the suburbs or the country dependent on the help of their friends and family, or expensive taxi services.

3. *Wireless will be everywhere.* In chapter 5, we described the geek pastimes of *war walking* and *war driving*, in which geeks equipped with laptops search neighborhoods for open wireless connections. But the fact is whether for fee or free, wireless connections are already ubiquitous with wireless signals available in McDonald's, Starbucks, Barnes & Noble, and Panera Bread, to name just a few wireless-offering chains. In addition, as of this writing, at least 57 percent of US colleges offer Wi-Fi on campus, a number that is rapidly growing.[5] This means that from here on out, graduating seniors will leave college accustomed to having the Internet everywhere around them, and will be disappointed if they find that it isn't that way in the "real" world. Meanwhile, municipalities such as San Francisco are working on deals that would provide free wireless access throughout the entire city.

One of the things we love about being technology writers is that we get to go to technology trade shows and collect all the fun doohickeys that vendors inevitably give away. Over the years we've collected yo-yos, rubber ducks, little plastic dusters for computer screens, cigarette lighter-size storage devices that plug into a USB port for transporting computer files, tiny FM radios, and special phone cords that retract like carpenter's tape measures into their own containers when not in use.

But this last item has virtually disappeared, as fewer and fewer travelers see any appeal whatsoever in plugging their laptop computers into slow-as-molasses dial-up connections. Instead, these are being replaced by a new device, the size of a business card case. If you push a button, the box will flash green if there's a wireless connection present, or red if there isn't. These items are extremely handy—we used one recently to determine that the Belvidere, New Jersey, public library was not a wireless hotspot, which was far easier than getting out our laptops would have been. We think these little devices are a good indication of wireless' standing at this writing—something sought after that will eventually become ubiquitous.

In a few years, these wireless-sensing devices, war walking and war riding, and the term "wireless hotspot" itself will all become obsolete. Consider mobile telephone service today: we don't refer to "hotspots" for our cell phones—we expect the inhabited world to offer cell phone service and when we come across a place that doesn't, we derisively call it a "dead zone." This is where we think wireless is headed—people will expect the high-speed Internet to be in the air everywhere they go.

The devices used to access this everywhere-Internet are changing too, as a growing number of products combine the benefits of both mobile phones and handheld devices. Then there are other, as yet experimental products, such as wearable Internet devices that incorporate computer functions into glasses, wristwatches, or even a denim jacket (Levi is already test-marketing in Europe a wearable computerized jacket, with an embroidered keyboard and speakers for making music).

Mobile phones themselves are already expected to do almost anything a computer could, including providing real-time voice communications— via the Internet. In a delicious bit of technological convergence, college campuses are testing mobile phones—already in use in Europe—that not only pick up a Wi-Fi signal if one is available, but actually use it to provide VoIP phone service. As with other forms of VoIP, the main attraction is reduced cost.[6]

Today, most people you pass on the street are probably Internet users. A few years from now, most people you pass on the street will likely be actually online as they walk by.

4. *Computing will move to the Web.* High-speed Internet available everywhere will help pave the way for another development that tech experts have been predicting for a while now: the rise of Web-hosted software and services. These days, software developers face a choice as they create new products: design them to run autonomously on an individual user's desktop, or build them on the application service provider (ASP) model. In the latter case, the software is actually hosted remotely on a server and accessed by clients over the Web, usually paid for by some sort of leasing arrangement. Increasingly, software companies like Gary Kruse's ECI (see chapter 13) are giving customers the choice, offering either a licensed or an ASP model of their product.

The benefits of hosted computing are many. It's less expensive than buying a license. The software provider can make changes to the software itself anytime, providing upgrades and patches, for instance, without the customer having the hassle of installing the improved version. Bugs are easier to identify and fix since the software is actually running on the host's server, and it's therefore easier for customer support staff to recreate malfunctions when customers describe them. And, of course, it simplifies IT for many companies, especially small and medium-sized ones that need fewer IT professionals on staff, since the software maintenance is done by the hosting company.

But in the long-term, perhaps the strongest argument for hosted computing is the hardware needs it eliminates. To date, the personal computer industry has had great success in instilling customers with the idea that they need a newer, faster desktop computer with greater storage capacity, chip speed, and RAM (random access memory) every two years or so. But the expense and inconvenience of constant upgrades, not to mention the difficulty in disposing of out-of-date computers (which contain large amounts of hazardous materials) are eroding customer willingness to continue the regular upgrades indefinitely. Hosted software offers a reprieve from this cycle: since the software itself is running on someone else's server, there's less need for constantly improving processor speed. With broadband Internet access available almost everywhere, the logic of Web-hosted software becomes even more appealing.

5. *As technology gets more complex, it looks simpler.* One result of technology's relentless spread is this seeming paradox: systems are getting more intricate and more user-friendly at the same time. Even as the infrastructure that supports our increasingly techno-logical world becomes so complex it's impossible for any one person, no matter how well educated, to understand more than a tiny part of it, it seems simpler and simpler for the people actually using it.

This paradox is perfectly expressed in a 2004 television ad for America Online's Computer Check-up service (available as part of AOL 9.0) in which parents stare in frustration at their nonfunctioning computer while their unnoticed toddler bangs away at the keyboard with a plastic hammer. As the adults debate whom to call for computer repair, the child accidentally hits the correct combination of keys and mouse to activate the service and the computer repairs itself before their astonished eyes.

It's a compelling ad and a very effective way to sell the service, but the subtler message it offers says something about the Geek Gap. For underlying AOL's intended message—that they take good care of their customers—what that commercial may also tell viewers is that you don't need technical expertise to make technology work. In a world so user-friendly that a baby can literally fix a computer, some may make a seemingly logical leap and wrongly wonder, then, how hard can it be for geeks to do their jobs? With ever more complex software that is ever easier to use, technophobes, including suits, need not appreciate the work, wisdom, and creativity that geeks use in creating computer systems and software, and keeping them in good working order.

A SHIFT IN POWER

This, then, is the technological backdrop against which geeks and suits will play out their relationship over the next several years. In many ways, that relationship is about issues of respect—many Geek Gap problems arise because technologists and business people fail to respect the importance of each other's jobs, and the knowledge required to perform them. But part of the problem is also the balance of power between geeks and suits, a balance that is in constant flux as the role and status of technologists in our society evolve.

So far, that status has looked something like an arc. Recall when technologists were called "nerds" and were relegated to chilly basements with their room-sized computers and generally considered too odd to partake in normal society. Bill Gates and his ilk changed much of this perception through the 1980s and 1990s, as the rest of the world slowly awakened to the fact that (a) technology was essential to running a business, and (b) people who started technology companies could make a lot of money.

The arc reached its zenith in the late 1990s, when the dot-coms were considered invincible. Skilled technology employees were so in demand that it was nearly impossible to hire one, and geeks were generally considered to have insider knowledge of the secrets of modern success. We remember reading magazine articles in those heady days about how the new young Internet entrepreneurs wanted to take their place among the decision makers in politics, and how technologists in general would have to be accorded the higher social status that their important skills so clearly merited.

But then came the dot-com crash of 2000 and it was as though the geeks had suddenly been shown to have feet of clay. Tech layoffs abounded over the next few years as many business leaders and technological experts turned their backs on each other in mutual disgust. Meanwhile, offshore outsourcing flourished, and businesses discovered having programmers on staff was not as essential as had once been thought. This led to more layoffs and deeper distrust between technologists and their business colleagues. The Geek Gap widened.

As discussed in chapter 11, we believe the trend to offshore outsourcing will only increase, as Corporate America (not to mention Corporate Rest-of-the-World) finds new ways to section off work into pieces that can be done elsewhere. Whether for good or ill, we believe this trend will be nearly impossible to reverse, as competitive pressures force even companies that don't relish the thought of offshore outsourcing to go this route to cut costs. The result is that the shape of IT careers is changing forever.

SHRINKING IT?

In May 2005 Gartner, Inc., a high-tech research firm, predicted that by 2010, the number of staff in IT departments overall would shrink by 15 percent, and that such departments in mid-sized and large companies would be reduced by at least a third.[7]

This process would take several years, the report said, but many IT professionals believed they were seeing it already: the transfer of employment to India, the Philippines, and other lower-labor-cost countries was already well underway. College students also seemed to read the writing on the wall, for enrollment in computer science majors fell across the country. According to the Computing Research Association, the number of college students declaring computer science as a major declined 39 percent from the fall of 2000 to the fall of 2004.[8] (This development, as noted, so alarmed Bill Gates that he took off on a tour of college campuses, campaigning for the benefits of pursuing a computer major.)

"RENAISSANCE GEEKS"

But even though there are fewer computer science majors, and even though IT departments may be smaller, the need for people with technological skills is likely to grow. This may seem like a contradiction, but it isn't. And it bodes well for the eventual lessening of the Geek Gap.

Throughout this book, we've divided the universe, or at least the workplace, into geeks, suits, and (in chapter 12) go-betweens who serve as liaisons between the two. But, to a growing degree, today's companies need people who are expert in both the technology that keeps the operation running and the business issues it faces. These staff members are not there to serve as a communications conduit from one department to another, but to use both types of expertise to help the business make the right decisions, based on both technological and business considerations. As more and more people use this wider set of skills in jobs incorporating both business and technology knowledge, the line between geek and suit will likely start to blur.

Indeed, this is the future that many of today's college students seem to be preparing for. Barbara Finer is adjunct professor of entrepreneurship at Babson College and entrepreneur in residence at the affiliated Olin College of Engineering, as well as a former engineer herself (see chapter 12). For those trained as technologists, she says, "I am now of the belief that if you don't have some sort of business background, experience or education, ultimately you're going to stay at a lower level position or fail."

With this in mind, she says, Olin College requires its students to take Foundations of Entrepreneurship, a course cotaught by Finer. Here, students learn how business works through software simulations and also by actually working at area companies. "I have students who say, 'I always thought marketing was just advertising, until I took this course,'" she reports.[9]

"On campuses today, the newest technologists have to become renaissance geeks. They have to understand computing, but they also typically need deep knowledge of some other field, from biology to business, Wall Street to Hollywood," notes a recent *New York Times* article on the new education for techies. "And they tend to focus less on the tools of technology than on how technology is used in the search for scientific breakthroughs, the development of new products and services, or the way work is done."[10]

This is the future envisioned by the Gartner study as well. For while it foresees actual IS departments shrinking, it also expects growth in the need for technological skills. (Gartner uses the term IS—for "information systems"—to refer to corporate departments that oversee technology, and IT—for "information technology"—as the actual work technologists do.)

"As IT becomes a more integral part of every business function, there will be increasing numbers of people outside the IS organization whose work involves IT, and as IT skills become a more important component of business professionalism, in-house IS staff will be displaced," the study notes.

Indeed, beyond the likely reduction in the numbers of pure technologists working directly for IS departments, the Gartner study envisioned a fundamental shift in the way these departments interact with the rest of their organizations, and that these could follow one of three possible models. One is to be what the study calls an "IT utility," which, of the three, most resembles what the typical IT department does today: providing technology services to the company as a whole in accordance with its needs. But, Gartner warns, this will be a difficult model to maintain successfully, not because of internal failings, but because of the increasing professionalism and efficiency of outsourced alternatives that will nearly always cost less.

A second possibility is for vastly reduced departments to become "IT services brokers," with expertise in contracts and negotiation as well as technological skills. These departments' main responsibilities will be to purchase and oversee IT work done by outsourcers, many of them offshore. Such departments will play an important role in managing these outsourcing relationships, the study says, but will have little strategic value.

The third possible business model is to become a "business change agent"—that is, a strategic element of the business that can help management steer the company. Gartner warned that today's IT departments should not undertake the shift to a business change agent unless they (a) have enough credibility within the company to become part of the decision-making process, and (b) have enough people on staff with the combination of technology and business skills to fulfill this role effectively. But for those who can, the rewards to the company at large may be substantial. Gartner predicts that organizations that fuse technology, business process design, and business relationships will outperform those that don't by at least 15 percent per year until 2010 at the earliest.[11]

This is the ideal future we envision for IT as well. No longer seen as a remote back-office department full of weirdos whose primary task is to make sure paychecks are mailed on time; IT will become a strategic player that helps shape nearly all interactions between a company and its customers, employees, shareholders, and the public. Ultimately, whether part of a formal technology department or integrated throughout the organization, we believe this is the role geeks will come to take on more and more—that is, those "renaissance geeks" who can expand their skills beyond pure technology.

As IT evolves in this direction, away from a marginalized utility and toward a player in organizational strategy, we should finally see some real narrowing of the Geek Gap. The balance of power discussed earlier in this chapter should shift again, not back to when technologists were considered to have godlike powers, but toward parity, where technologists stand on equal footing with their business colleagues because both possess expertise needed for their companies' survival, and because both will have acquired more knowledge and appreciation of what the others do.

"THE GEEK GAP AGAIN!"

People often ask us if we have a solution to the Geek Gap. Throughout these pages, we've offered tips for increasing understanding between geeks and suits, cautionary examples of how many managers and companies have worsened the Gap with their policies and practices. We also described—though these were much harder to find—a few examples of organizations that help bridge the business/technology culture clash and how they've managed to do it. But none of these amount to *the* solution. This is not a phenomenon that lends itself to a single approach.

In our introduction, we refer to the Geek Gap as "the elephant in the corner"—a problem everyone struggles with, and no one ever names. Recognizing that the business/technology culture clash is a real issue in nearly every organization is an important first step toward doing something about it. If you've read this far, you already know more than most people about why technologists and business executives so often miscommunicate, and why so many technology projects go astray.

As this book progressed, we found that it subtly changed our perception of the interactions between geeks and suits in the companies that we are familiar with. A technologist would describe an argument with a business colleague, and we could clearly see how the different ways he and his business counterparts look at the same problem led to frustrations and misunderstandings. "The Geek Gap again!" we thought. We're willing to bet many readers have had similar experiences.

What happens next is really up to you. Whether you're a business executive frustrated with technology, a techie aggravated at "the business side," or a manager who needs to bring the two together, you can find ways to narrow the divide. The right approach will vary depending on the situation and the nature of your organization.

The best way to bridge the Geek Gap, for everyone's ultimate success, is to learn more about the work of the other side, appreciate the thought and talent that goes into it, and respect all who contributed to the health of your organization. This will put you ahead of the competition.

PLEASE BE IN TOUCH!

We'd love to hear from you. The book came about because many geeks and suits in the trenches were willing to share their experiences, and we're always looking for more. Please tell us about any stories of frustration, successes, questions, or any comments you may have. You can find us at www.geekgap.com or authors@geekgap.com. We wish you luck and hope the tips in this book may serve as signposts to help you along your way.

NOTES

CHAPTER 1. WHAT IS THE GEEK GAP?

1. Standish Group International, "2003 CHAOS Report," http://www.standishgroup
.com (accessed April 9, 2006).

2. Diane Vaughan, *The Challenger Launch Decision: Risky Technology, Culture, and Deviance at NASA* (Chicago: University of Chicago Press, 1996), p. 2 (weather), p. 5 (diagram of o-ring system), p. 7 (flight duration).

3. Paul Hoversten, "Debate Raged Night before Doomed Launch," *USA Today*, January 20, 1996, p. A1.

4. Vaughan, *The Challenger Launch Decision*, p. 100. (Reproduction of Interoffice memo, July 31, 1985, from R. M. Boisjoly to R. K. Lund, with the subject "SRM O-Ring Erosion/Potential Failure Criticality." This memo has been reproduced in many other places, including at http://onlineethics.org/moral/boisjoly /MTImemo1.html.)

5. Ibid., pp. 2–6. (See also Ed Magnuson, "Nation: The Questions Get Tougher. NASA Draws Fire from Investigators for Its 'Flawed' Shuttle Decision," *Time*, March 3, 1986, p. 14.)

6. NASA, *Report of the Presidential Commission on the Space Shuttle Challenger Accident*, vol. 1, chap. 5, July 14, 1986, http://history.nasa.gov/rogersrep/v1ch5 .htm (accessed April 9, 2006).

7. Scott Adams, *Fugitive from the Cubicle Police* (Kansas City, MO: Andrews and McMeel/United Press Syndicate, 1996), pp. 20 and 29, respectively.

8. Paul Graham, *Hackers & Painters: Big Ideas from the Computer Age* (Sebastopol, CA: O'Reilly, 2004), p. 181.

9. Beth Cox, "RemarQ to Sell Keyword Links to Advertisers," *ClickZ News*, September 13, 1999, http://www.clickz.com/news/article.php/199441 (accessed April 9, 2006).

10. Minda Zetlin and Bill Pfleging "The Cult of Community," *Smart Business*, June 2002, p. 68. Soon afterward, RemarQ was acquired by Critical Path, which shut it down.

11. "US E-Commerce Growth to Significantly Outpace Total Retail Spending," *eMarketer*, April 19, 2005, http://www.emarketer.com/Article.aspx?1003358 (accessed April 9, 2006).

12. Todd Weiss, "Tech Job Losses Down for Quarter but Up Year Over Year," *Computerworld*, August 8, 2005, p. 44.

13. Edward Yourdon, *Death March: The Complete Software Developer's Guide to Surviving 'Mission Impossible' Projects* (New York: Prentice-Hall, 1999).

14. John Gray, *Men Are from Mars, Women Are from Venus: A Practical Guide for Improving Communication and Getting What You Want in Your Relationships* (New York: HarperCollins, 1992); John Gray, *Mars and Venus Starting Over: A Practical Guide for Finding Love Again after a Painful Breakup, Divorce, or the Loss of a Loved One* (New York: HarperCollins, 1998); etc.

CHAPTER 2. A BRIEF HISTORY OF THE GEEK GAP

1. J. J. O'Connor and E. F. Robertson, "Galileo Galilei," University of St. Andrews, Scotland, http://www.groups.dcs.stand.ac.uk/~history/Mathematicians/Galileo.html (accessed April 9, 2006).

2. Albert Van Helden and Elizabeth Burr, "The Galileo Project," Rice University, http://galileo.rice.edu (accessed April 9, 2006).

3. Galileo Galilei, *Dialogue Concerning the Two Chief World Systems* (1632) (translated from Italian by Stillman Drake), http://math.dartmouth.edu/~matc /Readers/renaissance.astro/ 7.0.0.html (accessed April 9, 2006).

4. J. A. N. Lee, "Charles Babbage," *Interactive Learning with a Digital Library in Computer Science*, Virginia Tech/Norfolk State University, September 1994, http://ei.cs.vt.edu/~history/Babbage.html (accessed April 9, 2006).

5. B. V. Bowden, *Faster Than Thought: A Symposium on Digital Computing Machines* (London: Pitman & Sons, 1953).

6. "Tesla Life and Legacy," *Tesla: Master of Lightning*, Public Broadcasting Service, http://www.pbs.org/tesla/ll/index.html (accessed April 9, 2006).

7. Ibid.

8. Margaret Cheney, *Tesla: Man Out of Time* (New York: Touchstone/Simon & Schuster, 2001), p. 73.

9. Ibid.

10. Ibid., p. 219.

11. Gene Dannen, "Leo Szilard—A Biographical Chronology" *Leo Szilárd Online*, http:www.dannen.com/szilard.html (accessed April 9, 2006).

12. Neal Conan, "Author William Lanouette Talks about Leo Szilárd," *Morning Edition*, National Public Radio, March 1, 1993.

13. Leo Szilárd, "President Truman Did Not Understand," *U.S. News and World Report* (August 15, 1960), http://www.peak.org/~danneng/decision/usnews.html (accessed April 9, 2006).

14. Robert S. Norris, *Racing for the Bomb: General Leslie R. Groves, The Manhattan Project's Indispensable Man* (South Royalton, VT: Steerforth Press, 2002), p. 235.

15. William Lanouette, *Genius in the Shadows* (New York: Scribner, 1993).

16. Conan, "Author William Lanouette Talks about Leo Szilárd."

17. Szilárd, "President Truman Did Not Understand."

CHAPTER 3. GEEKS GAIN LEGITIMACY

1. Kathleen Melymuka, "The Evolution of the IT Leader," *Computerworld*, September 30, 2002, p. 28.

2. Paul A. Strassmann, "Power Politics of the CIO," luncheon speech at Armed Forces Communications and Electronics Association (AFCEA), March 19, 2003, http://www.strassmann.com/pubs/fed/AFCEA-2003.html (accessed April 9, 2006).

3. Interview with Rod Fournier, January 1998.

4. Minda Zetlin, "Disinformation: What to Do When You Get Dissed," *Management Review* (July/August 1998): 34.

5. Ibid.

6. Interview with Dennis Wigent, director, internal communications, Kmart Corp., January 1998.

7. Zetlin, "Disinformation: What to Do When You Get Dissed."

8. Dean Takahashi, "Intel Apologizes for Pentium Mishap," *Knight Ridder/Tribune Business News*, December 20, 1994.

9. Ibid.

10. Rajiv Chandrasekaran, "How Did It All Go Right?" *Washington Post*, January 2, 2000, p. A1.

11. E-mail interview with Karin Albert, December 16, 2004.

12. Interview with Ian Hayes, September 4, 1998.

13. *Digital Planet*, World Information Technology and Services Alliances (WITSA), October 2005, http://www.witsa.org/digitalplanet, (accessed April 9, 2006).

14. Interview with Bruce Miller, January 12, 2005.

15. Amy Harmon, "Geeks Put the Unsavvy on Alert: Learn or Log Off," *New York Times*, February 5, 2004, p. A1.

16. E-mail interview with John Martin, January 4, 2005.

17. Interview with Jonathan Spira, January 6, 2005.

18. E-mail interview with Karin Albert, January 8, 2005.

CHAPTER 4. WHO'S TO BLAME FOR THE DOT-COM BUST?

1. "Dot-Com Failures Hit the Headlines Once Again," *M2 PressWIRE*, February 2, 2001, http://www.presswire.net (accessed April 9, 2006).

2. "Research Shows Dot-Com Boom and Bust Cost Investors over USD15bn," *Telecomworldwire*, September 23, 2002, http://www.m2.com (accessed April 9, 2006).

3. Douglas Rushkoff, "Who to Blame to the Dot-Com Failures," *All Things Considered*, National Public Radio, February 6, 2001.

4. Bill Lessard and Steve Baldwin, *NetSlaves 2.0: Tales of "Surviving" the Great Tech Gold Rush* (New York: Allworth Press, 2003), p. x.

5. Ibid., p. 45.

6. Mitchell Zuckoff, *Ponzi's Scheme: The True Story of a Financial Legend* (New York: Random House, 2005).

7. Bo Peabody, *Lucky or Smart? Secrets to an Entrepreneurial Life* (New York: Random House, 2005), p. 17.

8. Steven Levy, "Silicon Valley Reboots," *Newsweek*, March 25, 2002, p. 42.

9. Peabody, *Lucky or Smart?* p. 43.

10. "Internet Penetration Breaks the 50 Percent Mark in 21 U.S. Markets during September, according to Nielsen//NetRatings," *Business Wire*, October 16, 2000, http://www.businesswire.com (accessed April 9, 2006, via High Beam).

11. Scott Scheleur, Carol King, and Mike Shimberg, "Quarterly Retail E-Commerce Sales 4th Quarter 2005," February 17, 2006, US Department of Commerce, http://www.census.gov/mrts/www/ecomm.html (accessed April 9, 2006).

12. Fred Vogelstein and Doris Burke, "Google @ $165," *Fortune*, December 13, 2004, p. 98.

13. Chang-Hoan Cho and Hongsik John Cheon, "Why Do People Avoid Advertising on the Internet?" *Journal of Advertising* (Winter 2004): 89.

14. "Usage Statistics," SeatGuru, http://www.seatguru.com/adverts.shtml (accessed April 9, 2006).

15. Vogelstein and Burke, "Google @ $165."

16. Ibid.

17. Joannie Fischer, "The Dot-Bomb Survivors Club," *U.S. News & World Report*, March 19, 2001, p. 34.

18. Ibid.

CHAPTER 5. FUNDAMENTAL DIFFERENCES

1. Diane Dietz, "San Francisco-Based Environmental Group's Anti-Ford Campaign Courts Students," *Knight-Ridder/Tribune Business News*, February 23, 2004. (See also http://www.allyourbrand.org.)

2. Andy Goldberg, "Clan Gatherings to Wage War on Old Enemies; For Computer Game Addicts, There Is Nothing Better Than a LAN Party to Test Their Skills against Other Gamers," *Daily Telegraph* (London), December 14, 2000.

3. Marc Prensky, "Digital Natives, Digital Immigrants," *On the Horizon* (October 2001), http://www.markprensky.com/writing (accessed April 9, 2006).

4. Ibid.

5. Interview with Mark Oehlert, February 23, 2005.

6. Interview with Bill Brobston, January 16, 2005.

7. Paul Glen, *Leading Geeks: How to Lead and Manage People who Deliver Technology* (San Francisco: Jossey-Bass, 2003), p. 31.

8. "PringlesCantenna," Seattle Wireless, http://www.seattlewireless.net/index.cgi /PringlesCantennan (accessed April 9, 2006).

9. Paul Boutin, "Wi-Fi Users: Chalk This Way," *Wired News*, July 3, 2002, http://www.wired.com/news/wireless/0,1382,53638,00.html (accessed April 9, 2006).

10. Frank Hayes, "Thanks, Warchalkers," *Computerworld*, August 26, 2002, http://www.computerworld.com/securitytopics/security/story/0,10801,73784,00.html (accessed April 9, 2006).

11. "Welcome to the Largest Underground Hacking Event in the World," Defcon, http://www.defcon.org (accessed April 9, 2006).

CHAPTER 6. GRIPES ABOUT GEEKS

1. E-mail interview with Bruce Miller, February 23, 2005.

2. Interview with Clyde Steiner, April 14, 2005.

3. Interview with Ian Hayes, September 4, 1998.

4. Frank Hayes, "Chaos Is Back," *Computerworld*, November 8, 2004, p. 70.

5. Ibid.

6. Edward Yourdon, *Death March: The Complete Software Developer's Guide to Surviving 'Mission Impossible' Projects* (New York: Prentice-Hall, 1999; 2nd ed., 2004).

7. Paul Graham, *Hackers & Painters: Big Ideas from the Computer Age* (Sebastopol, CA: O'Reilly, 2004), p. 4.

CHAPTER 7. GRIPES ABOUT SUITS

1. Interview with Bruce Miller, January 12, 2005.

2. Paul Graham, *Hackers & Painters: Big Ideas from the Computer Age* (Sebastopol, CA: O'Reilly, 2004), p. 181.

3. E-mail interview with Karin Albert, December 1, 2004.

4. E-mail interview with Bruce Miller, February 23, 2005.

CHAPTER 8. GEEKS "GREP," SUITS "POTENTIALIZE"

1. G. B. Trudeau, *Doonesbury Dossier: The Reagan Years* (Austin, TX: Holt, Rinehart and Winston, 1984), p. 202.

2. "LART," Urban Dictionary, http://www.urbandictionary.com/define.php ?term=lart (accessed April 9, 2006).

3. Robert Heinlein, *Stranger in a Strange Land* (New York: G. P. Putnam's Sons, 1961).

4. Rudyard Kipling, "The Ballad of East and West," in *Rudyard Kipling: Complete Verse*, repr. ed. (New York: Anchor, 1989), p. 233.

5. R. Nichols et al., *Harvard Business Review on Effective Communication* (Boston: Harvard Business School Press, 1999), pp. 124–25.

6. J. H. Sheridan, "A Matter of Perspective," *Industry Week*, January 4, 1988.

7. William Lutz, "Life under the Chief Doublespeak Officer," *Free Republic*, http://209.157.64.200/focus/f-news/812924/posts (accessed April 9, 2006).

8. Scott Adams, *Fugitive from the Cubicle Police* (Kansas City, MO: Andrews and McMeel/Universal Press Syndicate, 1996), p. 74.

9. Elizabeth MacDonald and Asra Q. Nomani, "Unsuspecting Executives Become Fair Game in 'Buzzword Bingo,'" *Wall Street Journal*, June 8, 1998, p. A1.

10. M. Precker, "Buzzword Bingo," *Greensboro (NC) News & Record*, September 19, 1998.

11. Ibid.

CHAPTER 9. CYBERCRIME

1. Testimony of Peter A. Cavicchia, Special Agent in the US Secret Service, given before US Magistrate Judge Robert M. Levy, Eastern District of New York, March 14, 2000, filed at the Clerk of the Court Eastern District of New York, Docket Number M-00-0459.

2. Ann Harrison, "Programmer Rejects $70k Bonus, Is Charged with Online Attack," *Computerworld*, March 20, 2000, p. 8.

3. Testimony of Peter A. Cavicchia.

4. Lenny Savino, "E-Crime Is Confounding Police, Costing Companies and Consumers $1 Billion," *Knight Ridder/Tribune News Service*, August 30, 2000.

5. Harrison, "Programmer Rejects $70k Bonus, Is Charged with Online Attack."

6. "Man Goes Berserk," *Geek News*, March 17, 2000, http://www.geek .com/news/geeknews/jan2000/gee2000317000978.htm (accessed April 9, 2006).

7. Testimony of Peter A. Cavicchia.

8. "2004 E-Crime Watch Survey," *CSO* magazine, p. 14, http://www.cert .org/archive/pdf/2004eCrimeWatchSummary.pdf (accessed April 9, 2006).

9. Michelle Keeney et al., *Inside Threat Study: Computer System Sabotage in Critical Infrastructure Sectors*, US Secret Service and CERT Coordination Center/Carnegie Mellon Software Engineer Institute, May 2005, http://www.cert.org/archive/pdf/insidercross051105.pdf (accessed April 9, 2006).

10. Ibid., p. 11.

11. Dan Verton, "Analysis: Insiders a Major Security Threat," CNN.com, July 11, 2001, http://archives.cnn.com/2001/TECH/industry/07/11/insider.threat.idg/index.html (accessed April 9, 2006).

12. Keeney et al., *Inside Threat Study*, p. 14.

13. Interview with Jerrold Post, May 23, 2005.

14. Paul Graham, *Hackers & Painters: Big Ideas from the Computer Age* (Sebastapol, CA: O'Reilly, 2004), p. 18.

15. Keeney et al., *Inside Threat Study*, p. 37.

16. Ibid.

17. Keeney et al., *Inside Threat Study*, p. 14.

18. Ibid., p. 15.

19. Ibid.

20. Paul Glen, *Leading Geeks: How to Lead and Manage People Who Deliver Technology* (San Francisco: Jossey-Bass, 2003), p. 36.

21. Interview with Jerrold Post, May 23, 2005.

22. Keeney et al., *Inside Threat Study*, p. 16.

CHAPTER 10. PING-PONG VERSUS POWERPOINT

1. Christine Piotrowski and Elizabeth A. Rogers, *Designing Commercial Interiors* (Hoboken, NJ: Wiley, 1998), p. 14.

2. Darrin Zeer, *Office Feng Shui: Creating Harmony in Your Work Space* (San Francisco: Chronicle Books, 2004), p. 13.

3. Nancilee Wydra, *Feng Shui Goes to the Office: How to Thrive from 9 to 5* (New York: McGraw-Hill, 2000), pp. 19–21.

4. Ibid.

CHAPTER 11. OUTSOURCING THE GEEK GAP

1. "Gartner Says Outsourcing Will Continue to Be the Main Driver for Growth in IT Services," a press release from Gartner, Inc., published May 17, 2004, available at http://www.gartner.com/press_releases/asset_78848_11.html (accessed April 9, 2006).

2. *Dallas D. Register et. al. v. Honeywell Federal Manufacturing & Technologies*, LLC, 2005 WL 367319 (US Ct. of App., 8th Cir., 2005).

3. "Tacky?" a posting in the Career Discussion thread, *Tech Republic*, July 17, 2004, http://techrepublic.com/5208-11181-0.html?forum ID=6&threadID= 155700&messageID=1625780 (accessed April 9, 2006).

4. Ibid.

5. Ibid.

6. "Outsourcing Falling from Favor with World's Largest Organizations, Deloitte Consulting Study Reveals," a press release from Deloitte Touche Tohmatsu, published April 19, 2005.

7. Penny Lunt Crossman, "Justify Your Existence," *IT Architect*, February 1, 2005, http://www.itarchitect.com/showArticle.jhtml?articleID=57701952 (accessed April 9, 2006).

8. "Outsource Your Job to Earn More!" *Times of India*, July 7, 2004, http://timesofindia.indiatimes.com/articleshow/769493.cms (accessed April 9, 2006). Though it has been widely reported in many venues, the post is no longer findable on Slashdot.

9. Edward Yourdon, *Outsource: Competing in the Global Productivity Race* (New York: Prentice-Hall, 2004), p. 2.

10. Andrew Pollack, "Who's Reading Your X-Ray?" *New York Times*, November 16, 2003, p. 3.1 (late edition, East Coast).

11. Ibid.

12. Karl Schoenberger, "Legal Work Becomes the Latest White-Collar Job Being Offshored" *New Bedford (MA) Standard-Times*, January 18, 2005, p. L2.

13. Lou Dobbs, *Exporting America: Why Corporate Greed Is Shipping American Jobs Overseas* (New York: Warner Business Books, 2004), p. 34.

14. McKinsey Global Institute (McKinsey & Co.), *Offshoring: Is It a Win-Win Game?* August 2003, p. 7.

15. Interview with Ayush Maheshwari, June 21, 2005.

16. "Karma Yatra—Where It All Began," Big Indian, http://www.biginet.org /karmayatra.htm (accessed April 9, 2006).

17. DiamondCluster, *2005 Global IT Outsourcing Study*, p. 5., http://www .diamondcluster.com/Ideas/Viewpoint/PDF/DiamondCluster2005Outsourcing Study.pdf (accessed April 23, 2000).

18. Ibid., p. 7.

19. Manny Frishberg, "IT Protesters Outside Looking In," *Wired News*, February 27, 2004, http://www.wired.com/news/infostructure/0,1377,62462,00.html (accessed April 9, 2006).

20. Ellsworth Quarrels, "Fired!: The Press Plunges into the Outsourcing Debate," *Across the Board* (July/August 2004): 57.

21. Ibid.

22. Frishberg, "IT Protesters Outside Looking In."

23. DiamondCluster, *2005 Global IT Outsourcing Study*, p. 8.

24. Ibid., p. 4.

25. Frishberg, "IT Protesters Outside Looking In."

26. DiamondCluster, *2005 Global IT Outsourcing Study*, p. 11.

27. McKinsey Global Institute, *Offshoring: Is It a Win-Win Game?* pp. 13–14.

28. Paul Graham, *Hackers & Painters: Big Ideas from the Computer Age* (Sebastopol, CA: O'Reilly, 2004), p. 75.

29. Tom Peters, *Re-imagine!* (London: Dorling Kindersley Publishing, 2003), p. 73.

CHAPTER 12. SAME BED, DIFFERENT DREAMS

1. Bo Peabody, *Lucky or Smart? Secrets to an Entrepreneurial Life* (New York: Random House, 2005).

2. David F. D'Alessandro, with Michele Owens, *Career Warfare:10 Rules for Building a Successful Personal Brand and Fighting to Keep It* (New York: McGraw-Hill, 2004), pp. 13–14.

3. Jim Collins, *Good to Great: Why Some Companies Make the Leap . . . and Others Don't* (New York: HarperCollins, 2001), p. 21.

4. Leslie Jaye Goff, *Get Your IT Career in Gear! Practical Advice for Building*

a Career in Information Technology (Berkeley, CA: Osborne/McGraw-Hill), p. 35.

5. Ibid., p. 4.

6. "A Leadership Role without Direct Reports. Help or Hindrance?" post in Career Discussion Thread, *Tech Republic*, July 7, 2005, http://techrepublic .com.com/5208-11181-0.html?forumID=6&threadID=177473&messageID =1805110 (accessed April 9, 2006).

7. E-mail interview with David S. Fry, July 18, 2005.

8. Peabody, *Lucky or Smart?* pp. 6–7.

9. Collins, *Good to Great,* p. 109.

10. BlessingWhite,"Six Steps to Retaining IT Talent," http://www.blessingwhite .com/Library/Press/6StepstoReinITTalent.pdf (accessed April 9, 2006).

11. Arlyn Tobias Gajilan, "Palm Pioneers: The PalmPilot's Parents Created One of the Greatest Hits in High Tech. What the Heck Can They Do for an Encore?" *FSB: Fortune Small Business* (November 1999): 52, http://www.fortune.com/ fortune/articles/0,15114,374406,00.html (accessed April 9, 2006).

12. Crayton Harrison, "Palm-Handspring Merger Boosts Hopes of Phone-Organizer Combo," *Knight-Ridder/Tribune News Service*, June 4, 2003.

13. BlessingWhite, "6 Steps to Retaining IT Talent."

14. Rishab Aiyer Ghosh, "Interview with Linus Torvalds: What Motivates Free Software Developers?" *First Monday*, March 2, 1998, http://www.firstmonday .org/issues/issue3_3/torvalds (accessed April 9, 2006).

15. Interview with Mitchell Abramson, July 25, 2005.

16. Interview with Barbara Finer, June 8, 2005.

17. Interview with Cameron Herold, June 28, 2005.

CHAPTER 13. CLOSING THE GEEK GAP

1. Interview with Jordan Chanofsky, August 25, 2005.

2. Interview with Doug LaBoda, June 20, 2000.

3. Interview with Gary Kruse, August 19, 2005.

4. Ibid.

5. Interview with Barbara Finer, June 8, 2005.

6. Interview with Jay Heffernan, August 2, 2005.

7. Interview with Cameron Herold, June 28, 2005.

8. Interview with Roman Azbel, August 24, 2005.

9. Interview with Doug LaBoda, August 23, 2005.

10. Ibid.

11. Interview with Cameron Herold, June 28, 2005.

12. Interview with Roman Azbel, August 24, 2005.

13. Interview with Doug LaBoda, August 23, 2005.

14. Ibid.

15. Interview with Jordan Chanofsky, August 23, 2005.

16. Interview with Joseph Dans, September 1, 2005.

17. Interview with Michael Lane, September 1, 2005.

CHAPTER 14. THE FUTURE OF THE GEEK GAP

1. Claude S. Fischer, *America Calling: A History of the Telephone to 1940* (Berkeley and Los Angeles: University of California Press, 1992), p. 1.

2. "Forrester's Telecom & Networks Survey Reveals Demand for Mobile Data Increasing Faster Than Business' Planned," press release, July 11, 2005, http://www.forrester.com/ER/Press/Release/0,1769,1023,00.html (accessed April 9, 2006).

3. "VoIP: Coming Soon, Coming Everywhere," *eMarketer*, April 2006, http://www.emarketer.com/Article.aspx?1003913 (accessed April 9, 2006).

4. "Seniors Online: How Aging Boomers Will Shake Up the Market," *eMarketer* June 2005, http://www.emarketer.com/Report.aspx?seniors_jun05 (accessed April 9, 2006).

5. "Technology Trends—Campuses Go Wireless," *FAA Advisor* (Keybank), December 14, 2005, http://www.key.com/html/FAA-182.html#tech (accessed April 9, 2006).

6. Jim Wagner, "Colleges Test VoIP Cellphones," *Wi-Fi Planet*, August 19, 2005, http://www.wi-fiplanet.com/news/article.php/3528766 (accessed April 9, 2006).

7. "Gartner Predicts That by 2010, the Number of IT Staff in the Profession Will Shrink by 15 Percent," Gartner, Inc., press release, May 24, 2005, http://www.gartner.com/press_releases/asset_127764_11.html (accessed April 9, 2006).

8. Jay Vegso, "Interest in CS as a Major Drops among Incoming Freshmen," *Computer Research News* (May 2005), http://www.cra.org/CRN/articles/may05 /vegso (accessed April 9, 2006).

9. Interview with Barbara Finer, June 8, 2005.

10. Steve Lohr, "Computer Majors Adding Other Skills," *New York Times*, August 23, 2005, p. C1.

11. "Gartner Predicts That by 2010, the Number of IT Staff in the Profession Will Shrink by 15 Percent."

INDEX